MODERNISM THE MORNING AFTER

MODERNISM THE MORNING AFTER

Bob Perelman

THE UNIVERSITY OF ALABAMA PRESS
Tuscaloosa

The University of Alabama Press
Tuscaloosa, Alabama 35487-0380
uapress.ua.edu

Typeface: Minion and Futura

Manufactured in the United States of America
Cover image: *You Have to Be Lucid*, painting by Francie Shaw
Cover design: David Nees

Cataloging-in-Publication data is available from the Library of Congress.
ISBN: 978-0-8173-5889-1
E-ISBN: 978-0-8173-9109-6

This book is dedicated to Francie Shaw

Contents

Preface

Modernism the Morning After has taken a while. Its two-decade gestation is now inexorably woven into the book. An unambiguous benefit of such a long writing period is that it allows for a parallax view. Fixed stars move, et cetera.

Back in the twentieth century, after my first two critical books, I started a project on poetic fakes, but my interest in making a book out of it evaporated (though some of the original impetus shows up here in chapter 14). Meanwhile, there was writing, teaching, ad hoc critical activity: talks, articles, essay-poems; and poems like "Iflife" that were also poem-essays. And I had a title, "Modernism the Morning After," which suggested a perspective but kept mum about particulars. It became talismanic, an open-ended phrase that had room for whatever I was doing.

Now that the book is finally out, it's time to get more objective about what you will find here.

As writing, *Modernism the Morning After* dates from 1995–2016, particularly 2015–2016. Some chapters trace back to the nineties; some are new; but much of what you will read here comes from the last two years, as I wrote and reworked these pieces.

The title can evoke a wild party / regret scenario: modernism the exciting situation where wonderful things were said . . . but the morning after . . . totalitarianism, masculinism, otherism . . . what a splitting headache!

But there is no regret in *Modernism the Morning After*. While my skepticism about modernist dogmas (as well as about innovative ones) should be clear throughout, I am not privileging the moment of clear-eyed disenchantment. In what follows here, "modernism" and "the morning after" are interwoven: both are ongoing situations.

As I wrote and rewrote these pieces, I wanted to articulate a more capacious model of modernism, stretching back to Whitman, Dickinson, and Dunbar and extending to the present moments of writing and reception.

In *Modernism the Morning After* I am writing as a poet, teacher, and critic, addressing peers and beginners without choosing between them.

I owe the most basic thanks to Charles Bernstein and Hank Lazer, who pushed me to get this book done.

Acknowledgments

Earlier versions of some of these chapters have appeared in the following places:

1. "Canonicity." In *Jacket2*, ed. Jerome Rothenberg, Spring 2013, *http://jacket2.org/commentary/bob-perelman-canonicity*.

3. "Copying Whitman." In *Active Romanticism*, edited by Julie Carr and Jeffrey C. Robinson. Tuscaloosa: University of Alabama Press, 2015.

4. "Delivering Difficult News." In *21st-Century American Engaged Poetry: New Essays*, edited by Jeffrey Gray and Ann Keniston (2016).

5. "Homage to Pound's *Propertius*." In *Ezra Pound and Education*, edited by Steven G. Yao and Michael Coyle. Orono: National Poetry Foundation, 2012.

6. "Rachel Blau DuPlessis's *Drafts* and the Epic Moment." In *Jacket2*, ed. Jerome Rothenberg, Spring 2013, *http://jacket2.org/article/drafts-and-epic-moment*.

7. "Familiar Williams." In *The Cambridge History of American Poetry*, edited by Stephen Burt.

9. "Taste Test." In *Journal of the Poetry Society of America* (April 2000).

10. "The Pound Cage." In *Paideuma* (forthcoming).

12. "A Span for Burton Hatlen: From Pound to Flarf." In *Paideuma* 40 (2013).

13. "Bathos and Mind Reading." In *On Bathos: Literature, Art, Music*, edited by Peter Nicholls and Sara Crangle. London: Continuum, 2010.

14. "The Poetry Hoax and Poetic News." In *Foreign Literature Studies*, no. 2 (April 2005).

15. "A Williams Sound-Script: Listening to 'The Sea-Elephant.'" In *Jacket 2*, ed. Jerome Rothenberg, Spring 2013, *http://jacket2.org/article/williams-soundscript*.

16. "Alice Notley and Poetic Inheritance." In *Don't Ever Get Famous*, edited by Daniel Kane. New York: Dalkey Archive Press, 2006.

17. "Speech Effects: Talk and Transcription." In *Close Listening: Poetry and the Performed Word*, edited by Charles Bernstein. Oxford: Oxford University Press, 1998.

18. "Zukofsky at 100" and 19. "On 'The Jewish Question.'" Both in *Secular Jewish Cultures and Radical Poetics*, edited by Daniel Morris and Stephen Paul Miller. Tuscaloosa: University of Alabama Press, 2009.

20. "Dickinson – So –." In *The Emily Dickinson Newsletter* 15, no. 2 (2006).

Abbreviations

A	Zukofsky, Louis. *"A"*. Berkeley: University of California Press, 1978.
ABC	Pound, Ezra. *ABC of Reading*. New York: New Directions, 2003.
C	Pound, Ezra. *The Cantos of Ezra Pound*, 12th printing. New York: New Directions, 1991.
CB	Mullen, Harryette. *The Cracks Between What We Are and What We Are Supposed to Be*. Tuscaloosa: University of Alabama Press, 2012.
DWH	Notley, Alice. *Doctor Williams' Heiresses*. Berkeley: Tuumba Press, 1980.
GK	Pound, Ezra. *Guide to Kulchur*. New York: New Directions, 1970.
GS I	Stein, Gertrude. *Writings 1903–1932*. New York: Library of America, 1998.
GS II	Stein, Gertrude. *Writings 1932–1946*. New York: Library of America, 1998.
IM	Williams, William Carlos. *Imaginations*. Edited by Webster Schott. New York: New Directions, 1970.
P	Williams, William Carlos. *Paterson*. Edited by Christopher MacGowan. New York: New Directions, 1992.
PC	Pound, Ezra. *The Pisan Cantos*. Edited by Richard Sieburth. New York: New Directions, 2003.
P/T	Pound, Ezra. *Ezra Pound: Poems and Translations*. Edited by Richard Sieburth. New York: Library of America, 2003.
R	Mullen, Harryette. *Recyclopedia*. St. Paul: Greywolf Press, 2006.
RC I	Robert Creeley. *The Collected Poems of Robert Creeley 1945–1975*. Berkeley: University of California Press, 1982.
RC II	Robert Creeley. *The Collected Poems of Robert Creeley 1975–2005*. Berkeley: University of California Press, 2006.
RI	Williams, William Carlos. *A Recognizable Image*. Edited by Bram Dijkstra. New York: New Directions, 1978.

SP	Pound, Ezra. *Selected Prose 1909–1965*. Edited by William Cookson. London: Faber, 1973.
TTW	Mullen, Harryette. *Tree Tall Woman*. Galveston: Energy Earth Communications, Inc., 1981.
WCW I	Williams, William Carlos. *Collected Poems*. Vol. I. Edited by A. Walton Litz and Christopher MacGowan. New York: New Directions, 1986.
WCW II	Williams, William Carlos. *Collected Poems*. Vol. II. Edited by Christopher MacGowan. New York: New Directions, 1988.

MODERNISM THE MORNING AFTER

1
Canonicity

The good news now that I'm sixty-five is I can ride Philly buses for free. The more interesting news is that the balance of homeostasis and desire has become a touchy question. Keeping things recognizably the same is suddenly attractive, very attractive, impossibly attractive. All my writing life I've learned that semantics are open-ended, but I'm getting the feeling that some words will turn out to have only one meaning, which is not a totally pleasant thought. "Finite" is one of those words. I don't yet know what its one meaning is, but extraneous hypotheses are getting shorn away daily, even hourly, which I suppose is progress.

In one sense, the question of canons in poetry seems decidedly old school. It brings back memories of early postmodernist days, when the polemics were, as the etymology suggests, warlike: Marjorie Perloff's "Can(n)on to the Left of Us, Can(n)on to the Right of Us," Jerome Rothenberg's "Harold Bloom: The Critic as Exterminating Angel," Charles Bernstein's "The Academy in Peril: William Carlos Williams Meets the MLA." The battlemap was in crisp focus. This was when O'Hara's poetry could be compared to a small electric fan blowing out crepe-paper streamers, when Stein was a hoax and Language writing a dismissible fad, when Williams meant wheelbarrows (Perloff, *Frank O'Hara*, xii).

Traditional, gated, and fixed, the canon was on the other side of the field. Rothenberg writes of "a struggle between new vision & the literalisms of the canon-making mind" ("Harold Bloom," 24); "the struggles of . . . poets against repression, authority, & dogma . . . against the total apparatus of canon-formation both as a religious & secular phenomenon" (25). His opening salvo was pitched high, comparing Bloom to Josef Mengele, the exterminating angel of Auschwitz. But then you would also have to admit that Bloom started it when he wrote that he was "engaging in canon-formation, in trying to help decide a question that is ultimately of a sad importance: 'Which poet shall live?'" (5); and, in a different article, when he invoked the Holocaust to deny Jewish poets the possibility of being canonized: an ex cathedra pronouncement that too easily slips back to Wagner's anathema from 1848, *The Jew in Music*, where Jews, incapable of genuine creativity, can only imitate servilely or parodically. Who would want to be in that kind of canon?

The battle had a long history, with the interesting side almost never winning in any given present but always, with the passage of time, having won. There has been a long-running basic conflict in poetics between outlaw and classic (Stein), between iambic pentameter and the variable foot (Williams), between closed and open (Olson, Hejinian). Who wouldn't want to be on the interesting side of such choices?

But with the interesting side having repeatedly won—Loy, H.D., Zukofsky, Niedecker, and Tolson are in print, as are the first ten volumes of the Olson–Creeley correspondence, and *Against Expression: An Anthology of Conceptual Writing*, to name a few signal victories—doesn't this simply reproduce the dilemma of canon? The anti-innovative canon is dead, long live the—is this the right term?—innovative canon?

Rothenberg's essay would argue against this, using Blake's figures of the Devourer and the Prolific to dramatize the difference between rigid canon makers, fixated on elimination, and exuberant innovators furthering life in all its variety: "Unlike the Prolific—the producer—who revels in his own & others' excesses, the teacher / Devourer / critic is driven to despair & to canon-formation to relieve the stress" (10).

But faith, a secular faith, in the Prolific does not push the problem of canon formation very far away. While one can truly say that, in the poetic field at least, the Prolific has bested the Devourer—what better emblem than Rothenberg's big books, not to mention the Internet?—and thus that the exterminating angel has been bested by the recording angel, nevertheless, under these happy conditions, the Prolific runs right into its own anti-canonical, para-canonical, quasi-canonical dilemmas.

In writing, as in any art, everything that is produced needs to be fully received in order to exist in any fullness. Without the full-time cooperation of not just the recording angel but also the receiving angel, the Prolific does not exist. And it turns out that every receiving angel—and there are millions of us—is human. We have access, many of us, to storage and retrieval capabilities of great sophistication and tremendous scope, but our human powers of reception have not kept pace with our human-made proliferating machines. Thus canons, named or assumed, fixed or trending, are as loaded an issue as ever (dull pun intended), a blunderbuss of forward-moving writing—the modernist-to-postmodernist-to-postcontemporary shrapnel pointed fuzzily but accurately enough at the heart of what we do, disparate as we and our practices are.

The question is always choice (including choosing not to choose). Do we pick up this or that? Carry this along or not? Put this in circulation or not? In the portable archive of everyday practice—physical, social, poetic—instantaneous judgment is incessantly active. It is as ubiquitous as gravity.

The unfunny comedy of inclusion and exclusion never stops. Canons, sanctioned or prolific, are medium-term machines of reproduction—syllabi with their reading requirements, anthologies with their poets, schools with their fight songs, blogs with their names and blogrolls, gossip with its items. The question extends to finely granulated contexts of judgment. Think of the slider on digital maps, but applied to our human-cultural landscape, stretching from the personal to large institutional and historical effects. The question of what is interesting, the inclusions and non-mentions that indicate what is felt to be of note, what needs to be brought forward, all this—I'm trying to evoke a scale from ephemeral on up, from saying something in a conversation, to the larger actions of constructing a syllabus, to editing a once-a-decade update of a major anthology that has a strong, fairly stable market share, to going viral—all this depends on what could be called judgment, or taste, or desire, the pressure of conceived consensus, attraction across a wide gamut, what in the best light (theological, dialectical, geo-rhetorical) appeals.

Has this book been checked out in the last three years? If not, off it goes to high-density storage, from whence, they say, almost none returns.

The optimist answers: books are a shelf-bound storage/retrieval device; in the digital realm these constraints vanish, and while additional storage may not be too cheap to meter, as they used to say about nuclear power, digital storage space is still many magnitudes greater than the space on library storage shelves. You could say that digital storage changes everything. That all the drama adhering around canons was an outgrowth of print; that all the high-minded questions concerning value, as well as a great deal of the often more interesting lower-minded behavior of poets, spring from the constraints of print. What got promoted into permanence was a matter that everyone had to notice with the unalterable objectivity of everyday recognition: when there were only so many pages, not everyone got in. Today, you could say, the easy expandability of digital space makes such angst anachronistic, something of a costume drama. Still, the stoic has ongoing evidence that proliferation has not yet solved the problems of judgment. In fact, it seems to be exacerbating those problems.

Some of my first conscious moments concerning art date from my discovery of Pound's *ABC of Reading* in a bookstore at music camp: "We live in an age of science and of abundance. The care and reverence for books as such, proper to an age when no book was duplicated until someone took the pains to copy it out by hand, is obviously no longer suited to 'the needs of society,' or to the conservation of learning. The weeder is supremely needed if the Garden of the Muses is to persist as a garden" (17).

In view of the antiquarianism (to phrase it politely) of Pound's later career, one can almost imagine this in the voice of Maggie Smith: "The butler is supremely needed if Downton Abbey is to persist as a great house." But fear of the multitudinous is not confined to the Pound/Eliot axis; it is strong in a presentist like Stein, as the beginning of *The Geographical History of America* (nearly contemporaneous with *ABC of Reading*) shows: "In the month of February were born Washington Lincoln and I. . . . If nobody had to die how would there be room for any of us who now live to have lived. We could not have been if all the others had not died. There would have been no room" (367). This was written in the mid-1930s, a few years later than Canto 30 where Pound makes "clean slayne" (i.e., hygienic weeding/killing) exciting and necessary (Pound, *Cantos*, 147).

Act so there is no use in a canon—didn't Stein write that? But didn't she also write that in English literature in her time she was the only one? And hasn't the Library of America issued a two-volume canonical selection of her work on thin, strong, acid-free (eternal) paper?

Space: I write it in standard orthography because it is a basic constituent of our choices: how much space is there on shelves, in bandwidth, in brains? The finitude of active use makes for not-large groups of things.

We may now live in post-canonical times, but more than ever we live in the long century of the example, the clickable, the trending, the viral.

Typical cruxes of aging (partial list): de-accessioning; frequent urination; making lists, then forgetting them; making lists where the desire to cross the item off and never have to think about it again is greater than the desire that impelled the writing down of the item in the first place; always having to look up what Nietzsche said about history—are you supposed to forget it or remember it?

Critics are crucial to poetic market share. It's the old song: poet-critics creating the poetics by which the poetry is to be enjoyed. To model the reading world in which one writes: Wordsworth did it, as did Stein. But poetry is venal as well as, on occasion, powerful, and there are still non-poet critics, interesting ones like Jameson, who writes of how Baudelaire might be received: "Then there is the hardest of all Baudelaires to grasp: the Baudelaire contemporary of himself (and of Flaubert), the Baudelaire of the 'break,' of 1857, the Baudelaire the eternal freshness of whose language is bought by reification, by its strange transformation into alien speech." I want to stop him here, and start showing some ever-fresh language, fresh from the bonds of reification, but the paragraph concludes: "Of this Baudelaire, we will speak no further here" (223). Alas.

New senses are always needed. At least this has been my experience as I've grasped it via everyone I have known and heard of. Senses of gender; senses of humor; senses of carbon; senses of the global. Newborn senses are not well developed; teaching, modeling, some sorts of systematic reinforcement are always needed, as well as generous anti-systematic rupture of same (use as needed). Technocratic avant-gardism will not thrive if it does not nourish attentiveness and make frame switching and mind reading interesting.

The religious trappings of canonicity have always creeped me out. It is the unsubtle whisper of violence. The pun on "cannon" comes back insistently. Cannon are old-fashioned: the Civil War, *War and Peace*, freshly painted cairns of fused cannonballs in city parks. Then, too, the human cannonballs: what a lousy way to make a living, or so I imagine. More than thirty human cannonballs have died on the job, I learn from Wikipedia.

Judging how art feels and what it does is a lifelong process. (Although more and more it's looking like the ones who said art is longer than life were right.) Still, trying to get right with the canon is a dull endeavor.

Writing (the practice, the activity) is for the living, and reading is something the living do. As a kind of self-pep talk, I'll close with lines from my quasi-elegy for Derrida:

> We poets
> (it must be written) really don't know,
>
> are prohibited (structurally) from knowing
> what we write before it's written, and,
>
> in a back-eddying double-whammy,
> can't really forget what's come before
>
> the most recent word.
> In that we model both the alert insouciance
>
> of the newborn (with its millennia of entailments,
> but still in-fant, unspeaking) and
>
> the fully aged fluent inhabitant
> of language flowing
>
> around a life. (67–68)

The moment of desire! The moment of desire! Blake wrote it twice to tell himself and the future that it takes two to tango: read-write is the name of the game, and the game changes.

2

Time Management

Marianne Moore, Ted Berrigan, and the Geniune

To pronounce too thoroughly on what is genuine in poetry is to reach for the dunce cap that time always holds poised.

But in the meantime, to give up on the question is not a lively option. In poetry as elsewhere don't things get more interesting after a few basics are squared away? Aren't some things actually the case? Isn't it still true that Ern Malley was made up? That Ted Berrigan had a sense of humor? That Marianne Moore meant what she wrote?

In what follows, I will be taking poems as sites of intended exactness (*those* words, *these* poetic gestures) and will be noting how reception introduces difference. I will trace this dynamic through two quite different realms—classroom logistics and publication history—focusing on the particular trajectory of a Ted Berrigan poem in my classroom and on Moore's "Poetry" in its various instantiations from its original publication in 1919 to its notorious 1967 three-line version. Teaching innovative poetry to neophyte readers is quite different from Moore adjudicating her life's work, but in both situations there are transmission issues: a student will miss Berrigan's full-bore irony; Moore will mutilate the adventurous contingency of her original "Poetry." Taking poems as both what the poet writes and as what readers read means seeing them not as autonomous verbal structures, but as pragmatic frameworks activated via uneven temporal investments, from the blank immediacy of unfamiliarity to the deep nuance and even fatigue of thorough expertise.

Expertise does not always make one a good reader. Moore, on the evidence of her final version of "Poetry," became an obtuse if not a phobic reader of the earlier poem. The bold gesture of its title promising to tell what poetry is or, more heroically, to simply *be* poetry; the crushing opening line seemingly concluding a real-life conversation about how lame poetry is; the rest of the poem paradoxically demonstrating how poetically interesting real life is (when recombined in Moore's deft phrasing and run through arbitrary line breaks, that is)—it is a sublimely confident performance. After a life's worth of writing and revision, all this becomes:

POETRY

I, too, dislike it.

Reading it, however, with a perfect contempt for it, one discovers in
it, after all, a place for the genuine. (Moore, 36)

Like other admirers of Moore's work, I dislike this final version. Its dreary concluding moral thump—"the genuine"—is what sparked this essay. Why people should read poetry (if they don't already like it, that is) remains a vexing question for poets and teachers; but bringing forward "the genuine" as an answer strikes me as particularly ungenerous. Isn't that the response of an antiques expert? The purveyor of this three-line version of the poem dislikes "Poetry" and perhaps poetry in general. A gatekeeper no longer interested in opening the gate.

Then again, "genuine" is gesturing toward something I can't simply abandon. While the full-length version of "Poetry" may not be the genuine poem, it is much better than the sour three-line deformance. But substituting "better" for "genuine" doesn't avoid the troubling crux of poetic value. Protean and multiply-construed as such a thing is, the question of poetic value underlies both the teaching and the writing of poetry.

I will not be considering poems here as machines made of words: a poem's words are only one part of the situation; the varying temporal investments of writer, teacher, reader, student are an equally important dimension. Over the last decades poems have been celebrated as machines producing difference, polysemy, indeterminacy; here, I will focus instead on meaning (the sending of the bundle of signals that is the poem) and intention (how the signals are to be received) and on how precarious such transmission is.

Meaning is not singular: poems are events saturated with intentions and aspects. A welter of different meanings emerges as a poem circulates among writers, readers, teachers, students, editors.[1] Nor, as a poem circulates, do its words necessarily stay the same. Poets rewrite poems (editors do too), students encounter them at various angles of legibility, anthologizers and teachers abbreviate drastically. In other words, it is no use pretending that generalized literacy is not some unending comedy of errors. Nevertheless, there can be situations of fundamental misconstrual.

As an example of a poem that is not reducible to its words and where intention seems primary, consider this untitled poem by Ted Berrigan:

With
daring
and
strength
men

like
Pollock,
de Kooning,
Tobey,
Rothko,
Smith
and
Kline
filled
their
work
with
the
drama,
anger,
pain,
and
confusion
of
contemporary
life.

Just
like
me. (Berrigan, *Collected Poems*, 568–69)

Some years back, a student interpreted this poem in a final paper as Berrigan earnestly affirming his poetic stature. It was quite a good paper, showing in detail how the form helped articulate what was being said. But for me, the poem was thoroughly ironic: thus, it felt like the student and I were reading the same words but different poems.

I had crammed Berrigan's work into one of the final class sessions, and we had only had time for *The Sonnets*—and when I say *The Sonnets*, I mean two of them: the first ("His piercing pince-nez") and fifteenth ("In Joe Brainard's collage its white arrow": the scrambled elegy to William Carlos Williams and Marilyn Monroe). We had not discussed "With / daring"; it was in the penumbral "exploratory reading" bin. Thus, the student encountered the poem in a freer zone than usual. It was great to see a paper on a poem that we had not discussed: if teaching poetry means expanding reading repertoires, I couldn't have asked for more. In my comment I praised the paper, its careful reading and courage in going beyond restatement of class discussion; I also gave a quick synopsis of my sense of Berrigan's humor, but it was too late for continued teaching: the class was over. I don't know if the student read my comments; I didn't keep the paper—a typically incomplete pedagogical exchange.

As an emblem of such pedagogic distances, here is a dialogue from a linguist observing two pre-adolescents as they are learning a second language:

Observer: Where is the book, Alej?
Kevin: [He takes over the questioning] Where is the book? Touch the book, Alej.
Alej: Touch the book.
Kevin: Touch the book, the book! Here's the book: touch the book.
Alej: Touch the book.
Kevin: Touch it!
Alej: Touch it!
Kevin: Don't say touch it—touch it!
Alej: Touch it! (Fillmore)

I'm heartened by the chance echo of Whitman's credo of poetic immediacy, "this is no book, / Who touches this touches a man" (Whitman, 611); by Kevin's enthusiastically assuming the role of teacher; and by Alej's earnest attempts to demonstrate his understanding. However, my point here is that these more-or-less identical utterances—

Kevin: Touch it!
Alej: Touch it!

are profoundly disconnected.

This is too simple a model for reading poetry. Kevin asking Alej to touch the book is a pragmatic moment; poems, acting on multiple readers across times and social spaces, are very much more complicated. Then, too, what Alej does by accident—ignoring the semantic content of words, misapplying ordinary pragmatic cues, etc.—poets often do on purpose; nevertheless, the exchange does make for a good emblem of the problems of transmission.

With Berrigan's poem, the student missed the irony. The transmission problem in the case of "Poetry" is more difficult to name. That Moore continued to have clashingly incommensurate ideas of the poem can be seen in her numerous rewritings. I find something both emphatic and floundering in the array of different versions; they strike me as quite outside the tradition of deliberate indeterminancy (say from Dickinson's variant words to Cage's methods and beyond). It feels like Moore keeps trying to get it right.

On the page authorized by Moore, "Poetry" is now a three-line poem consisting of twenty-four words. That this is to be taken as her firm intention is the point of her famous epigraph to the 1967 *Complete Poems*, "Omissions are not accidents," which insists that the three-line version is a determinate act. But that act has not determined how the poem has been received. Moore herself presented the older 29-line version of the poem in the notes (in smaller type) to the 1967 book (266–67); and it is this version which circulates as "Poetry."

The gap between the three-line version and the twenty-nine-line version is notorious, but if we scan through the poem's many reprintings, we can see some persisting problem. Moore always made changes, but there is no teleological shape to her activity: sometimes the adjustments were minute and sometimes the recasting was drastic.

"Poetry" first appeared in the July 1919 issue of *Others*, guest-edited by William Carlos Williams; it was then reprinted in Alfred Kreymbourg's anthology *Others for 1919*, in Moore's 1921 *Poems* (assembled by H.D. and Bryher), and in Moore's self-assembled 1924 *Observations*. Each time, the changes were relatively small and the poem is more or less like the familiar version that appeared in her 1951 *Collected Poems* and in the notes to her 1967 *Complete Poems*. While Moore's quasi-Darwinian attention to detail can invite one to dwell amid the myriad verbal distinctions, I would like to borrow psychoanalyst Donald Winnicot's idea of the "good-enough mother," and to consider the twenty-nine-line poem Moore prints in her 1967 notes a "genuine-enough" version of "Poetry." To simplify complex matters, when I refer to "Poetry" here I mean the long version; I'll call the final three-line printing the short version.

But before comparing the long and short versions, I want to reiterate that Moore's problems with the poem are not confined to the final disavowal in 1967. In the 1925 second edition of *Observations*, she rewrites the poem almost as drastically as in 1967, reducing it to a thirteen-line, flush-left, free verse stanza (Schulze, *Becoming Marianne Moore*, 205–7). She abandons her own pioneering lineation and seems clueless about what the poem is saying. The conclusion is dull, insisting on clarity as the sole criterion of poetry: "It may be said of all of us / that we do not admire what we / cannot understand; / enigmas are not poetry" (*Becoming*, 205–7).

The seventeen-line version she published in the 1932 *Poetry* magazine anthology, *The New Poetry* (this is what Zukofsky uses in *A Test of Poetry*), is a bit more generous toward the longer version, but still seems uncomfortable with it. The 1932 ending is as obtuse as the 1925 one, but in a different way: "This we know. / In a liking for the raw material in all its rawness, / and for that which is genuine, there is liking for poetry" (Zukofsky, 151). The impersonal stance at the end—"there is liking"—obliterates what made the opening line so good, how deftly it evokes the interpersonal. In "I, too," the adverb is crucial, with "too" implying agreement in some conversation that is already ongoing. Imagine if the first line were "I dislike it."

"Poetry" first appeared in the July 1919 issue of *Others*, where Williams, in order to voice his contempt for the direction the magazine had taken, placed the poem immediately after his opening editorial calling for the end of the magazine (*Becoming*, 467–68). It was a crude use, typical of Williams's literary behavior in that period: "Poetry" // I, too, dislike it = *Others* // I can't stand it. If crudeness is one of Williams's stereotypical qualities, fastidiousness is often associated with Moore. Williams, in the prologue to *Kora in Hell*, was one of the first to sound this note, when he quotes her as saying, "My work has come to have just one quality of value in it: I will not touch or have anything to do with those things which I detest" (10). Whether or not we want to take fastidiousness as a central descriptor of Moore's writing procedures in general, it makes for an economical explanation as to what motivated the final, three-line version of "Poetry" in her 1967 *Complete Poems*. If poetry is something one not only dislikes but detests, then it should be touched as little as possible. Hence, all the "poetry" of "Poetry" (remember, I'm intending "Poetry" to refer to the long version) must be omitted: for the transcendently fastidious, only the genuine may be granted a place in the poem.

In 1967 most readers of Moore's *Complete Poems* would have known her work and would have considered the three-line "Poetry" a sad aberration. But there would have been others who would not have known her work. From such a vantage, akin to that of a neophyte student reading Berrigan, how would the short "Poetry" read?

The unusual lineation shows at a glance, but careful reading will not clear things up. Perhaps our neophyte reader would have heard that Moore counted syllables and sometimes used rhyme. But here the syllable count (five, nineteen, eleven) displays no regularity. There is rhyme, if one looks for it: "in" and "it" are near eye-rhymes, and "in" rhymes, in the stealthy way that Moore often favored, with "genuine." (But if "it" and "genuine" rhyme in some sense with "in," they do not rhyme with each other.)[2] The endstopping of the first line amplifies the force of implied speech, but the emphatic enjambment of the second and third lines, "in / it," has nothing to do with speech. The first line is a great first line, but the next two give the impression that "Poetry" is not poetry at all but simply prose that has been lineated. Such an impression would be strengthened by the fact that, outside the title itself, the word "poetry" does not appear, as if the title proclaimed a topic too distasteful to be mentioned directly. Instead, the little word "it" obtrudes, almost obsessively—out of the twenty-four words, it appears four times.

It's impossible to miss the radical chastisement this three-line version exacts. Where are the Sappho-like lines describing the rapt body: "Hands that can grasp, eyes / that can dilate, hair that can rise / if it must"? Where is the terse, variegated catalog of natural-social-poetic material: bat, elephant, wild horse, flea-bitten critic, et al.? The imaginary gardens with their real toads? Where is all the poetry? The capacious mini-encyclopedia of poetic delights—hair-raising, sobering, polemical, abstract—has been sacrificed on the altar of the genuine.

Nevertheless, this short version holds, in a crabbed sense, to the plot of the long one. Both versions begin by rejecting poetry and both resolve into what might be called a happy ending, though in the short version it is a parsimonious, didactic one in which we are told that poetry—dislikable, contemptible, unmentionable poetry—is not utterly unredeemable but can be compatible with the genuine. On the questions of what the genuine might be and whether poetry itself can be genuine, the three lines are resolutely silent, unless their presentation as what appears to be poetry implicitly answers their own explicit contempt.

In the long version, poetry is vindicated in a virtuoso display of frame shifting and verbal and tonal precision, and on a more elemental register as well. I will use this register—a kind of fairy tale built around the word "poetry" as the protagonist—to structure my reading of "Poetry." If we follow the trajectory of this protagonist, the word "poetry," from the title to the very end of the poem, a familiar (fairy) tale will emerge: initial deficit and eclipse resolving into fully validated presence.

The title, the honorific "poetry," pronounces the full name of our protagonist. But instantly ogreish opposition arises: the disliking, perfectly contemptuous "I" who, as if casting a spell, diminishes "poetry" into "it." Our protagonist, "poetry," will not fully reappear until the final word of the poem; for now, "it" appears in disguise (disgrace). But "it" has an efficacious talisman: "the genuine." The body, the social world, and the natural world (bats, horses, hair standing on end, elephants, critics, statisticians)—everything testifies for "it." Near the beginning of the fourth stanza, imposters appear: the "half poets." These produce a simulacrum of poetry—that is, the word "poetry" appears in the text, but only in the negative: "the result is not poetry." The next stanza and a half seems to push the happy ending into the future: when "the poets among us" will show us imaginary gardens with real toads, then "shall we have / it." But this is not the ending. Even with those gardens and toads we will not then have the presence of our protagonist in the poem, only "it." The ogre's spell is still in force: "poetry" remains disguised as "it."

Notice the perilous (thoroughly "unpoetic") line breaks forced upon our protagonist-in-eclipse: at the beginning, lines 2 and 3, when the spell is being cast ("one discovers in / it") and here at the end of the penultimate sentence ("shall we have / it"). But it is this second perilous line break that ushers in the presentiment of a happy ending, the reemergence of "poetry." We had been in a not-yet-realized future, when the poets would present the happy synthesis of the mental and the physical—theology and Darwin, perhaps. But now in the concluding stanza we are back in the present, "In the meantime," with a fully energized "you" making the two proper demands: (1) "the raw material of poetry"; and (2) the "genuine." (Could this be the modernist equivalent of the fairy tale's generic three wishes?) If you the reader make this double demand, it brings our protagonist quite close: when you read "the raw material of poetry" you are almost in the presence of "poetry." But "the raw materials of poetry" are not, by themselves, enough; without the "genuine," the raw materials presumably remain raw, dislikable, the kinds of thing half poets drag in. It is only when materials and the genuine are united that "poetry" appears plain, unadorned, fully present, ending the poem happily ever after: "then you are interested in poetry."

Fairy tale endings are assertions of plenitude: lovers united, kingdoms regained. This is not what happens at the end of "Poetry." Though the final stanza takes place in the present and the poem ends in rhetorical triumph with the reappearance of the protagonist word "poetry," poetry is not exactly present. What is present is your interest: "you are interested in poetry." But perhaps your interest in poetry will be like Vladimir and Estragon's interest in Godot. If poetry is not that unknowable, at least it is something that you seek, not something that you have. For all its superb modernist spikiness, "Poetry" concludes with a Romantic tableau, akin to Keats's unheard melodies or his half-heard nightingale "buried deep / In the next valley-glades" (209). Poet and reader are united in questing for poetry: that's as much presence as we get.

But in the long version at least poet and reader are united. In the short version, the verbal circuit uniting "I" and "you" is muddied. The effective opening remains, with the "too" of "I, too" implicitly invoking that ongoing conversation ("Yes, I know what you mean. I, too, . . ."). But then in mid-sentence the grammatical subject changes to the opaque "one," suggesting a settled universality: "one discovers in / it"—what "one" discovers sounds like what is present to be discovered. The three-line version ends by pronouncing a transcendent dogma; universal opinion has subsumed the enthusiastic, interested, seeking "you" of the long version.[3]

*

Moore's endings, happy or glum, do not fit neatly into the classroom. Getting through the poems assigned for class, covering the territory outlined on the syllabus—these are mere simulacra of completed actions. Teaching poetry, at best, activates open-ended processes that students can make into their own or can reject. Where Moore finds resolution, I hear the stresses of our contemporary pedagogic situation most strongly. Her earlier version details poetic excitement and asserts "these things are important not because a // high-sounding interpretation can be put upon them but because they are / useful" (266–67). No defense of teaching innovative poetry will amount to much if it cannot imagine such values. Having your hair stand on end can be, both in the short and in the long run, quite useful.

Moore's "genuine" and "useful" call up a basic structural opposition. Of course innovative poetry is useful in the classroom; let's not keep recycling the received idea that it is an obscure luxury. But the useful effects that Moore describes, the excitement innovative poetry can arouse in its readers—these immediacies are the results of innumerable processes through which poetic knowledge gets activated in individuals and in a community. Such conditions have to be reproduced to some extent in the classroom before the poetry will be of much use. But does being reproduced entail being the same? The sense that the teachable is always static is widespread; throughout the varieties of innovative poetry antagonism to academic routine is one constant: whatever the vectors claimed for genuine innovation, they all point away from the classroom.[4] An extreme version would be the claim that whatever can be taught is not genuine—a negative version of the trajectory Stein celebrated, from outlaw to classic.

Optimism of the pedagogic will asserts that with enough time, energy, tact, flexibility, any student can become receptive to any poetry, but it is hard to banish the suspicion (courtesy of the pessimism of the experiential intellect) that the gradient of receptiveness can be steep, and the best use of resources is to teach those who are already primed with some interest in the matter. But allowing this (extremely reasonable) suspicion its full rein leads to the conclusion that poetry is not for everyone and is, in fact, a specialty, with innovative poetry a sub-specialty, so why not narrow the focus of the old double imperative? If poetry should delight and instruct, let that happen where it wants to; stop hoping general instruction can create universal poetic delight. To quote two of my favorite poets: "Poetry, as other object matter, is after all for interested people" (Zukofsky, *Complete Short Poetry*, ix); "Nobody should experience anything they don't need to, and if they don't need poetry bully for them" (O'Hara, 498). But then again, there are innumerable places in the work of both of these poets that affirm the pleasures and importance of poetry; those two quotes, in fact, are taken from a textbook on poetry and a manifesto. If poetry is for those who are already interested, where did that interest originally come from? If we push skepticism of teaching to an extreme, we get the conclusion that readers of poetry are born, not made.

Poems overwhelm classroom schedules: they need attention, discussion, sounding out, comparison to other poems, historical contextualization. Meanwhile the minutes have elapsed and we haven't gotten to Ashbery. Read *The Tennis Court Oath* and *Girls on the Run* for Monday. This is a standard academic narrative; the standard remedy is abbreviation. *Tender Buttons* becomes one or two of the shorter pieces out of 108 and these few become not

> Suppose An Eyes
> Suppose it is within a gate which open is open at the hour of closing summer that is to say it is so.
> All the seats are needing blackening. A white dress is in sign. A soldier a real soldier has a worn lace of different sizes that is to say if he can read, if he can read he is a size to show shutting up twenty-four.
> Go red go red, laugh white.
> Suppose a collapse in rubbed purr, in rubbed purr get.
> Little sales ladies little sales ladies little saddles of mutton.
> Little sales of leather and such beautiful beautiful, beautiful beautiful. (Stein, *GS I*, 475)

but a literary version of Cubist portraiture, with some sentences from "Portraits and Repetition" receiving notice, as well as issues of domestic space and lesbian erotics versus surveillance.

An opposing impulse is to insist that each poem be actually read, those exact words and contours: experience, not knowledge, is the goal. Basil Bunting, teaching late in life, went for this, in a kind of despair. As the anecdote is told,[5] he grew tired of talking about poetry, and would simply read; occasionally, trying to awaken the cadence-deprived ears of his students, he would play a record of the Goldberg Variations.

But if there is a Gordian knot of logistics involved in trying to transmit context, history, poetic literacy in one immediately perceived present, in trying to teach an ear for poetry, then John Cage's work aims to cut through such a knot. Reading and writing change from terminally encumbered demonstrations of competence or failure into happy activities where perception and knowledge coincide. Like Bunting playing Bach, the goal is experience; but unlike Bunting, the difficulties in forming aesthetic judgment seem to have vanished.

In conversation with Cage, Joan Retallack tells of getting her students to write down a question and a statement independently. She then shuffles the two batches and asks students to pick a question and an answer randomly. "The first reads the question at the top of her pile, the second reads the statement '*as if*' it were the answer; and of course it *is* the answer. My students are always amazed" (*Musicage*, 53). This procedure gives students "a sense of trust in *their* ability . . . to make meaning." Meaning is no longer external, lodged in the writer's intention and skill; it does not entail learning a body of prior work, or practicing and mastering specific procedures. Instead, meaning results immediately from open attention. The angst of logistics, reading lists, the impossible Parnassus of taste and flexible literary judgment—all this disappears in the present moment of the students' democratic, empowering, unjudged experience.

There is no longer any charged boundary between art and world: both are made of the same materials. Cage, still in conversation with Retallack, speaks of coming out of a Mark Tobey show: "I was waiting for the bus and I happened to look at the pavement I was standing on and I couldn't tell the difference between that and the Tobey. Or I had the same pleasure looking at the pavement" (54).

Perception is knowledge (and perfect aesthetic taste). The contrast with Pound is clear. Pound loathed poetic ignorance. London poetasters were like children who hear a concert pianist then immediately try to give a concert themselves: "the ordinary piano teacher spends more thought on the art of music than does the average 'poet' on the art of poetry" (*Prose*, 31). At fifteen, Pound said he would know more about poetry by the age of thirty than anyone else. Olson takes the imperative to knowledge in a slightly different direction: it is not the poetic field that the poet needs to master directly, but the material-historical world, and through that, the poetic. But the ground of poetry is still the same as Pound's: expertise.

> Best thing to do is *to dig one thing or place or man* until yourself know more abt that than is possible to any other man. It doesn't matter whether it's Barbed Wire or Pemmican or Paterson or Iowa. But *exhaust* it. Saturate it. Beat it.
> And then U KNOW everything else very fast: one saturation job (it might take 14 years). And you're in,
> forever.
> (Olson, *Prose*, 306–7)

While some of Pound's pronouncements seem to make learning potentially available to all, the sense of the exceptional, the inner sanctum of expertise—"And you're in, / forever"—eventually predominates, as in Pound's last characterization of *The Cantos* as "the great ball of crystal" (809). The line between inside and outside is sharply drawn. As enabling as senses of being "in" are for those students who experience them, the alienation for those on the outside is just as strong.

The contrast between the Pound-Olson-Bunting tradition and a Cagean poetics is blatant; but a Cage procedural work can be as baffling to students as Pound or Olson. In both cases work has to be done to connect with the words, animate and inter-animate them. The student has to identify to some extent as an artist, or at least have become curious about the enterprise of art.

Without such prior or emergent identification with art, the following two items are equally closed. The first is a line from Cage's "Writing through the Cantos"; the second is the lines in *The Cantos* themselves from which Cage derived his line:

Public destrOyed de vaUx 32 millioN exhumeD with
("Writing Through the Cantos," 28)

———

as I recall it there was no such thing as public
opinion (Vienna)
Metternich destroyed Maria Theresa. Maremma
Hroosia,
"tranne nella casa del re"
B. Mussolini
to some chap from Predappio
not yet, so far as I know, written down.
Lugubrious Knole,
Capture of Warsaw
Paris, at Palais Royal
"where they are rather badly off for society"
de Vaux talked of nothing but bullfights
not only 32 million subjects, but
pretend to govern all Europe
That he (the Archbishop) had not quite the grasp
St Leu, Beauharnais, Tascher
given to M's'lle Hortense by the Citizen Talleyrand
"a sapphire, and a bit of the cross
true cross, exhumed with Charlemagne's skeleton. (753–54)

To read—or better, to *want* to read—either of these passages, one needs to know something of the aesthetics that motivated the procedures that produced the words. This means giving some sense of the careers and art narratives involved. Students do want to learn things, and narratives about other people's lives are easily learnable. Cage says that all that is necessary to do is to "brush information against information" (*Musicage*, 54)—but what makes information *information*? Certainly the more one knows, the more textured and connected the information. At best, more knowledge means better focus, sharper excitement. But of course, the terms make a kind of Möebius strip: better focus and the excitement necessary to fuel complex perceiving are prerequisites, so to speak, for activating more knowledge.

Cage continually urges his listeners and readers to pay attention to all parts of their environments equally, not valuing any one part over another, but in fact his own procedures stay firmly loyal to friends and admirable ancestors: Pound, Duchamp, Joyce, Thoreau, et al. Cagean procedures do not preclude using everyday materials, but their poethical[6] approach is thoroughly an aesthetic endeavor. Cage's practice of non-intentionality developed in a sophisticated art environment, and while the results were addressed to any and everyone, they were performed, displayed, published in sophisticated venues. In no way am I criticizing this as "elitist." But I am underlining his devotion to art and the happy success and energy that buoyed it. Cage's activities are those of a most blissful artist. He imports information (stuff, material, charismatic art) into his work effortlessly, seemingly duty-free; but the direction is from world to work. Cagean perception is grounded in art, its ethos and its histories. This is clear in the continuation of the anecdote of his seeing the sidewalk after leaving the Tobey exhibit. While he "had the same pleasure looking at the pavement" as at the paintings, he first had to have seen the paintings. "And yet I was, I was determined—I was very poor at the time—and I was determined to buy the Tobey, on the installment plan, which I did. I paid five dollars a week for about two years. And yet I had learned from Tobey himself, and then from his painting, that every place you look is the same thing. You don't really need the Tobey (*laughs*). But you need it to tell you that I guess" (*Musicage*, 108). The social and aesthetic ramifications are very different, but Cage's work in fact resembles Pound's in that both are predicated on a canon of artistic values. Cage, though, is not invested in major form—in hierarchy—the way Pound is, so Cage is able to enjoy changing his mind.

To return to Berrigan. One has to invest quite a bit of time to hear the unpredictability of his tonal changes. Reading his work widely helps, as well as knowing something of his doings (the written record and the oral teaching). Take, for instance, his fake interview with John Cage. From our twenty-first-century vantage, it has an excitingly preposterous edge, at times cringe-inducing. For example, "Cage" speaking of his mother says: "She lay on top of me when I was tied to the bed. She writes me all the time begging me to return. Why do we have to speak of my mother?" (Berrigan, "Interview"). But at the time (1966) the interview was taken at face value by, among other jurors, Susan Sontag, and won a thousand-dollar prize. When Cage was told of the hoax, his response was to ask if Berrigan was "for me or against me" (Berrigan, *Collected Poems*, 719–20). That's a request for basic information; but Berrigan's ironic intentions often evade such basics.

An early version (1970) of "With / daring" lacked its final stanza; it's a big difference:

With
daring
and
strength
men
like
Pollock,
de Kooning,
Tobey,
Rothko,
Smith
and
Kline
filled
their
work
with
the
drama,
anger,
pain,
and
confusion
of
contemporary
life. (Berrigan, *Collected Poems*, 195–96)

—especially when placed next to other word-a-line pieces, which clearly amounted to lineated prose; for example, this clinical description of sexual arousal:

Before
the
orgasmic
platform
in
the
outer
third
of
the

vagina
develops
sufficiently [. . .] (194)

With such examples in my head, I couldn't help sensing that in "With / daring" Berrigan was, as he often did, writing wrong. We are meant to hear this as sententious art prose. The one word a line rubs it in our ears.

But the later version—the poem ending with the set-off stanza "Just / like / me" that my student wrote about—performs a complex twist via the addition of those three lines: they allow for both sarcastic critique and earnest assertion. If Berrigan didn't aspire to a serious poetic vantage point on the pain and confusion of the present, no one did. So he *was* like Pollock, Kline, and Tobey, and so the student was quite right to read the whole poem unironically. Back then, in the midst of that class, I was sorry that the student didn't catch Berrigan's ventriloquy/critique of art-speak; but now I am glad the student showed me the genuineness of the poem's statement.

The final three lines added on—"Just / like / me."—enact a topos of proud humility. What had been the entire poem is now the first "verse paragraph"; it is still the same long drip of words, but a big gulf in social tone has been established, by contrast. "With / daring / and / strength," etc., is now heard as the lofty puffery that needs to exist for serious investment to occur. The paintings of Tobey, Pollock, and de Kooning are serious financial objects. But when the conclusion is added, suddenly we have a jejune outsider. A twelve-year-old could be talking.

But the poem is now putting the two together: by presenting the financial-aesthetic world for critique, one becomes capable of entering it. The poem is now saying, By the concentrated deadpan sarcasm of my utterance, I am as serious as these masters who have been translated into the empyrean of capital. Tobey, Pollock, and de Kooning, the famous and the dead, can no longer avoid such descriptions, which I can mock, distilling the historical distances between them and me into a few banalities, so painful in their verbal devaluation, and by deftly conveying this pain-at-a-distance I *am* just like them: one of the big ones.

Have "the / drama, / anger, / pain, / and / confusion / of / everyday / life" been overcome? Yes, by this very high humor. But also, no: the poem sharply registers the distance between museum/high-end gallery world (where heroic stories are expensively wafted onto pristine walls) and the St. Mark's poetry world (where the poet has to do all the work of registering and propagating his own aesthetic success on a postcard[7] circulating beneath the museum's radar).

Not to draw too taut a distinction here: the postcard series is now a recognized high-art strategy; Berrigan had detailed connections with the New York art scene. And with the poem appearing in the elegant 700-page University of

California Press edition of his *Collected Poems*, such questions are, at least for the moment, moot.

In another postcard poem, Berrigan shows himself tasting worldly success, but in a number of ways he undercuts this:

> *Eureka!*
>
> I left the bookstore stunned & giggling
> between Baudelaire & Betjeman my books
> in print took up nearly a foot. —I
> walked several blocks to my car—
> glowing at having reduced the competition,
> not to mention John Ashbery & John Berryman,
> after all, how many Johns does one poem need?,
> to mere, forlorn, lonely manifestations
> of the lame, the limp, the loud, and one Knight. —
> got in, put it in reverse, and backed up
>   a block and ½. I was home. Odd
> having a car in Manhattan! Now home,
> stretched out on the bed, I'm working on #233
> of my next work, "500 American Postcards."
> Now I've stopped, to do this one, #13 today!
> Oops! Wait a minute. Will this fit on a
>   Postcard? Joseph Conrad, here I come ▲ Ted Berrigan 4 Apr 1982
> (*Sunlight*, n.p.)

This poem, not included in the 2005 *Collected Poems*, is fascinating. "*Eureka!*" is typical of the way Berrigan ended up working, with personal life and public poetics impossible to distinguish. In the St. Mark's Poetry Project scene, he became the embodiment of poetic knowledge, a kind of modern Samuel Johnson modeling a poetic literacy that was not so much anti-academic as exo-academic. That this poem is printed in a facsimile of his handwriting is an emblem of his literary immediacy (most of the other poems in *Sunlight* are typeset).

"*Eureka!*" is a funny poem, in both senses. Berrigan's literary triumphalism—a foot of books in the St. Mark's Bookshop, an ongoing project, utopic productivity (thirteen poems a day)—collides against the "Oops!" which the picayune reality of pen on paper triggers. The staged megalomania is then allowed to take over again: this thin postcard-poem threatens to shoulder Conrad off the shelves.

There are nests of irony here. Berrigan is teasing himself, but under the cover of comedy, taking pride not just in the success of what he has written but also in the panache of the poem he is now writing. It's as if his pen inscribing the postcard is simultaneously—magically—placing that writing on the shelves. He very much wants to be a player on major shelves, taking his place beside Baudelaire.

The inclusion of Ashbery in the hosts of the beaten competition is typical of Berrigan's shifting irony. Throughout Berrigan's work it's a given that Ashbery and, even more so, O'Hara, are unquestionable masters. How is this information transmitted? You have to know. How do you get to know? In my case it was by reading what he wrote and by social contacts—by following both written and oral traditions.

On occasion Berrigan's work foregrounds the aggression of literary judgment. The goofy and more or less good-humored quality of "*Eureka!*" vanishes at the lines castigating the "mere, forlorn, lonely manifestations / of the lame, the limp, the loud," which is as aggressive as anything in *The Dunciad*. Part of Berrigan's appeal comes from making his aggression funny, but it's not just funny:

> Poem
> for Larry Fagin
>
> You are lovely.
> I am lame. (Berrigan, *Collected Poems*, 329)

These words could read (straight) as a note of abject apology. However, once Berrigan's deadpan subject switching is admitted as a poetic device, the poem becomes a minimalist poetic minefield. Cage's question about Berrigan's fake interview comes to mind: is Berrigan for or against the you? It could be a tiny homage and then again it could be a nugatory anti-gift. It could refer to some third and fourth parties, an in-joke Berrigan is sharing with Fagin. Biographical reference tends to fall away, leaving the imbalance between the "I" and the "you" as emblematic of a poetic fact: some poetry is lovely, some is lame, a fearsome, crucial perception for ambitious art.

A poem is concentrated time, variously activated. There is the accessibility of immediate perception, but medium and long-range consequences of literary and social history sound in the most immediate of poems. One can present this as poetic history, as cultural studies, as developing an ear. In all cases there's a ratio of what the students can use immediately and what may not be useful for days or years. Neither the mercurial aspect of fashion nor the scarifying eternity of Parnassus can be left out. "It is necessary to be absolutely modern," writeth Rimbaud, in the dawn of avant-garde alienation (89). Cage's motto, "our ears are open," does not bypass these temporal, perceptible, historical processes: sound is immediate, and the various personal and social long histories begin unfolding immediately as well.

The individual poet's relationship with the times animates Berrigan's poems: or say, rather, that the real thing, the genuine, the poem, is time-proof. "*Eureka!*" is a comic enactment of Eliot's "Tradition and the Individual Talent," shouldering its way onto the "ideal order" of the bookstore shelf. Berrigan wasn't interested in Eliot's canon, but he was interested in being in his own canon, and his place in that canon was not something that slipped his mind when he wrote.

Admitting poetic judgment is akin to admitting aesthetic falsifiability, insisting that, even though poetry can use any material and any stance, there are uses that aren't very interesting. Allowing negative judgments is to admit to taste—taste as something simultaneously immediate and long range. As Berrigan's two-line poem puts it: "It is important to keep old hat / in secret closet" (*Collected Poems*, 351). That it's obvious doesn't detract from its astringence.

But what does it say to students? What does Berrigan's deployment of the language of Charlie Chan sound like? Does it sound simply offensive? Can it be heard as taking the aggressive thrust of stereotype and flipping it in a more capricious direction?

Students don't yet know which hats are new and which are old; in fact, many are enthusiastic about slightly used hats—which is fine. What did Hegel say? All hats are new at dawn?

Delight instructs.[8]

3
Copying Whitman

A few times I've turned into an anti-Bartleby of sorts and typed out the work of other writers. I do it both for pleasure and to practice, somehow or other, the craft. In this case I opened up the Library of America *Whitman* in the middle and started typing the last section of "Passage to India," a poem I hadn't read for decades.

At least it was typing practice, which I always need. I have a fantasy of typing quickly, effortlessly, with the fluency of Kerouac (120 wpm), the impossible ego-ideal. To have no conscious interference, but simply to allow the impulse to be articulated in sequentially appearing letters on the screen, the words gathering to say what they already, unbeknownst to me before that extending moment, actually are saying—the analogy is with music, feeling it under your fingers as you're hearing it.

The scratchier truth is that, after all these years, I'm a fairly lousy typist, better than I was back before there were computers, but hardly reaching mediocrity in my better stretches. This forces me to think and rethink, assert and reframe, typing a few strokes then lifting my fingers off the keys as I stare at the cursor blinking from its little rut of error. It's a toss-up whether I then abandon incipient formations whose beginnings lie on the screen in mistyped botches, or delete a bit, back up, and soldier on. The overall activity of my typing/writing is a mix of keystrokes, staring, thinking, deleting, starting over, getting frustrated, giving up, printing up the offending draft onto the distancing paper, which I later hover over with a pencil or pen, before going back to the keyboard.

It strikes me that such a practice is closer to Neal Cassady than to Kerouac. Cassady, the story goes, would never correct typos, but instead change what he was writing to match the typed letter. It's not an account that makes perfect sense, but schematically it makes for a useful pairing: at one end Kerouac the fluent typist, keystrokes blurring into instant transcription, and at the other, lunging, stuttering, each crashing keystroke an intention-twisting blow, Cassady. I don't give over my initiative to typos to that extent, but my spotty typing must be a formative cause of what I write (of what gets written).

Beyond this literal (letteral) level, typing out the work of others is a kind of old-fashioned compositional practice borrowed from painting, where it used to be a standard learning tool. I have occasionally seen people in the more relaxed museums with their easels, copying.

I wouldn't have thought of applying such an exercise to writing except that I read somewhere that Robert Louis Stevenson, in the limbo between rejecting the family business (lighthouse lenses) and becoming an author, copied out passages from writers he admired. In a commonsense way, this sounds hopeless. Yes, copying is writing in the purely physical sense, but isn't it exactly *not* writing in the sense of writing something new?

Stevenson wanted to *be a writer* (to be the originator of words typesetters would then set up, printers then make copies of, people then read). He didn't want to merely (physically) *write*.

Copying has drastically different imports. It is drudgery: think of the outsourced keystrokes that underlie much published writing. Not knowing the language being typed, some say, makes for faster, more accurate typing, which in turn makes for cheaper commodity costs. Knowing what you're copying can make it worse, as Joyce makes clear with Farrington, the copyist from *Dubliners* ("Counterparts"). First, via the copyist's slow attention (he really needs a drink), we get a glimpse of some of textuality's little pleasures:

"The man returned to the lower office and sat down again at his desk. He stared intently at the incomplete phrase: In no case shall the said Bernard Bodley be . . . and thought how strange it was that the last three words began with the same letter."

But quickly the onus of the business reasserts itself:

"The chief clerk began to hurry Miss Parker, saying she would never have the letters typed in time for post. [Sentences spelling this out.] . . . His body ached to do something, to rush out and revel in violence" (Joyce, 86).

Alienated copying is a specter whose all-too-physical manifestations (ennui, rage, carpal tunnel) the contemporary environment for writing is designed to banish, thoroughly and at the smallest level. The cut and paste functions in word processing, macros, the basic correctability of computer files, not to mention optical character recognition (OCR) programs—but these niceties do little against the onslaught of the endless keystrokes.

At another extreme of copying is the reproduction of sacred text, where, in theory, the copyist is transmitting and thus sharing the verbal embodiment of divine power.

An intriguing distinction here comes from Paul Gehl, who contrasts "orthodoxy" and "orthopraxis" (as related by historian of rhetoric Mary Carruthers in *The Craft of Thought*). Orthodox believers seek orthodoxy, which is "to reproduce the experience of learning from the teacher, whose teaching lives on in authentic texts" (1)—letter-perfect copying of the Torah, say. With orthopraxis, on the other hand, the believer wants "to achieve an immanent experience of the divine equivalent to that of the founder, usually by following a devotional practice presumed to be similar." Carruthers goes on to elaborate the subtle interplay of orthodoxy and orthopraxis, noting that they "often co-exist in the same religion." But we can also use these notions more bluntly so that they become portable emblems of basic binaries: spirit/letter, writing/copying, innovation/convention, new/settled.

When we move from religion to art, we can see that orthodoxy with its stability and familiarity is often exactly what needs to be overcome to achieve orthopraxis. Make It New. But then again, orthopraxis is firmly attached, Möbius-strip fashion, to orthodoxy. When Make It New becomes the orthodoxy, the orthopractic need is to make Make It New new.

Stevenson could be imagined as engaged primarily in an orthodox pursuit when he was copying something out. He was getting the words right, accurately reproducing a bit of stylistic doctrine. But he was also learning a craft via rehearsal of some of its parts, learning scales, a passage, a complete mood—in other words, hoping that orthodox might become orthopractic, that he would make direct contact with the authorial spirit whose letters he was reproducing.

I write you, in some backward-and-forward-moving transitive sense, with subject and object changing roles. What had been *You write, I copy* becomes *I copy out your writing* becomes *I copy you writing* becomes *I write you* which then reads *I write.*

Whitman was my first inkling of writing, age twelve. Thus for me, since bodily experience of words is never fully erasable, Whitman is, among other things, perpetually adolescent. And thus, according to my idiosyncratic use of the term, romantic. Romantic = adolescent, semantically and historically promiscuous, impervious to strict definition, its always-ersatz appeal ever rediscovered (by adolescents and the young at heart). To avoid unuseful ambiguity here, I should say that this is not a putdown but a friendly expansion of the job description.

While a case can be made for Whitman as a romantic poet in the standard literary sense (identification with the world; expanded class sympathy; political urgency of self-expression), as likely a case can be made for him as a modernist (thoroughgoing formal iconoclasm; his claim that *Leaves of Grass* is "experimental" [Whitman, 657]). But categorizing such a sui generis writer is no easy matter—and certainly not to be accomplished by such a piece as this. No, the romanticism in what follows lies in its refusal of critical distance. While I copy

Whitman I am enacting his claims of immediacy by replacing them with mine. Whitman repeatedly claims that he is present in his writing; here I am claiming that, copying his words, I am writing them. Thus, in what follows, I will mostly avoid quotation marks around words that Whitman originally wrote.

For my use of *romantic* here, I can only offer one precedent, and that far-fetched: Stendhal, when he wrote "Moliére was romantic in 1670, because the court was full of Orontes and the châteaus in the provinces were full of very discontented Alcestes. Actually, ALL GREAT WRITERS WERE THE ROMANTICS OF THEIR DAY" (Stendhal, 145). Romantic, modernist, avant-garde, adolescent—some names for Baudelaire's eternally present new (Baudelaire, 102–8).[1]

What follows is what happened when I typed some half-good thing—the last section of Whitman's "Passage to India"—from a writer I care about permanently.

I opened the Whitman in the middle without thinking, as a form of *sortes Virgilianae* (Virgilian lots, making a book such as the *Aeneid* or, later, the Bible prophetic when opened at random: *sortes Whitmani*).

Come to think of it, such a procedure splits the difference between orthodoxy (stable text, printed book, authoritative edition) and orthopraxis (need for the new, accurately open to the present).

What follows is that typing, which I have edited (interrupting the interruptions, retyping the thinking and rethinking the retyping), aiming for the whole flavor of reading and writing mixing. Both are irreplaceable motions of any transcription.

What of the *trans* in transcription? Something is going between things, but what, and what about the between? Re-inscribing goes across what? Doesn't the *trans* invoke some continuum, some condition bordering both things but common to neither? Neither reading nor writing, that is. (And not wreading either.)

Now to type out the whole thing. Section 9 of "Passage to India": type the monstrous koan.

> Passage to more than India!
> are thy wings plumed indeed for such far flights?
> O soul, voyagest thou indeed on voyages like these?
> Voyagest thou indeed on voyages
> nobody but Whitman.
>
> Whitman: Vietnam. Vietnam: Whitman. Whitnam. Vietman.
> Disportest thou in places like these? voyagest thou indeed on voyages
>   like these?

Wait, I got it wrong. It's not *these*, but *those*:
O soul, voyagest thou indeed on voyages like those?

Those not *these*, means it's not here, not felt, not a live report. O soul, voyagest thou indeed on voyages like those means the voyages are over: he's just thinking about feeling it. Lots of poetry is like that. Thinking about feeling something.

But it's not as if feelings are transparent. For instance, why, copying Whitman, am I suddenly conscious of the desire to read those old compilations. Scalinger, Quintilian. Why? Why set up those antique spaces? If you copy *those* enough times will it become *these*?
It's a plan, if not a theory.

Soundest below the Sanscrit [sans crit, *poésie pure*] [—but who doesn't, at some level, *hate* puns?], and the Vedas?
Then have thy bent unleash'd.

Type that to get into head:

Then have thy bent unleash'd.
Then have thy bent unleash'd.
Then have thy bent unleash'd.
Then have thy bent unleash'd.

Then have thy bent unbent—
Then have thy bent unleash'd.
Thy bent, have unleash'd.
Then have, then have.

Unlearn'd, thy bent has thee.
Learn thy bent.
Learn, unlearn, unleash.
Unleash'd when unlearn'd.

Learn thy bent lest thy leash stay taut. True enough. Type that into head.

Whitman, walking Basket, lets him off his leash. The large poodle immediately runs away. Stein, furious, has to get another Basket, then another, and another. (See the biographies.) All of this is in the continuous present, but still, it gets *annoying* when it happens over and over and *over* . . .

Passage to you, your shores, ye aged fierce enigmas!
Passage to you, to mastership of you. Whitman's writing during the not-

yet-finished transition from slavery to post-slavery. Think of other aimless gestures of reconciliation. Todorov, the love the conqueror must feel for the conquered. Rape, conquest, pillage as history's Happily Ever After, dear dear Other, will we ever reach post-slavery?

Passage to more than Whitman's India.
Passage to Afghanistan. A package from Pakistan: for you.

Passage to you, to mastership of you, ye strangling problems! Ye fucking incompetent parallel parkers taking up two spaces! Ye goddamn Verizon voice-outsourcing, throwing up verbal baffles from India under the nom de voix of Frank Fernandez!
Passage to India!
Passage to you, to mastership of you, ye strangling problems!
You, strew'd with the wrecks of skeletons, that, living, never reach'd you.
Actual other dead bodies, lives, trained senses, shortcuts, loving aspirations and just shouldering the load, dig the graves and you have to find someplace to put the dirt, the tree names of streets to remind the supposed you of home. Actually dead. Got nowhere.

Passage to more than India!
O secret of the earth and sky!
Of you O waters of the sea! O winding creeks and rivers!
Whitman the materialist!
all water is actually in the end wet
Of you O woods and fields! of you strong mountains of my land!
Whitman the nothing-but-autobiographer. Specific woods and fields
Of you O prairies! of you gray rocks!
O morning red! O clouds! O rain and snows!

Sometimes it's Of, sometimes it's O.
When the secret is most salient, it's Of. When the surface sense is, it's O.

O day and night, passage to you!
O sun and moon and all you stars! Sirius and Jupiter!
Passage to you!

Passage, immediate passage! the blood burns in my veins!
We leave the vocative, now it's a demand for immediate access. Give me my ticket. My language is my credit card. My language is worth the world. Whitman is imperialist, but he's writing with his body again. That's why you've got to hand it to him. But, still, we each only get one body.

Away O soul! hoist instantly the anchor!
Consider instantly Whitman and word order.
What is problem his?

Cut the hawsers—haul out—shake out every sail!
Have we not stood here like trees in the ground long enough?

In 1878, about ten years after "Passage to India," Whitman wrote "Thoughts Under An Oak—A Dream" (816): *June 2.*—This is the fourth day of a dark northeast storm, wind and rain. . . . I have now enter'd on my 60th year. Every day of the storm, protected by overshoes and a waterproof blanket, I regularly come down to the pond, and ensconce myself under the lee of the great oak; I am here now writing these lines. . . . Seated here in solitude I have been musing over my life—connecting events, dates, as links of a chain, neither sadly nor cheerily, but somehow, to-day here under the oak, in the rain, in an unusually matter-of-fact spirit.

But my great oak—sturdy, vital, green—five feet thick at the butt. I sit a great deal near or under him. Then the tulip tree near by—the Apollo of the woods—tall and graceful, yet robust and sinewy, inimitable in hang of foliage and throwing-out of limb; as if the beauteous, vital, leafy creature could walk, if it only would. (I had a sort of dream-trance the other day, in which I saw my favorite trees step out and promenade up, down and around, very curiously—with a whisper from one, leaning down as he pass'd me, We do all this on the present occasion, exceptionally, just for you.)

Have we not stood here in the ground like trees long enough?
Have we not grovel'd here long enough, eating and drinking like mere
brutes?
But has Whitman not been the poet of happy eating and drinking?

Have we not darken'd and dazed ourselves with books long enough?
Sail forth—steer for the deep waters only,

Reckless O soul, exploring, I with thee, and thou with me,
For we are bound where mariner has not yet dared to go,

or as it is said now on the reruns
to boldly go where no man has gone before

and we will risk the ship, ourselves, and all—even the ratings
because *all* literature is reruns eventually!

O my brave soul!
O farther farther sail!

O daring joy, but safe! are they not all the seas of God?
O farther, farther, farther sail!

So we reach bombast at the end, bombs bursting in air still the national pastime. Jets drones smart payloads—what are a few civilians between allies?—cheaper than ground forces, and no local casualties filtering back to the withering hometown papers

References

Baudelaire, Charles, "The Painter of Modern Life," in *Modernism: An Anthology of Sources and Documents*, edited by Vassiliki Kolocotroni, Jane Goldman, and Olga Taxidou, 102–8. Chicago: The University of Chicago Press, 1998.

Carruthers. Mary, *The Craft of Thought*. Cambridge: Cambridge University Press, 1998.

Joyce, James, *Dubliners*. New York: Penguin, 1993.

Perelman, Bob, "That Deep Romantic Chasm," a review essay on Jeffrey Robinson's *Unfettering Poetry*, in European Romantic Review 22.1 (February 2011).

Stendhal, *Racine and Shakespeare*, translated by Guy Daniels. New York: Crowell-Collier Press, 1962.

Whitman, Walt, *Walt Whitman: Poetry and Prose*. New York: Library of America, 1982.

4
Delivering Difficult News

Stephen Colbert [*at his main desk*]: Welcome back, everybody. My guest tonight has a new book called *Seven American Deaths and Disasters*. Hey! Seven's my lucky number! Please welcome Kenneth Goldsmith.

This is the beginning of the transcription I made in July 2014 of an Internet clip of Kenneth Goldsmith appearing on *The Colbert Report*. The firestorm surrounding Goldsmith's performance of "The Body of Michael Brown" in 2015 casts an unavoidably ironic light on what follows here, and I supply a brief coda reflecting on this.

The six-minute conversation, originally broadcast on July 23, 2013, contains a number of incommensurate situations: conceptual poet who skewers authenticity meets mainstream broadcaster with his own trickster agenda; avant-garde transgressor-poet appears on mainstream talk show to hawk his new book; talk-show comedian maneuvers avant-garde transgressor into asserting a Wordsworthian poetics of speech as well as the moral imperative of poetic witness; the rhythms of public entertainment talk are forced to share air time with the strikingly distinct rhythms of poetry. These are compressed descriptions of what I trust will become manifest via my transcript and comments. Ultimately, I am suggesting we see Goldsmith and Colbert as enacting a comic, serious debate on how art can best face the glare of the present.

My transcript, in boldface, is in part documentary: this is what Goldsmith and Colbert said to one another, with pauses, half-words, and some cross talk omitted. But verbal transcription cannot catch the assertions and transactions that take place via the tones and micro-rhythms of conversation and via costume, posture, and gesture, though to a close observer these things say at least as much as the explicit words. Here, my bracketed additions, also in boldface, will be an attempt to say what the conversation looks like and sounds like, and what it feels like is happening.

To the reader who can watch the clip over the Internet, I'm asking for corroboration: in the very beginning of the segment, doesn't it not sound like Goldsmith is trying to change the agenda, and that Colbert has momentarily stopped speaking in persona? For those without access to the clip, the following is meant as a script with stage directions. It is realist to an extent—based on a true story, as they say—but at the same time it is an investigative allegory of poetics, in the form of a masque with simplified figures: KG (Poet) and C (Broadcaster). I should emphasize that KG and C refer only to the on-screen protagonists of the six-minute conversation; they are to be distinguished from the off-screen persons Kenneth Goldsmith and Stephen Colbert. The readers of this script are invited to activate their mental theater and watch poetry in action.

I will be interrupting the script, turning off the boldface to offer what I will call comps. In the real estate world a comp indicates a comparison where there is at least one element in common, even if much else is quite different. In the case of this script, ultimately there are no good comps—Goldsmith appearing on *Colbert* is a one-of-a-kind situation—but as an instance of mainstream-media-asking-scandalous-artist-for-an-explanation, their conversation can be comped to Mike Wallace grilling William Carlos Williams in Book 5 of *Paterson*. And Williams as a documentary poet (e.g., the Marcia Nardi letters in *Paterson* Books 1 and 2) is an obvious comp to Goldsmith, though a more frequent comp is the Reznikoff of *Testimony*. But then again the breadth of Goldsmith's public reach (from *Colbert* to the White House) suggests Stein of the thirties as a better comp than either Williams or Reznikoff.

As will be evident, my comps are interruptive, and often quite speculative. It is good to remember that while these comps come from my stopping the flow of the script and comparing things, the speakers had to be continuously performative. The boldface of the script is a reminder of how rigorously the conversation had to enact the present tense: it was six-plus minutes of airtime on *Colbert* where the bar was set high: no wasted half-seconds, things must be presented clearly and at the same time made comic. Consider how briskly C's opening salvo, quoted above, carries out both tasks. In between naming topic and guest, C's manic Colbert persona pops up and makes itself perfectly audible: "My guest tonight has a new book called *Seven American Deaths and Disasters* [topic]. Hey! Seven's my lucky number [manic C interruption]! Please welcome Kenneth Goldsmith" [guest].

[C leaves main desk and runs across stage to the interview desk; as the camera follows him, it pans across KG sitting at one side of the desk. We see KG wearing a straw hat, solid pink blazer, pink-striped shirt, striped bowtie; his legs are crossed, revealing, above the black and white

saddle shoes, one red and one green sock. After the initial pan, a second shot settles on C and KG seated across from one another, and we see KG only from the waist up.]

C: Hey, Mr. Goldsmith, thank you for coming on.
KG: So glad to be here.
C [referencing KG's waist-up outfit]: Later we can play some *Dixieland jazz*, or churn some fresh *buttermilk ice cream* . . .

KG's whole ensemble down to the clashing socks signals an avant-garde/bohemian lineage (Mayakovsky's yellow shirt; Pound's green velvet pants), but its initial presentation flashes by quickly; the second shot, where we see KG with blazer, shirt, and bowtie as the sole costuming code, reinforces C's sudden recasting of KG in a parodically retro Americana frame. Thus the interview begins at an absurd slant—absurd for KG that is; buttermilk ice cream and Dixieland jazz are perfect props for C's hyper-conservative persona. It is a powerful comic maneuver: C begins by misidentifying KG, addressing him not as a major new poetry provocateur—which is of course why he is on the show—but as an example of Americana shtick, like some character in *The Music Man* who had wandered onto the wrong stage set.

KG: [smiling at C's gesture] . . . or recite some poetry.

KG deflects C's parodic frame and reasserts his position as a poet who is here to talk about his new book. By completing C's sentence with a third item of his own (Dixieland, buttermilk, poetry), KG enters C's frame on his own terms, equating poetic recitation to fresh buttermilk ice cream as an equally imaginary consolation.

C: We could. We could do that now.
KG: We could do it together.
C: Whaddaya got? Whaddaya want to start with?
KG: Oh . . . how about "Oh Susanna"?

When I first watched the clip this seemed very much like a rehearsed turn in the conversation and that a plan to recite Stephen Foster had been agreed on backstage. But Goldsmith, when I asked him, said it was spontaneous. In any event, the choice of "Oh Susanna" as the poetry to recite is apt both for C's parodic persona and for Goldsmith's poetic position, even though it means opposite things for the two. (Note my switch to Goldsmith; there will be more to follow about his poetic difference from the on-screen KG.)

Goldsmith is an artist with a highly visible, charged position that he has been presenting over the last two decades. As a leading exponent of conceptual poetry, and thus of provocation and a narrative of avant-garde poetic advance, he has repeatedly marked his separateness from many non-new poetic traits: creativity, inspiration, the recognizably "poetic." A corny old ditty like "Oh Susanna" makes a good stand-in for the naive assertions of presence that conceptual poetry defines itself against.

For C's persona, on the other hand, what better opportunity to enunciate his parodic hyper-conservatism than "Oh Susanna": an antebellum song obliquely celebrating plantation life and making something spritely and amusing out of slavery.

C: . . . [declaiming, emphasizing each syllable] Oh, don't you [KG points his index finger at C in approval, begins to recite along with C] cry for me [audience laughs with recognition] / I come from Alabama / With a banjo on my knee.

KG: Absolutely. It's a . . . [this is a gambit to return to the speech rhythms of conversation]

C: [overriding KG's gambit, continuing the poetic declamation] I had myself a dream last night, / when everything was still [KG stops trying to recite; rapidly, he swivels sideways to C, crossing his legs and resting a hand against his head, the ensemble of gestures polite but signaling a half-patient impatience, waiting out C's recitation]. / I dreamed that I saw my girl Susanne, / she was comin' round the hill. / Oh the buckwheat cake was in her mouth, / a tear was in her eye. / I said that I come from Dixieland, / Susanna don't you cry. [Audience whoops and cheers as the second stanza is completed.]

KG: You know it [i.e., you know this obscure other stanza; KG points his index finger at C, laughs]

Here, it is as if C becomes "the poet" in some old-fashioned sense. After the initial stanza KG seems to have heard enough. (And who could blame him? If you get invited onto *The Colbert Report* to discuss your new book you want to discuss it, not spend the finite seconds of airtime reciting Stephen Foster.) C, on the other hand, seems tinged with the oracular, fulfilling a ritual obligation to recite.

When I first watched the clip, I found the second stanza very odd (crying while holding a pancake in your mouth?); if KG didn't know it, I certainly didn't either and thought that C must be making it up without a break in the rhythm, which would have been an impressive bardic feat. But to my surprise, looking it up later, the words are Foster's.

C: You are the poet laureate of the Museum of Modern Art. You've got ten books of poetry; you teach writing at the University of Pennsylvania, and you've got a new book called . . . ***Seven American Deaths and Disasters.*** **[Holds up book] Did you write this?**

KG: Absolutely not. I never write any of my books. [audience laughs]

C: You didn't actually write this, you . . . ***collected*** **it?**

KG: I ***transcribed*** **it. [laughter]**

KG presents himself as provocateur, instigator of new turns in poetic history: conventional poetry is *written* by conventionally inspired poets; my work is premised on breaking these expectations: I didn't *write* this book, I *transcribed* it.

But six minutes of airtime doesn't allow for the presentation of the long-range complexities of Goldsmith's work: the acts of high art *impossibilitas*; uncreative writing; the indifference to content; the commitment to avant-garde provocation and excitement; the productively unstable position between the art world and the scene of innovative poetry—there is no time to mention any of this.

Provocation/unreadability: "You really don't need to read my books to get the idea of what they're like; you just need to know the general concept" ("Being Boring").

Provocation/excitement: *Day*—in which Goldsmith retyped the September 1, 2000, issue of the *New York Times* onto nine hundred pages of uniform type size—is, for most readers, unreadable. But for the writer (and the writerly reader) it is a portal to avant-garde excitement. Goldsmith describes the writing process: "If it could be considered text, I had to have it. Even if there was, say, an ad for a car, I took a magnifying glass and grabbed the text off the license plate. . . . it was the most fascinating writing process I've ever experienced" ("Boring"). Outraging the staid reader and exciting the writerly mind: they aren't always two sides of the same coin, but often enough they are.

Content as a matter of indifference: "Most of us spend hours each day shifting content into different containers. Some of us call this writing" ("Boring"). *Sports*, in which Goldsmith transcribes a broadcast of the Boston Red Sox playing the New York Yankees, is a good example of poetically indifferent content. One comp here would be Mallarmé's call for a book about nothing. The anthology *Against Expression* that Goldsmith co-edited with Craig Dworkin includes, in a related gesture, Mallarmé's "falsified writings on fashion" (374–79).

Differing histories of the art world and the innovative poetry world. In the (visual) art world, avant-garde scandal is pretty much a lost art; but imported into poetry it still has legs: "Art has long ceased to shock. . . . [T]he poetry world [is] so conservative, that we can still get people upset. . . . [Y]ou can still have a bit of a scandal" ("Kenneth Goldsmith in Conversation").

None of this is shown on-screen. The six minutes only allow for the KG we see in front of us, discussing this one book.

C: Because this book itself is actually transcriptions of real-time reporting of deaths and disasters, as they happened in the United States.
KG: Absolutely.
C: You start with JFK . . .
KG: Absolutely.
C: . . . and it's a little radio station in Dallas. [looks down at the page in question]
KG: KLIF.
C: KLIF, that's Dallas's news leader. And they are . . . it's just a morning in 1963 and they are talking about, Buy Hamm's beer, and you're going to want a nice turkey this Thanksgiving because we're talking November 22 here, and slowly it dawns on this guy that this little shooting downtown turned into one of our greatest national tragedies. Why did you want us to hear every word of this?

The off-screen Goldsmith could have supplied a provocative answer: you don't need to hear *any* of it, the particular words don't matter, you just have to know the idea of the piece. But the on-screen KG says something quite different.

KG: Well, because radio sounded so *different* back then than it does now. And that's what happens throughout the book: there are different eras in the last fifty years and every transcription has the mark of its own era on it. So this is a beautiful naive fantasy time that is punctuated by an assassination, or a shooting at that point, of a president. And it shatters the entire illusion of pre-Thanksgiving holidays.

Neither KG nor C is indifferent to the content of *Seven*; far from it. The unconsciously historical November 22, 1963, is the place where before and after meet, where the naive totality—"Hamm's beer and a nice turkey" in C's image, and "beautiful naive fantasy time" in KG's—is shattered by death and disaster.

And so these guys that are broadcasting this are not prepared in any way for this to happen. And suddenly they are improvising; they are riding by the seat of their pants and they're making it up as they go along. And this happens again and again and again. The World Trade Center chapter of the book is remarkable in this way because these guys are AM morning shock jock guys, who go into work that day figuring

they're going to do their shtick and then a plane goes into a building. They're stuck in the studio narrating something that they have no idea about. And this is incredible, how they have to make it up as they go along. What's amazing to me is that there have been hundreds of books written about 9/11 and to my knowledge nobody went to listen to the way those events were described.

C: Maybe they listened to it, but then, [slightly dropping his persona] they did additional work. [audience laughs]
KG: Well, that work . . . but, you see, artists are dumb.
C: Artists are dumb?
KG: Artists are dumb. We do things that you shouldn't do. What I'm doing is too *easy* for an investigative reporter to do. And by doing something that is *that* simple, we're uncovering something that no one else has actually ever thought of: the poetic quality of what was unfurling linguistically at that moment.

One comp for "the poetic quality of what was unfurling linguistically at that moment" would be Keats's "If poetry comes not as naturally as the leaves to a tree it had better not come at all" (Keats, "Letters to John Taylor," 536). Clearly KG is departing radically from Goldsmith's Duchampian position where, just as (advanced) art shouldn't be retinal, (advanced) texts needn't be read. In contrast, here KG focuses on how interesting *Seven*'s language is. The claim is that unaltered transcription, rather than a provocative aspect of uncreative writing, is a tool for displaying the natural eloquence of crisis-charged emergent popular language.

Perhaps KG's answer is so different from the *impossibilitas* of Goldsmith's prior projects because *Seven American Deaths and Disasters* is itself fundamentally different, containing seven short pieces that are quite readable, even engrossing.

In my initial compressed description I referred to KG proposing a Wordsworthian poetics, celebrating the power of everyday speech. But that comp only stretches so far: Wordsworth celebrated the long-lasting certainties of an unruffled rural language ("the real language of men") while deploring the daily shocks of news that bombarded urban centers: "For a multitude of causes . . . are now acting . . . to blunt the discriminating powers of the mind . . . reduc[ing] it to an almost savage torpor. . . . [T]hese causes [include] the great national events which are daily taking place, and the increasing accumulation of men in cities, where the uniformity of their occupations produces a craving for extraordinary incident which the rapid communication of intelligence hourly gratifies" (Wordsworth, "Preface to *Lyrical Ballads*," 484). Long story short, Wordsworth loathes news. KG, in contrast, is celebrating the real language of shocked broadcasters.

From this perspective, the deaths and disasters themselves have the quality of avant-garde breakthrough into a newly made present. Another comp for KG's praise of *Seven*'s language would be Stein's "Composition as Explanation." For Stein, the opposition is stale routine vs. the presentness of genius. Routine: "It [bad art; old-fashioned battle plans for World War I] is prepared and to that degree it is like all academies it is not a thing made by being made it is a thing prepared"; genius: "the few who make it as it is made" (*GS I*, 520). For KG, the routine is the shock jocks who are "going to do their shtick"; in contrast, the genius of the present is: "And suddenly they're improvising; they are riding by the seat of their pants and they're making it up as they go along."

C: You've got seven of these. It's the reporting on the death in real time of JFK, RFK, John Lennon, the Columbine tragedy, September 11, the Challenger disaster, and Michael Jackson's death. All these things, these seven different events, we know what's happening when we read this. These people who are just livin' their lives, thinking it's an ordinary day, don't know it's coming. [out of persona here] When I read this I feel like I am some sort of time-traveling aesthete, who is coming in to sample other people's shock and tragedy. I'm tasting their disbelief and the way it's changing them forever. I'm tasting it while I read it and it feels vampiric.
[slight pause]
KG: Umm.
C: Are you giving us a feast of other people's blood?
[audience and KG laugh briefly, thoughtfully]

KG is, here, far from the Duchampian provocateur and instigator of the new. Goldsmith's work has been premised on indifference to content and to readerly identification. For a reader expecting to identify with what is written, Goldsmith has insisted on a basic displacement: I didn't *write* this, I *transcribed* it; this isn't poetry, you're not reading my eloquent thoughts and feelings, this is a transcript of the Red Sox playing the Yankees. Such displacements have been, up to now, the point of Goldsmith's work.

And C is far from his persona, which is built on a continuous dismissal of trauma (evoking it only to run roughshod over it, e.g., "*Seven American Deaths and Disasters* . . . Seven's my lucky number!"). Here, he has dropped the persona and is speaking earnestly of the vivid pain the book causes him. He finds this pain morally suspect: he's not joking when he calls *Seven* vampiric.

At this point, both KG and C are admitting that the trauma presented by *Seven American Deaths and Disasters* is all too real, and both are contemplating it.

KG: These are the tragedies that mark our lives . . .

KG counters C's charge of vampirism: I am not a time-traveling vampire ransacking the *past* for aesthetic pleasure: these disasters are part of our *present* condition.

C: But must we go back to them? Why can't we just . . .
KG: We go back to them all the time. [Both voices are rising in pitch a bit, and the timbre and rhythm of exchange are more intense.]
C: . . . forget they happened, just forget they happened [dialing down the volume, fully back in persona], so we can move on to happy days again.
KG: [not joining C's switch back to the conversational, still intense] And then we have things like the Boston Marathon bombing, which could have made an eighth chapter in this book. They never go away.

In fact, three months before this interview, Colbert had presented an eloquent, though still quite funny, response to the Boston Marathon bombing (Colbert 4/16/13).

C: Of course they never go away, so what's the point of going back to look at them? There's always going to be another one for us to experience.
KG: Yeah, right. You know, why don't you write the next book of the next eight or nine of these that happen? This book can go on forever.
C: All right . . . [abruptly quite soft, acting out a faux-therapy mode] You seem mad. [pause; audience laughs at the quick switch]
KG: [still agitated] I'm upset about it: we live in a . . .
C: [continuing the faux-therapy voice, expanding his previous remark, softly ignoring what KG's saying] You seem mad at my desire to not think about sad things. [audience laughs]

Again, we have C being "the poet," rhyming "mad" with "sad"—both negative words disavowed by C and applied to KG.

KG: You must think about sad things. [still agitated]

Rilke's "You must change your life" is possible as a comp, but Pound's Hell Cantos are a better one.

Seven's JFK chapter has been described briefly on-air but no word of it has actually been read.[1] This can be explained by the six-minute time constraint, but it is also possible that C, who appears to have read *Seven* (at least some of it) and, as I say, seems to have been knocked out of persona by it, found the mentions of JFK too grossly real to read. The JFK that the KLIF broadcasters name is the real president, and it hurts to read about the actual assassination in such unfiltered form.

Pound's Hell Cantos are in this sense a comp. Lloyd George and Woodrow Wilson in Canto 14 are the prime minister and real president and Pound's presentation is as gross as he can manage: ". . . . e and . . . . n, their wrists bound to the ankles, / Standing bare bum, / Faces smeared on their rumps, / wide eye on flat buttock, / Bush hanging for beard, Addressing crowds through their arse-holes" (*C*, 61). But the Hell Cantos are cringeworthy due to the childish violence of Pound's editorializing, and they foreshadow all too clearly his upcoming broadcast follies on Radio Rome, where his delusional pretensions to Dantescan powers of judgment are sadly obvious. "Poetry is news that STAYS news" may have been the slogan, but after WWI Pound registered contemporary events with paranoiac rigidity.

Another comp: "Wichita Vortex Sutra," where Ginsberg transcribes his own speech, peppered with occasional phrases from the car radio. The basic similarity to *Seven* is the transcription of real-time voices: both poets are showing how poetry can be expanded by use of new recording technologies. The basic difference is the politics. Ginsberg is denouncing LBJ and the Vietnam War as contemporary facts he wants to change; *Seven*, on the other hand, is inescapably elegiac. KG's "You must think about sad things" is proposing that his book and its method be considered a means of purified remembrance. Perhaps the better comp is "When Lilacs Last in the Dooryard Bloom'd."

C: Why must you think about sad things?
KG: Because sad things *happen*.
C: "Put on a happy face." [in a rhythmic chant which makes the audience laugh]

There is a familiar frame in which poetry is seen in a zero-sum position, defined against ordinary language use. Here, such a frame might show C as "winning," since his persona has reemerged, made the audience laugh, and knocked KG out of his initial position. But the conversation does not resolve in such a standoff.

KG: People . . .
C [arms outstretched, chopping hands marking the beat emphatically]: OH SUSANNA, OH DON'T YOU CRY FOR ME! [KG, recognizing this as a conclusion, joins in at the end, reciting and hand-chopping somewhat

tentatively. When the recitation is finished KG points his index finger at C in approving pleasure for the apt citation of the line; then C and KG clasp hands in rhythmic coordination.]

Again, in the zero-sum frame this could be taken as the triumph of C's persona: let us forget the disasters and celebrate a transhistorical America; let the indestructible "Oh Susanna" enunciate and erase slavery; let avant-garde hijinks yield to anodyne comedy.

But consider the physical actions of the moment: KG's immediately recognizing the wit of C's sudden citation of "Oh Susanna," his joining in the recitation, his index finger pointing in appreciation at the end of the line; then KG and C reaching forward and clasping hands in rhythmically entrained fashion to signal the conclusion of the interview. The wordless total of these actions suggests that a zero-sum reading is shortsighted: the moment can be seen as KG and C both affirming a place for poetry in the present world. Over the course of the interview, they have agreed that there are disasters (quasi-unmentionable as they are), and here both are buoyed by their mutual recognition of the aptness and power of the citation. They are agreeing that poetry is one answer we can make in the face of unceasing disaster.

But what are they agreeing on as poetry? Do we have to choose between Stephen Foster's "Oh Susanna" and Kenneth Goldsmith's *Seven American Deaths and Disasters*?

No: it's not a matter of particular items. As a start, let's say this consensus of poetry involves basic displacement. Here, at the end of the interview, a line from "Oh Susanna" has been wrenched from its antebellum associations. But such displacement is only blurrily comped by the n + 7 method:[2] it is not a matter of the appearance of the unexpected; rather, multiple appropriateness is the point. "Don't you cry for me" works as the end of the interview, and it also has a larger application. It's a stoic anthem to be chanted in the midst of ongoing, traumatic history, something akin to "pessimism of the intellect; optimism of the will." How can we talk about the disastrous present? With a buckwheat cake in our consuming mouths and a tear in our networked eyes? Possibly; but it's not a static content that counts, but rather the mutual recognition that the words have moved in order to speak to the present moment. It's a poetry of the present, using whatever is around; this is poetry in the old Greek sense of *kairos*, where all vocabulary, to work, must be opportune, mutually audible, mutually enacted. KG and C's rhythmically entrained handshake is an emblem of the poetic moment.

Two last comp questions. First, is Kenneth Goldsmith a comp for KG? Or does what KG says about *Seven*—and the fact of *Seven* itself—signal a large departure from his poetics of the prior two decades?

Second: is C a comp for KG? Is C a conceptual poet? If both are poets—in the wordless sense enacted by the handclasp that I have just tried to articulate—then does that mean they are both poets of displacement?

Throughout the interview, C has demonstrated his quickness with displacement (the buttermilk ice cream moment, for example). As we have seen, C's persona uses displacement continuously. But in addition to displacement, Colbert has developed a method that is more powerful: embedding—a species of exaggerated agreement, as opposed to the estranging effect of displacement. Does C's (and Colbert's) use of embedding rather than displacement give C a wider political articulation than KG?

Ten years after the US invasion of Iraq, "embedded" remains a poisonous word for leftists: the propaganda relayed as if it were news by reporters "embedded" with the military continues to emit toxic consequences. The standard comp is Judith Miller, front-page reporter for the *New York Times* in 2003. It was only because Miller was embedded that *Times* readers were able to read up-to-the-minute dispatches from the search for WMDs, spurious as we now know those searches and dispatches to have been.

However, in a redeployed sense, "embedding" is an apt word for much of what Colbert does. The results are the opposite of reports like Miller's: it is impossible to miss his critique of what his character pretends to be praising. Many of his effects can only be achieved from an embedded position. Take, for instance, Colbert's statement to President George W. Bush at the 2006 White House Correspondents' Dinner: "no matter what happens to America, she will always rebound—with the most powerfully staged photo ops in the world . . . . Over tax cuts, WMD intelligence, the effect of global warming: we Americans didn't want to know, and you had the courtesy not to try and find out" (McGrath). Or when he ran for president, created a Super PAC, and almost persuaded the South Carolina Republican Party to accept the $400,000 the Super PAC had raised in exchange for renaming the primary the Stephen Colbert Super PAC South Carolina Primary. Such statements have wide political reverberations (McGrath).

Perhaps Kenneth Goldsmith, sitting across from Stephen Colbert, is not so much displacing as beginning to embed.

C: Kenneth Goldsmith. The book is *Seven American Deaths and Disasters*. We'll be right back.

**

Coda (from 2015)

I wrote this piece in 2014; one year later, Goldsmith's place in the landscape of conceptual poetry is markedly different, sparked by the outrage over his reading of "The Body of Michael Brown" at a poetry conference (and the related outrage over Vanessa Place tweeting *Gone With the Wind* accompanied by racist imagery). The controversy is taking place via digital media, which will rapidly outstrip and outflank the slow-to-emerge, monologic print medium I am using. What I write here is emphatically time-bound.

Goldsmith read the poem at a conference in March 2015. The reading was a mostly verbatim presentation of the autopsy report on the police shooting of Michael Brown on August 9, 2014, during a confrontation after Brown stole cigarettes from a convenience store in Ferguson, Missouri. In one sense, Goldsmith was doing much the same thing he did in *Seven*, transcribing public words that describe a terrible event; however, how he went about fashioning the poem was significantly different, as were the poem's immediate reception and the ensuing consequences.

Beginning during the reading itself and spreading out exponentially, there was an eruption of comment on social media condemning Goldsmith's appropriation. His response was various, but he defended the piece primarily on poetic grounds: he is a conceptual poet and had been doing such things for years. Still, his poetic claims have not stilled the storm of protest. Comment has ranged from disapproval of a thoughtlessly invasive appropriation to accusations of simple racism. It was not literary appropriation—transcribing some official's prose—that sparked the rejection. Instead, the plane of discussion shifted to his actions. He has been seen as a white avant-gardist with major publicity privileges swooping in to a scene of maximum trauma: a poetic ambulance chaser. Meanwhile, Place's tweets have kept the flames of outrage stoked.

To my knowledge, Goldsmith has not apologized for the poem, but in response to the general agitation he did donate his conference fee to the Brown family and has taken the clip of the reading—and thus the poem itself—out of circulation.

As of this writing, the reading-and-disappearing of "The Body of Michael Brown" seems to mark a watershed in Goldsmith's work.

Before, his figure was that of heroic innovator, dandy, trickster. Oscar Wilde's hostility toward what mattered to ordinary people ("a little sincerity is a dangerous thing, and a great deal of it is absolutely fatal"); Duchamp's paradox pieces (this snow shovel, and only this, is an utterly advanced work of art); Warhol's stance of indifference to meaning—these would be comps. Before, Goldsmith was a very successful innovator, with the CV-for-TV of a quasi-celebrity: poet laureate of MoMA, teacher at UPenn, ten books, new book just out (and we can add in his appearance at the White House). Before, Goldsmith's mode was emphatically open. His website UbuWeb had for decades hosted links to hard-to-find avant-garde work that it made available without asking for permission—the militant assumption was that a free avant-garde cultural commons was a greater good than copyright.

Afterward, much is reversed. *Seven* was thoroughly public and widely publicized; "The Body of Michael Brown" has been removed from circulation. Goldsmith's joke/provocation that his pieces need not be read is now literalized; the poem cannot be read and only circulates in anecdotal details. Where conceptual poetry had flaunted indifference to content, now it is defended as the technique of rigorous truth telling.

Goldsmith's statement on Facebook in defense of the poem mixes elements of these before-and-after situations. On the one hand he writes that "The Body of Michael Brown" was like his other conceptual work: "Many of you have heard me read from [*Seven American Deaths and Disasters*]. This reading was identical in tone and intention. This, in fact, could have been the eighth American death and disaster." The verbatim nature of the appropriation is emphasized: "I didn't add or alter a single word or sentiment that did not preexist in the original text, for to do so would be to go against my nearly three decades' practice of conceptual writing." But the purity of conceptual appropriation is not kept up: "I altered the text for poetic effect; I translated into plain English many obscure medical terms that would have stopped the flow of the text; I narrativized it in ways that made the text less didactic and more literary" (Facebook post).

This signals a profound change in stance. Content, rather than a matter of indifference, is now something that has to be communicated. The end of Goldsmith's Facebook statement is emphatic: "Perhaps people feel uncomfortable with my uncreative writing, but for me, this is the writing that is able to tell the truth in the strongest and clearest way possible."

On its face, this sounds like Reznikoff's procedure in *Testimony*: editing court transcripts to ensure legibility. But when Goldsmith writes that he "narrativized" the report, his phrasing obscures a major change that has become an infuriating detail for many detractors. Instead of copying the autopsy report sentence by sentence, he moved one sentence, which described Brown's genitalia as "unremarkable," to the end.

I am not privy to Goldsmith's intentions here, but I can imagine this ending was meant as critique: reactionaries in the United States are consumed with fear of black masculinity; the tacit moral of the concluding sentence might be that each of us is merely human. But such an interpretation, in addition to being thoroughly universalizing, requires ironclad faith in the power of critique, as if terrible truth needs painful form in order to be communicated adequately.

Goldsmith is receiving no such allowance of critique. "The Body of Michael Brown" may have been presented as art, but it is being received as a gesture in an ongoing crisis, like something someone says at a rally, with many impatiently listening. The artfulness of the poem has dissolved, in its reception, into the content of what the person reciting the poem was saying.

The poem has been a public relations disaster for Goldsmith; among poetic communities it has galvanized aesthetic vigilance and been the occasion for high-ratcheted aggression. The poem may have been drastically weak for the forces it was trying to critique, but in response some of the outraged voices are exercising a depressing vigilance on the border between who speaks and what gets said.

Goldsmith's work expresses a lineage; framed by that lineage, it is part of a sequence of radical innovation, and it is all art. Thus it presupposes free access to public space.

At the moment, certainly, many disagree. Goldsmith may have been called a time-traveling aesthete on *Colbert*, but both C and KG tacitly agreeded that JFK was a monumental figure at a temporal distance, needing to be properly mourned. For the immediate audience for Goldsmith's poem on Michael Brown, and for the poem's subsequent detractors, there was no time travel, and the abysses between immediate social spaces were too painfully present to transcend: no visas were being granted for travel from MoMA to Ferguson. "The Body of Michael Brown" was not an eighth American death and disaster, nor was it part of any innovative series. It was heard in the context of a long series of violence against people of color in the United States, an ongoing, crowded series: Trayvon Martin (February 2012); Walter Scott (April 2014); Eric Garner (July 2014); Michael Brown (Aug 2014); Tamir Rice (November 2014); Freddie Gray (April 2015); the nine members of the Bible study group at Emanuel African Methodist Episcopal Church in Charleston (June 2015).

5
Homage to Pound's "Propertius"

1.

Now if ever it is time to translate modernism into a contemporary idiom,[1]
into "something to read in normal circumstances"[2]
to quote "Homage to Sextus Propertius," one of the few moments when
Pound's poetry
was fully contemporary, when he felt the distentions of writing time
most generously
and thus most accurately.

2.

In "Propertius" Pound was able to write as though
the present had a past and that past had a future
which wasn't just a reproduction of the original present
because he was changing it with the very words of the poem
finally breathing the actual air of modernity
first sniffed in Baudelaire, temporarily eternal modern air.[3]

So the equations that scored social space into such exacting drawing
rooms
could open out into a workable public surface.

It looked like there might be room for more than one generation
a bit of an age-playground for human noise rather than soundtrack music
—for once Pound escaped
that timeless tone or at least managed some time off.

There was room for women and men.

For once Pound turns his back on heroism
and makes women (though he calls them girls) the primary audience.
In the words of a scolding Apollo:

> "Who has ordered a book about heroes?[4]
> "You need, Propertius, not think
> "About acquiring that sort of reputation.
> "Soft fields must be worn by small wheels,
> "Your pamphlets will be thrown, thrown often into a chair
> "Where a girl waits alone for her lover."

3.

1917, who needs a book about heroes?
Chronology is always a sore spot with Pound.
"Propertius" is dated 1917 in *Personae* but it sounds like 1915,
with Gaudier still invincibly alive in the trenches,[5]
thus allowing our poet to greet the war with an elegant stage yawn:

> "Out-weariers of Apollo will, as we know, continue their Martian generalities."

Pound then shows said generalities rolling out their blood-red carpets
to receive the tread of imperial distension:

> "Tigris and Euphrates shall, from now on, flow at Caesar's bidding,
> Tibet shall be full of Roman policemen."

The snappy insouciance of that couplet is part of the best of Pound's legacy. In the first line he simultaneously sounds and skewers the tedious formalism of the sycophantic-prophetic, where the poet is to mouth the divinely sanctioned godlike power of the state: "Tigris and Euphrates shall, from now on, flow at Caesar's bidding"; he then quickly untunes this in the next line via mismatches in diction, history, and geography, which are puzzlingly instructive as they lighten up the ear: "Policemen," an anachronism and an Americanism; "Tibet," utterly unrelated to the Roman Empire. But beyond simple incongruity Pound is constructing a witty equation. Propertius had been sarcastically assenting to Augustus's world rule: there would be Roman legions in the utterly far-away provinces, Parthia or Britain. Thus, in Pound's time travel, contemporary London gets to hear itself described as "Tibet," the exotic end of all known things. Though the message of the couplet is ultimately tame—empire rules the world, we are told—its wit displays itself as the fastest thing around. And today Pound's prophetic bridge between past and present still stands: American soldiers are still in Afghanistan.

4.

Write in two times, two languages
neither of them simply new or simply old.
Think, tongue, notebook open by the warm bed.
Hold hands, Pennsylvanian, under the table, Bride Scratton's hand, say
explore the logomelopoesis of sticking close to women.
You hadn't done it much before and you hardly—if ever—did it again.
For once you heeded Oppen's later warning: "Only one mistake, Ezra!
You should have talked to women" (Oppen, xii).

5.

Imagine a world without Homer, Pound, without Virgil, without Mussolini

6.

"Propertius" compliments itself on being soft, on its sexy slither:
    "you ask on what account I write so many love-lyrics
    And whence this soft book comes into my mouth.
    Neither Calliope nor Apollo sung these things into my ear,
        My genius is no more than a girl.

        . . . if hair is mussed on her forehead,
    If she goes in a gleam of Cos, in a slither of dyed stuff,
    There is a volume in the matter . . .
        And if she plays with me with her shirt off,
        We shall construct many Iliads. . . .
        We shall spin long yarns out of nothing.
    Thus much the fates have allotted me."

Pound and so-called Cynthia are their own fates
spinning their own thread of days
The Empire can mind its own business

            "if, Maecenas,
    I were able to lead heroes into armour, I would not,

Neither would I warble of Titans, nor of Ossa spiked onto Olympus. . . .
Nor of Thebes in its ancient respectability."[6]

7.

The Empire was ankle-deep in fresh-flowing blood, the top salons
weren't absolutely closed, and you had discovered
that it was possible to talk about women
(plural and with a small w) in the same language that could also
encompass
arma virumque.

In one breath
you could point with disdain at the wars along the distended
assumptions of empire and without having to inhale

you could move over the articulate smoothness
of a body that very much
wasn't yours. Then it would be time
for a new breath.

8.

It's hard to breathe well when there are gods around
floating in the azure air, bright gods and Tuscan,[7]
recumbent on Miltonic adjective postpositional,[8]
back before dew was shed.

In that dry Mediterranean climate
the gods have no homework

they wear, when they choose
loose-fitting attractive clothes

there are no references to look up
no conference papers

only the pleasant present
good on the skin
and unlimited supplies
of hors d'oeuvres and fresh gossip

but the gods turn out to be
hard acts to book.

They'll appear (briefly) in big set pieces
costing an arm and a leg
(Canto 2—can't afford to do *that* too many times!)[9]

but to get the gods to actually impart some information
there's about as much hope of that
as of cashing a check written in water[10]
A Draft of XXX Cantos
a thousand and one cantos
whatever the going rate, you acted like you could pay it
rushing forward to pick up the bill each time
stuffing them in your pocket
because, anyway, the gods were going to pay.

But the gods don't pick up checks
they display perfection
from the source, easy to drink from

but difficult to find. Impossible really, unless one of them shows you.
And the question is: Can the route be taught?

Taught in a poem? taught
to many, to only a few?
or is it that no one can simply *learn*
how to gain access? Pound, you learned things and

you taught. But can that which you teach
be detached from your own practice of teaching?

Or is "teach" no more than an intransitive, godlike verb?
the sound of judgment echoing and reechoing

over everything that is new
upon which dew
simply must not fall?

Perhaps that was what you heard the gods teaching
as you walked "sheer into 'nonsense'"

and saw "two eyes like the eyes of a wood-creature"
peering at you "over a brown tube of wood" (Pound 1932)

But if anything can neutralize the new it's the gods.
So that your predicted history grew monstrously encumbered

and never arrived in any form you could ever get your benighted listeners to recognize.

9.

Will *The Cantos* outlast the Pound industry?
Or have they made it so that any poetry, to be read outside its group
must manufacture its own industry?

Do the scholiasts' clarifications
do more than add to the rubbish at the base camps?

Heat-soured milk
overburdened verbal habits
the cold peak beckoning.

Still, Pound,
it is not with your demi-gods I would walk
nor would I suggest others sign up for that endless afternoon hike
neath sun-beat tho it be.[11]

I won't make a pact with you[12]
just as you didn't make one with Propertius

not that I'm unmindful of what you did there
staging a new kind of battle of the Moderns vs. the Ancients

playing on both sides of the net, frigidaire patent in one hand
party invitations in translationese in the other.

"Though my house is not propped up by Taenarian columns from Laconia
(associated with Neptune and Cerberus)"[13]

—that is *not* something someone "in the throes of some particular emotion"
would actually *say*.[14] It's something you

wrote. For pleasure

in flimsy exception
to general war.

6

Rachel Blau DuPlessis's *Drafts* and the Epic Moment

1. Creeley Sidestepping *The Cantos*

"Homage to Pound's 'Propertius'" is not quite saying that it's too bad Pound wrote *The Cantos*, but it does stage the wistful thought experiment of imagining a Pound who didn't wander onto the epic stage sets of mytho-religious assertion. I am of course in no position to pronounce infallibly on where or how Pound went wrong: this book shows his achievement thoroughly informing my own poetics, and "Homage to Pound's 'Propertius'" is Exhibit A.

Rachel Blau DuPlessis's *Drafts* is a project whose very name makes *The Cantos* a central concern.[1] Before turning to her work, I want to present a contrast: Robert Creeley's non-epic Pound. This paratactic figure made of moments furnishes a useful negative to the intense cross-structuring through which DuPlessis constructs *Drafts*.

Creeley never mentioned Pound without praising him as central to his poetic "company."[2] Nevertheless, it's interesting to see his desire to sidestep Pound's epic project. A Pound without *The Cantos* is obviously non-empirical; but this non-epic, momentary figure makes a useful emblem of a widely influential paratactic impulse in innovative American writing, which started with Creeley's own *Pieces*, which in turn inaugurated the long-poem strand of Language writing stretching from Robert Grenier's *Sentences* to the new sentence and modular works of Ron Silliman, Lyn Hejinian, and Bruce Andrews, among others, and onward to a great array of twenty-first-century procedural writing.[3] While *Drafts* does exist in the same general innovative quadrant as *Pieces* and *Sentences*, it is doing something quite different. *Drafts* is anti-momentary, insistently relational, cross-referenced at every turn.

I will delineate Creeley's non-epic Pound via a reading of "Olson and Others: Some Orts for the Sports," a prose piece where the conflict between Creeley's Poundian approach to poetry and his avoidance of *The Cantos* is particularly clear. "Orts," as I will refer to it, resists categorization: it is hardly an essay, and certainly not a review. As it begins, it will only self-identify as "a few sentences":

> Where writing will go to, what comes next, or the answers to any of those profoundly speculative questions bred of Saturday afternoons in comfortable surroundings—god alone knows. Where it's all come from is another question, and a few sentences may serve as well to answer it as any more documented or descriptive account. For example, in 1950 Cid Corman, the subsequent editor of Origin, had a radio program called This Is Poetry, which by a fluke of air waves I heard one night in Littleton, N.H. (*Essays*, 106)

Readers not used to such genre-less directness might find this disorienting. These sentences show us, to repurpose Wordsworth's phrase, a writer speaking to writers. This is the default rhetorical situation of Creeley's prose; it is a mode he got from Pound. With Pound as with Creeley, no matter the ostensible occasion, the subject is always writing: each sentence is both an act of the moment and a move in the poet's lifelong battle for poetic values. Such sentences need close attention as much as poetry does.[4]

Creeley's first sentence begins by proposing the entire future of poetry, but, halfway through, dismisses the largeness of the question with deep sarcasm. It is hard to pinpoint where the change happens: "profoundly speculative questions" seems at first to be meant in earnest, but the mention of comfortable Saturdays retroactively characterizes such deep thinking as the shallow pontification of the armchair poet. The overall import of the first sentence is that a cozily knowable future is an exasperating proposition.

But the past, the second sentence tells us, is another matter. "Where it's all come from"—that is, the entire history of live writing as it has sparked the individual career—is of the greatest interest. The entirety of writing announces itself in single, and thus eccentric, chunks such as the fluke airwaves of the third sentence, wafting Cid Corman's radio program from Boston to Creeley in rural New Hampshire.

This is the kind of oblique epiphany Pound continually celebrates: the big vista arriving via a singular encounter. These poetic/pedagogical moments cannot be categorized since each is unique: Agassiz's fish at the beginning of *ABC of Reading* (the single fish the student is told to stare at); the quiet assertion at the end of Canto 81: "To have, with decency, knocked / That a Blunt should open / To have gathered from the air a live tradition" (81, 168–70). These are specific knocks allowing Pound to catch the scent of live poetry. Traipsing across Freiberg to understand *d'noi ganres*; if Pound hadn't sought out "old Levy" he would never have awakened to the sensory intelligence encoded in the Provençal phrase (Canto 20, 89–90). In Canto 82 the transmission of poetic fact is emblematized by a reference to Aeschylus's *Agamemnon*, where the fall of Troy is relayed around the rim of the Aegean via a series of bonfires:

> The news was quicker in Troy's time
> a match on Cnidos, a glow worm on Mitylene (Pound, *Cantos*, 539)

Poetic knowledge arrives via channels which are always unpredictable—fish, aristocrats, pedants, bonfires, fluke airwaves.

ABC of Reading is nominally a textbook and does contain pedagogic lists (a feature Creeley imitates in "Orts"), but these never remain objective. At one point Pound will put Whitman in a list (79), but will later dismiss the work in completely personal terms: "From an examination of Walt made twelve years ago the present writer carried away the impression that there are thirty well-written pages of Whitman: he is now unable to find them" (192). To read *ABC* is not to study a textbook but to have an audience with Pound.

Here he imparts a large point via an anecdote from Yeats:

> The gulf between Homer and Virgil can be illustrated profanely by one of Yeats' favourite anecdotes.
>
> A plain sailor man took a notion to study Latin, and his teacher tried him with Virgil; after many lessons he asked him something about the hero.
>
> Said the sailor: 'What hero?'
>
> Said the teacher: 'What hero, why, Aeneas, the hero.'
>
> Said the sailor: 'Ach, a hero, him a hero? Bigob, I t'ought he was a priest.' (*ABC*, 44)

Yeats may have been merely telling a joke in dialect, but in Pound's presentation we are meant to hear an authoritative judgment. Pound uses the sailor's authentic speech (the real language of men) to dismiss the *Aeneid* as dull state rhetoric.

Creeley's prose is Poundian in this overall sense that I am suggesting. Writing is made of specifics but is responsible to a larger, embattled, emergent tradition: any one detail can mean everything.

Twice in "Orts" this diffused Poundian quality is made to focus on Pound himself. First, in the midst of a reminiscence on Christopher Logue, Pound's books suddenly surface as a rock-solid currency: Logue, Creeley writes, "showed me his Pound books (which are as much a currency in some areas as dollar bills in others)." The second instance is the end, where "Orts" concludes with Pound in a markedly unstable way: "The issue is the poem, a single event—to which, as to the Battle of Gettysburg, or the Pan American Highway, many men may well contribute—'*aperiens tibi animum*. . . . Like, you dig the 85th Canto? Like—that's all'" (*Essays*, 109–10).

Again, a reader new to Creeley's prose might wonder what is being said. I take the large swings in rhetoric (from incantatory Latin to hep talk) and the wide jumps in reference (the poem, the Civil War, the Pan American Highway, *The Cantos*) as Creeley ramping up the scale of his discourse, wanting to end "Orts" with a bang, with live writing being a fact of world-historical importance and *The Cantos* as the crowning example of live writing. But, at the same time, he flinches away from them, as if from a sun he cannot look at: "Like—that's all."

Whether praise or evasion, the scale is epic: the Battle of Gettysburg and the Pan American Highway are world-size facts rife with loss. With the italicized Latin, we are suddenly handed an opaque prestige object (the last line of Canto 85, the opening poem of *Rock-Drill*, which would have been the latest installment of *The Cantos* at the time Creeley was writing "Orts"). Creeley, having taught Latin, however bumpily, in New Mexico, would recognize the meaning of the words: roughly, "opening his soul to you," or perhaps, "opening your soul for you." Is this a poetic benediction, or just a pleasant mystery, a moment of hieratic otherness for the common reader, something to doze over on Saturday afternoons in comfortable surroundings? Is this Latin like the church Latin the younger Creeley once satirized: "And the poor love it / and think it's crazy," to quote the end of "After Lorca" (*RC I*, 121)? However the Latin is taken, Creeley suddenly pauses, then ends "Orts" by turning to hep talk (another superseded language), simultaneously mentioning and praising *The Cantos* and dropping them like a hot potato.

This is not to say Creeley didn't know Pound's work: his incisive grasp on it can be seen in a small moment from his introduction to an anthology of Whitman. There, Creeley aligns Whitman with Pound as not using enjambment, against the ever-enjambing Williams (Creeley, *Essays*, 12). It is a quick aside, but it makes a large, accurate point. Pound's lack of enjambment is rarely mentioned, but once noticed it seems fundamental to his poetry. Consider such different work as *Cathay*, "Propertius," "Mauberley," *The Cantos*: there is hardly any enjambment.

Such familiarity with and reverence for Pound did not, however, make *The Cantos* useful to Creeley[5]; as he writes in 1965, "my own limits made the *Cantos* intimidating to me" (*Essays*, 26). That is Creeley being polite. In his poems he is more aggressively anti-epic:

EPIC

Save some room
for my epic.

*

Absence makes
a hole

*

Any story
begins somewhere

and any other story
begins somewhere else.
(*RC II*, 82)

This is the method Creeley inaugurated in *Pieces* (1971), where patches of lines, mostly short, are loosely connected via a simple system of dots: one dot marking a new section, three marking the completion of a poem. However, in the experience of reading such work, the distinction of section from poem, of continuity from completion, seems nominal: the reader encounters a stream of short pieces.

By 1980, this is how Creeley was describing *The Cantos*, as a continuity of moments: "As Ginsberg says, first poet [i.e., Pound was the first poet] of our accessible time to reclaim poetry as sound. Also Ginsberg's emphasis, on hearing of Pound's death: that the *Cantos* are the first articulate record/graph of mind/emotions continuous over fifty years" (*Essays*, 29). Ginsberg and Creeley's habit of abbreviated syntax is Poundian. Here is Pound using his abbreviated style to justify abbreviation: "Narrative not the same as lyric; different techniques for song and story. 'Would, could,' etc.: Abbreviations save *eye* effort. Also show speed in mind of original character supposed to be uttering" (*Letters*, 322). Such brusqueness is the mark of a man with no time to waste: it is an essential feature of Poundianism.

This dissolution of *The Cantos* into a sequence of moments also dissolves the conflict between Creeley's Poundian instantaneity and his refusal of Pound's epic dimension: the epic moment makes it possible to take *The Cantos* as doing what *Pieces* does.

2. Pound's Own Epic Anxieties

Looking back from our vantage point, we can see Pound himself initially flinching from *The Cantos*: the so-called ur-cantos express his own anxieties as he faced the challenge of the long poem. Lines like these from the original first canto, "I walk Verona. (I am here in England.) / I see Can Grande. (Can see whom you will.) / You had one whole man? / And I have many fragments, less worth?" are, to say the least, very nervous.[6] A lesser-known instance of Pound's worry is a chatty and revealing footnote from *Gaudier-Brzeska*:

> Note
>
> I am often asked whether there can be a long imagiste or vorticist poem. The Japanese, who evolved the hokku, evolved also the Noh plays. In the best "Noh" the whole play may consist of one image. . . . I see nothing against a long vorticist poem.
>
> On the other hand, no artist can possibly get a vortex into every poem or picture he does. One would like to do so, but it is beyond one. . . . (94)

The first paragraph looks like Pound trying to imagine *The Cantos* but not being able to decide whether that means writing a long poem or a single, all-intensive moment. The second paragraph admits at least temporary defeat: "it is beyond one." Perhaps one cannot always rise to the level of writing epics, but there are, for this "one" (the urbane man of letters), other pursuits. The footnote, atypically for Pound, goes on to imagine a few:

> [. . .] but it is beyond one. Certain things seem to demand metrical expression, or expression in a rhythm more agitated than the rhythms acceptable to prose, and these subjects, though they do not contain a vortex, may have some interest, an interest as "criticism of life" or of art. . . . [A]nd a vorticist or imagiste writer may be justified in presenting a certain amount of work which is not vorticism or imagisme, just as he might be justified in printing a purely didactic prose article. Unfinished sketches and drawings have a similar interest. (*Gaudier-Brzeska*, 94)

As his career progressed, this urbane stance became less and less available to Pound: all secular, urbane perspectives and genres evanesced to the point where there was no longer an outside to the epic enterprise. *The Cantos* became insistently paratactic: every moment was the epic moment. A clear emblem of this occurs in *The Pisan Cantos* when Pound notates the birds (turning them into notes in the epic song) as they flit on and off the wires which furnish the music stave:

in
discourse
what matters is
to get it across e poi basta
5 of 'em now on 2;
on 3; 7 on 4

thus what's his name
and the change in writing the song books
5 on 3 aulentissima rosa fresca
so they have left the upper church at Assisi
but the Goncourts shed certain light on the
french revolution
(Pound, *Cantos*, 500)

Each line here is momentary and momentous: each epic moment is enough "to get it across," where "it" means both the one thing being said then and everything else. The French Revolution can be understood in an instant (at least by those who have read the Goncourts).

3. DuPlessis: Outlasting the Epic Moment

As I was writing a talk in 2011 for DuPlessis's retirement, I emailed her to check my memory-image: "Do you remember when I asked you if with *Drafts* you were going for 100? And, as I remember, you said yes, as if you had decided at that moment?" She answered: "I sure do remember! it was (I am sure) after an Ann Lauterbach reading at Temple. . . . We were having the readings at 1515 Walnut then . . . and it was not the world's loveliest room. . . . If it was 1993, this is before Jena (I think), so maybe Susan S. was around, maybe Gil";[7] and she referred me to a passage from *Blue Studios*: "Somewhere during the exfoliation of *Drafts*, I think in around 1993, but possibly just after *The Trouble with Genius* appeared in 1994, Bob Perelman asked, not quite casually, 'how many of them there would be.' I hadn't considered the question consciously, but unconsciously I was ready. So I answered, '100, like Pound's *Cantos*.' We both sort of gasped. I am grateful that he asked, because his question . . . catapulted me into facing my actual ambition. It was the first time I had said the number aloud" (*Blue*, 246). This reactivated my own slightly different memory. I did hear myself asking if calling it *Drafts* meant there would be 100 of them and then, after a small pause, DuPlessis answering, Yes, wary but not unconfident. In my version the names of Pound and *The Cantos* are too charged to mention; but whether the names were spoken or repressed, anxiety over the epic is the point of both our memories.

This might be taken as something like an epic moment, the big vista opening instantly. But now that *Drafts* has been completed and the panoply of its formal exfoliation and cross-referenced construction is fully available, it seems clear that the epic moment is a masculinist-universal subject position that *Drafts* has been written to challenge. To create a female epic subject position is not the work of a moment. DuPlessis's methods court multiplicity, not singularity.

I should reiterate that the epic moment is an ad-hoc phrase I'm using here to keep a large context in mind; it is not a term, but a loose glomeration of historical patterns and impingements that I'm evoking to narrate how I read DuPlessis's work.

As an initial example, compare how DuPlessis and Pound handle deixis—the gesture of pointing unambiguously to what is being talked about. Deixis is sacred to the epic moment: "5 of 'em now on 2": Pound is pointing to those birds, on those wires, at that moment. As a counterpart to such charismatic singularity, compare this stanza from "Draft 33: Deixis":

Say "I." Say "here."
    Say "now," "then,"
        "recently," "soon," "today."[2] (220)

Footnote 2 is printed at the bottom of the page, as part of the poem. (Most of the drafts, including "Deixis," have endnotes at the end of their particular volumes; the footnotes in "Deixis" are distinct from these—they are a poetic device.) Footnote 2 reads as follows: "2. This list of words from John Lyons. And this definition: 'By deixis is meant the location and identification of persons, objects, processes and activities being talked about, or referred to, in relation to the spatiotemporal context created and sustained by the act of utterance and the participation in it, typically of a single speaker and at least one addressee.' John Lyons, *Semantics: 2* (Cambridge: Cambridge University Press, 1977), p. 637. I am grateful to Muffy Seigel for this reference." There are a number of anti-deictic gestures here: the singleness of the deictic word is undone by the seven examples of deictic words, all of them are in quotation marks; we are given the source of the list—a linguistics textbook—with complete academic provenance; and with mention of Muffy Siegel the web of scholarly friendship is respected. "Deixis" polemically sets the poem within a critical, intellectual, social web.

When DuPlessis and I had our brief talk in 1993, she had already been writing *Drafts* for some years. In a 2006 essay, written when the poem was half completed, reflecting on the poem's genesis, she lists seven inceptive moments, stretching from 1964 to 1986. Besides providing biographical background, these multiples polemicize against the notion of a single origin; each is introduced by the same phrase followed by a date: "*Drafts* began in 1964," "*Drafts* began in 1984," etc. These key moments were: reading *Spring and All*, *Paterson*, and *The Pisan Cantos* in graduate school; teaching *The Waste Land*; reading Beverley Dahlen's *A Reading*, which modeled "tracking the intricate meanings of one's own accidents"; teaching Creeley's *Pieces* and hearing that he never revised; writing on the "luscious paper" of an Italian notebook she got from Kathleen Fraser; working on George Oppen's *Selected Letters* and contemplating a sentence of his: "You have your own pencil and your own piece of paper and you're on your own word by word from scratch," on which DuPlessis comments, "It was true."[8]

Invigorating as Oppen's stoic advice can be—and what poet has been more invigorated by Oppen than DuPlessis herself?—it does not help make sense of *Drafts*. Oppen's page is blank—heroically blank, one might say—awaiting the word of the poet. But as DuPlessis's criticism has emphasized, this is not the case for the woman poet, whose page is pre-inscribed by the masculinist poetic inheritance from Pound among many others. For Pound, DuPlessis writes, "forms of modern maleness . . . depend, as subject positions, on proposing and maintaining a dehistoricized, despecified female figure" (*Blue*, 124).

It was not just Pound proposing an unusable subject position for a female writer. The following passage shows DuPlessis confronting a millennia-old tradition of such proposals, equally as old as the Tradition which Eliot, that self-effacing Individual Talent, celebrated, and to which Edgar Allan Poe adds his wisdom:

> What happens when you are an actual-historical woman, whom the poetic ideas of Woman have molded, entranced, partially colonized . . . . Lyric poetries certainly build on female inspiration, those invertebrate muses, love objects, wraithes, haunting figures with armes long and small. Armes of the woman, I sing. Satirical poetries build on suspicious objects, the Juvenalian deceits celebrated in certain works of Swift, T. S. Eliot, and Coleridge. The muse/beloved or antimuse/cautioned and reviled is a central (though not exclusive) discourse of poetry and art-making based on the structures of difference organizing persons asymmetrically by gender. What happens when you are a female poet wandering in the museums of, the mausoleums of, poetry—given that the most poetical subject was said—albeit by Poe—to be the death of a beautiful woman. . . . Do you turn away? Does turn away mean stop writing? (*Blue*, 76)

This is an excellent fusillade against the masculinist regime; at the same time, some of its most effective resources are rather Poundian. Certainly the range of poetic reference (Juvenal, Wyatt, Swift, Coleridge, et al.) is as wide as Pound's; and the polemical vividness of tone matches Pound in granular immediacy. You have to move lithely to catch the impact of "Armes of the woman, I sing," which pivots from one word of Sir Thomas Wyatt's "They Flee From Me"—"armes," with all its loaded resonances (erotic immediacy, with "her armes longe and smalle," though she enters the poem as a tamed deer)—into a parody of the first line of the *Aeneid*: *arma virumque cano*, "arms and the man I sing." Virgil had been the center of imperial poetic pedagogy for centuries: both Keats and Rimbaud translated the *Aeneid* as teenagers.

The opening page of *Drafts* is pre-inscribed with a paternal negation:

Draft 1 : It

N.

N.

= =

Three pages later in the same draft, we begin to get hints that these mysterious *N*'s or mountains are posing the question of epic:

CANO, can o,   yes   no
conno-
tations of impurities fill the fold.
(*Drafts*, 4)

"CANO" quotes the just-mentioned beginning of Virgil's *Aeneid* and is the classic verb of epic singing. It then dissolves into "can" and "o," the separated syllables suggesting two quite opposed things: *O* the epic apostrophe (O Zeus, O Achilles), and the modal verb *can*, which both asserts ability and allows/refuses permission (I can do this; Can I do this? You can't do this). Can o, can I sing? am I allowed to sing epic? The answers yes and no are both then proffered, but doesn't the second syllable of the original "cano" point to "no" being the authoritative epic pronouncement?

In "Draft 20: Incipit," we get more of the backstory:

The beginning was, as these things go,
negation. But
'twas also setting forth of signs to read or tell.
Moonlit refraction by a strange heap
counted on base "N" and on base "Y."
Yes and no. Both and and.

And inside that beginning
the no no no set out, unrolled
its grave and merry way (131)

This suggests we reread the beginning of *Drafts* with the *N*'s explicitly spelled out as *No*'s. But there are now two distinct speech acts: the paternal veto denying the woman epic privilege and, simultaneously, the stuttering beginning of the woman's own epic language. As *Drafts* gets written, this stuttering will transmute into a cornucopia of formal invention and canny gestures of self-difference.

Drafts is an epic whose language operates in "base 'N'" and "base 'Y'"—something like base No and base Yes. The estrangement should be noted. Base 10 is natural to us and therefore, naturally, 100 is the culminating epic number. Imagine having to count in base 6. After minutes of trial and error I think an equal number of Poundian cantos would be expressed in base 6 as 244.

When it first appears, the yes/no opposition seems destabilized by the following phrase: "Yes and no. Both and and." Then, the next three lines deploy a little triplet of no's that seem to be stripped of the power of negation, so that "the no no no set out, unrolled / its grave and merry way." And in other places in *Drafts* DuPlessis will simply toy with the paternal "no":

                D
wor <
                K
in a No No No

                tebook

(*Torques*, 136)

But such moments of productive play with prior masculinist vetoes do not amount to happy feminist endings. Having written *Drafts* does not mean that the problem of a woman writing a poem such as *Drafts* has been solved: the force of refusal that the "no" has directed toward women is not undone by any one act of critique. Even though DuPlessis herself writes, in an essay after the poem was completed, that "*Drafts* . . . as a whole ruptures the binaries that might contain it" (*Surge*, 2), and even though *Drafts* exhibits a plethora of gestures that destabilize the distinction between sameness and difference (strict numerology that includes an exception; continual rupture of the line between poem and gloss, poetry and criticism, poetry and feminist action); nevertheless, I think that to see *Drafts* as dissolving binaries is to miss something fundamental about what the poem is doing.

Drafts contains a through-line of gender: the long history of the dichotomous male/female situation is sounded and challenged throughout. The "no" of the epic moment is both consistently critiqued and persistently present. But if the problem of prior masculine determination and negation is never to be solved by poetic fiat (the method of the epic moment), the obstacles it presents also form occasions that fuel the inventiveness of *Drafts*.

Here is a passage from "Draft 33" that presents and critiques the decorative position that has long been proffered to women in the poetic field and invents poetically out of that situation. The final word of the second stanza, "'dove-grey,'" besides being in quotes, is footnoted (footnote 15). First I will discuss the words alone:

> —I was no daughter of
> unpronounceable Mnemosyne—
>
> and being the woman writing, anyway,
> Master of the Female Half-Lengths
> I was ambivalent in re:
> the beautiful and its "dove-grey."[15]
>
> (*Drafts*, 228)

The classical muses are "the daughters of memory," and the goddess of memory is Mnemosyne (*nee-mo-su-ne*). For Eliot, the classics are universal and their memories must be found in the body of the poet, who is simultaneously Eurocentric, male, and timeless;[9] for an outsider like Reznikoff, the classics are so desirable that he begins to learn Greek only to also learn that Greek is built on scorn for barbarians like him;[10] for DuPlessis, the classics are the site of ancient and long-lasting gender confinement. Euridipes's *The Bacchae* may have played to a mixed audience, but in the Athens of that time women were generally confined to their fathers' or husbands' houses. Being a muse within that cultural arrangement is not a role DuPlessis aspires to; the name of the mother of those muses is all Greek to her.

"Deixis" touches on, among other things, the story of DuPlessis beginning to write as a woman dissatisfied with the prior rewards and attributes she was, as a woman, automatically in line for. Being "Master of Female Half-Lengths" suggests feminine rhyme and, on a wider social scale, the species of gender confinement packaged in the condescending complement of making woman ruler of domestic space.

The last line, "the beautiful and its 'dove-grey,'" is deployed in multiple ways. On the one hand, its adjectives are examples of conventionally feminine decorativeness and are presented for critique. On the other hand, it is part of a stanza that is anti-decorative, almost a pastiche of Pound's *Mauberley*:

The tea-rose tea-gown, etc.
Supplants the mousseline of Cos,
The pianola "replaces"
Sappho's barbitos.
(*P/T*, 550)

and being the woman writing, anyway,
Master of the Female Half-Lengths
I was ambivalent in re:
the beautiful and its "dove-grey."
(DuPlessis, *Drafts*, 228)

Note the similarities: syllables closely weighted with semantic import; words in quotes; use of stenographic abbreviation (Pound: etc.; DuPlessis: in re); frequent rhyme, given the low syllable count; unusual rhyme (DuPlessis: anyway, in re, "dove-grey"; Pound: Cos, barbitos).

DuPlessis goes Pound one better in formal complexity. Besides participating in gender critique and a signifying rhyme scheme, "'dove-grey'" is also quoting Pound (more precisely, it is quoting Pound quoting: Pound puts the adjective in ironic scare quotes) and it is footnoted as part of the poem "Draft 33." The text of the footnote reads as follows:

> 15. Pound speaks against the "viewy" and the "dove-grey" in "A Retrospect" (1913–1918), *The Literary Essays of Ezra Pound*, ed. T. S. Eliot (London: Faber & Faber, 1954), p. 7 and 5. Of course, many of his modernist criteria (hard, "no emotional slither") are implicitly antifeminine, despite originating in praise of H.D. (*Drafts*, 228)

DuPlessis here is moving even farther away from feminized romantic post-Victorian lyricism than Pound does in "Mauberley": if Poundian-Eliotic modernism is intellectual, then a poem including footnotes in its text is even more modernist, less "dove-grey."

The inventiveness is polemical. We need to distinguish Pound's anti-feminine poetics, which posit elemental traits, from DuPlessis's anti-masculinism, which opposes the epic moment throughout the poem.

Invention can be a necessary reflex arising from original displacement, as we see in the following from the "Preface" to the final installment of the project: "So Je est un Author: like Dante, Pound, Oppen . . . But there is a difference. Je est that other kind of autre/ other/ author as a conceptual act of disturbance and cultural recalibration. I am then a female author." But this position is not a culmination: the displacement continues into an energetic series: "then I am inauthentic; a pretender; a fake . . . ghost, revenant, plagiarist copyist, chameleon, never doing things as well as those male others" (*Surge*, 10).

While this is telling the long story of the cultural impoverishment of women, it is also full of polemic energy: the pun of other/author articulates the problems and possibilities of the inheritance DuPlessis received, along with many other poets, from Pound. But to put things schematically, Pound was a poet-critic whose poetry and whose poetics were indissolubly drawn inward to the service of his epic project; DuPlessis, on the other hand, wrote *Drafts* as a poet-critic for whom criticism extends beyond the precincts of epic and of poetry. His work is charismatic; hers is searchable.

There are no happy endings. Working to produce effective critique is a step along the way. As opposed to the epic moment's instantaneity, the problem of H.D.'s name is never solved. In *An End to Torment*, H.D. narrates her baptism:

> "But Dryad," (in the Museum tea room), "this is poetry." He slashed with a pencil. "Cut this out, shorten this line. 'Hermes of the Ways' is a good title. I'll send this to Harriet Monroe of *Poetry*. Have you a copy? Yes? Then we can send this, or I'll type it when I get back. Will this do?" And he scrawled "H.D. Imagiste" at the bottom of the page.
> (18)

This naming is not unfriendly: Pound is effectively helping a fellow poet begin her career. But it is also an enduring trauma. It places the woman in the lyric position and we never hear another word from Hilda Doolittle. And, to reiterate, the title of H.D.'s memoir of Pound is *An End to Torment*. In *Helen in Egypt* the Pound figure, Achilles, performs a scarifying reading of Helen, attempting to strangle her and insisting she is a hieroglyph.

DuPlessis is an efficacious poet-critic. As she writes in "Haibun": "Speaking as a scholar, it's not so much the belatedly understood influence of H.D. on me but (don't get me wrong) my influence on H.D. This peculiar position is true of several other feminist critics who wrote on H.D. very early . . . notably Susan Stanford Friedman, Adelaide Morris, and Alicia Ostriker. . . . We were inventing an H.D. We influenced her work—how it was read, what parts of it were read, why it was interesting. We made it matter for this generation" (*Blue*, 226).

This is not unnaming H.D., but working against the consequences of Pound's naming. DuPlessis's critical readings have fundamentally challenged that fundamental tenet of critical decorum, disinterestedness, since she writes as a committed feminist. Her readings of H.D., of Loy, of Williams, of Creeley, et al. are refreshingly accurate while remaining wide-focused, not in spite of, but because of the ubiquity of gender. It is as if DuPlessis were reminding us that gender is one of the (social) senses, one that had been systematically crimped.

Take this moment from "Draft 101: Puppet Opera," a semi-comic, semi-manic dialogue between a she- and a he-puppet. The invention is, as always in *Drafts*, complex. The impetus for the puppets comes from a jotting from Marcel Duchamp's Green Box DuPlessis used in a prior draft: "perhaps introduce it / in the hung / suspended woman" (*Surge*, 41). From this, DuPlessis exfoliates a play where the she- and he-puppets discuss, from many different angles, the problem of the woman's being suspended. Their initial names are H/SW and AP, M (hung/suspended woman; another puppet, male). At one point, the he-puppet renames them:

> Now you will be Pond-Dew Fee-melle. I will be A. Larrey Dore.
> Pond-Dew: That's a change? Why are you giving me my name?
> A. Dore: Don't you love that I love you? Don't you love that I adore you?
> (*Surge*, 51)

While DuPlessis (unusually) supplies no notes to "Puppet Opera," I cannot help but read this as a replay of Pound's Adamic naming of H.D., née Hilda Doolittle. The binaries are scrambled a bit: the she-puppet now almost has Pound's name—the first five letters of Pond-Dew are PondD—but she still is given "dove-grey" attributes: the evanescence of pond-dew, the mellifluousness of honey, the secondariness of being a fee-male (a gender with a debt to pay).

While *Drafts* is unified—is, in fact, rife with internal pattern—it is also fundamentally open-ended, and not just because of the incommensurability DuPlessis has built into it. It is open-ended because it is of a piece with DuPlessis's larger project of many decades, which started before *Drafts*, continued alongside it, and continues after it.

This consideration of the epic moment has been a schematic construction. I want to exit its binaries with the caution that there is much more than Ezra Pound in *Drafts*, just as the multiplicious careers of Pound and Creeley furnish ample qualifying and contradicting examples to the models I have presented here. It should be added that DuPlessis's inventiveness and her encyclopedic formal display are also inheritances, modified to be sure, from Pound.

4. Coda: Poets in Libraries

Nothing is more antithetical to the epic moment than a library. Here are our three poets in libraries.

For Pound, the need to eliminate the excess stored in libraries is basic: as his early epiphany in the British Museum reading room attests, books en masse were numbing.[11] His later dismissals of swaths of history—"and then for 180 years almost nothing" (*Cantos*, 534)—are a genteel version of the Futurists' proposal to "destroy the museums, libraries, academies of every kind, . . . fight moralism, feminism."[12] Pound is not that systematic, nor does he disdain scholarship. But Marinetti, the main author of the first Futurist manifesto, remains an attractive poetic model for Pound, who in Canto 72 summons Marinetti's ghost to support the fascist cause. Pound, we might say, is a Futurist with a shelf of overdue library books.

Creeley, describing to Olson the first time he tried to act on the endless reading lists in Olson's letters, narrates a slightly comic freak-out: "The last time I tried (Dartmouth, & you should have come along, personally, with that $4) I was led to the stacks, pushed in, and came out with a book I had already read. I could never get up enough guts to try it again. . . . they scare the hell out of me : libraries" (*Correspondence*, 19).

DuPlessis uses libraries—books and journals, physical and digital—with professional precision. Her writing is activist, feminist, and the knowledge, sociability, and authority of scholarship is not to be laid aside: even when formally innovative, the citations and overall scholarly engagement are normative. If the woman being kept out of the Oxbridge library at the beginning of *A Room of One's Own* is a key episode in human development, DuPlessis's career furnishes a heartening moment along the way.

7
Familiar Williams

"But that sounds just like my husband! . . . You mean to stand there and tell me that *that's a poem*?"—a teacher enrolled in a poetry workshop in the 1970s has just been introduced to what many readers will recognize as the erstwhile kitchen-table note William Carlos Williams scrawled to his wife, Flossie. It has become one of Williams's most familiar poems. First, the confession:

This Is Just To Say

I have eaten
the plums
that were in
the icebox
(*WCW I*, 372)

The second stanza displays a bit of sympathy for the wronged party, who was "probably / saving" the plums "for breakfast." The final stanza starts with a bare-bones apology: "Forgive me," but then shifts to a recollection of the guilty pleasure: "they were delicious / so sweet / and so cold."[1]

The teacher's reaction to the poem is a small moment situated well outside the circles of critical expertise, but it makes a telling emblem of the current situation of Williams in the twenty-first century. The anecdote appears in an essay concerned with teaching poetry in the schools (Zavatsky); it involves a reader who is neither poet nor critic, and her reaction is out of sync with the standard critical histories. But this is appropriate for Williams, who himself was out of sync with the reigning paradigms of his day. He remains anomalous with regard to contemporary poetic expectations, though this is masked by his ubiquitous influence on poets and his presence in anthologies and on syllabi. In accounts of American poetry Williams is a basic marker of the development of modernism, of the avant-garde, and of a democratic art of everyday speech. However, while he has become important to each of these literary chronologies, he fits awkwardly into them all. The imagery from one of his own typically off-the-cuff critical remarks can be applied to his current reception: "Forcing twentieth-century America into a sonnet—gosh, how I hate sonnets—is like putting a crab into a square box. You've got to cut his legs off to make him fit" (Wagner, 30).

The teacher in our opening anecdote is not thinking in terms of literary-historical categories, but she is, in a way, reinventing them, reinscribed in a democratic (unprofessional) context: to her, the poem seems scandalously unpoetic, simply a scrap of real life masquerading as art. Such a reaction could put us in mind of earlier, more notable shocks. *Time* magazine, reviewing *The Waste Land* (1922) in its initial issue, quoted the last eight lines as if they were self-evident nonsense and concluded, "It is rumored that *The Waste Land* was written as a hoax."[2] If we emphasize the origin of "This Is Just To Say" as a kitchen-table note, the closer parallel might be a Duchamp readymade, where a snow shovel, bottle rack, or, most famously and provocatively in the case of *Fountain* (1917), an upside-down urinal was exhibited as art.

A strict chronological perspective would disallow such comparisons. The minimalism and undisguised everydayness of "This Is Just To Say" might, in 1970, have surprised a neophyte like the teacher, but even at its publication in 1934 it would have looked, to a knowledgeable reader of the day, merely "modern" (unrhymed, unpunctuated *vers libre*). By 1970, the poem had become a literary chestnut. Kenneth Koch's affectionate parody, "Variations on a Theme by William Carlos Williams," published ten years before in *The New American Poetry* (1960), assumes the Williams poem as an obvious reference, otherwise Koch's violent humor loses much of its bite: "We laughed at the hollyhocks together / and then I sprayed them with lye. / Forgive me. I simply do not know what I am doing" (Koch, 135). The poem is currently being used as a writing prompt for eighth-graders.[3]

Naive as the teacher's reaction must seem from an informed perspective, it shows us a quality of Williams's work that has affected its reception for many decades: its unstable mix of the ordinary and the new. If we attend carefully to what the teacher says—and Williams is the poet who has been crucial in showing how everyday speech can be a primary material for poetry—we will find more than some dim echo of avant-garde or modernist impacts. In fact, what first strikes her about the poem is its utter familiarity: "But that sounds just like my husband!" For her, the shock of the new arises reflexively from what we might term the shock of the familiar.

In the pedagogical context in which the anecdote appears, the teacher is no longer a half century behind the times. Rather, she becomes a figure of the expansive future of Williams's work: her reaction in the 1970 workshop remains a teachable moment on the twenty-first-century website of the Academy of American Poets. A myriad of similar events has enabled Williams to outflank the larger reputations that, during his writing life, were always ahead of him. A laggard according to modernist calendars, Williams's staying power is better measured in terms of social breadth rather than via tropes of aesthetic advance. It participates in multiple chronologies, making its relation to literary history labile. That "It Is Just To Say" can be a writing prompt for eighth-graders is not a sign of backwardness. Far from it: eighth-graders are not easy to reach.

This does not make the work, in any sense, timeless. Often the ever-widening gap of actual years is quite clear: as in the widely taught "The Young Housewife" (1916). The questions that poem raises about male voyeurism are vivid in the twenty-first century, but the following lines, which present the object of the doctor's fantasy coming into actual view, also present a puzzle to the contemporary reader: "Then again she comes to the curb / to call the ice-man, fish-man, and stands / shy, uncorseted" (*WCW I*, 57). What were corsets, ice-men, and fish-men at the moment the doctor-poet was driving by? Many things, clearly; but contemporary readers will have only a fuzzy sense of them. Williams's success in addressing his present with appropriate poetic quickness remains apparent, but it is also clear that the poem is a century old.

The poetic horizon that Williams often evokes—a primal opposition between a young United States and an adult Europe, pitting a jejune chaos against a culture of varied sophistication—is now a dated trope twice over, since it is prior to both American midcentury hegemony and the post-Vietnam phase of American decline. And for all of Williams's complaints about being stuck in New Jersey, we should remember that New York City was close, and that Williams kept up assiduously with the artists and poets, from Stieglitz and Duchamp to Pollock, Loy, Freytag-Loringhoven, and Ginsberg. In addition, as a doctor with a full-time general practice, he had access to a greater variety of people, classes, and types of events than any other American poet. One example: "The girl who comes to me breathless, staggering into my office, in her underwear a still living infant, making me lock her mother out of the room" (*Autobiography*, 361). This is not meant as a dramatic climax; it is mentioned as part of the daily routine. Williams's combination of wide social experience and artistic sophistication is, in hindsight, remarkable.

But the narrative that mattered to Williams involved a frustrating pursuit of those who, he felt, were ahead of him: Pound and Eliot, primarily—though Duchamp merits mention here as well. Late in life Williams said, "Before meeting Ezra Pound is like B.C. and A.D." (*IW*, 5). From their meeting as teenagers, Pound—younger, confident, and knowledgeable—assumed the role of teacher, a pattern which was to continue for half a century. Williams soon saw through some of Pound's intellectual pretentions: in *Kora* Williams outs Pound, so to speak, by quoting him as saying, "It is not necessary . . . to read everything in a book in order to speak intelligently of it. Don't tell everyone I said so" (*IM*, 10). Nevertheless, Williams remained daunted. Three decades later in *Paterson* he quotes pedagogic letters that he was still receiving from Pound: "Read all the Gk tragedies in / Loeb.—plus Frobenius, plus Gesell" (138). Williams made irregular progress toward emancipating himself, declaring in one of his last poems, "To My Friend Ezra Pound" (1956), "Your English / is not specific enough / As a writer of poems you show yourself to be inept not to say / usurious" (*WCW II*, 434)—the last word a knowing thrust naming the cardinal sin in Pound's poetic politico-theology.

Williams was not a figure like Eliot, Pound, or Duchamp, who could declare, authoritatively, what mattered and what did not. This authority was effected by their creative work but just as significantly by their critical dicta: Duchamp's rejection of what he termed "retinal art"; Pound's division of poetry into *melopoeia*, *phanopoeia*, and *logopoeia* (Pound, *ABC*, 63); Eliot's pronouncement that Joyce's "mythical method" was something that "others must pursue after him" (Eliot, *Selected Prose*, 178–80), or that "poetry in our civilization, as it exists at present, must be *difficult*" (65). Such statements, regardless of how accurate or prophetic they turned out to be, were powerful in setting the terms for inexorably forward-moving aesthetic chronologies.

Williams's despair at the publication of *The Waste Land* is well known: "It wiped out our world as if an atom bomb had been dropped upon it. . . . I felt at once that it had set me back twenty years" (*Autobiography*, 174). A less remarked encounter with Duchamp produces a similar result. "I finally came face to face with him as we walked about the room and I said, 'I like your picture' . . . . He looked at me and said, 'Do you?' That was all. He had me beat all right, if that was the objective. I could have sunk through the floor, ground my teeth, turned my back on him and spat" (137). Williams did not react to these defeats in similar fashion. He paid the most serious attention to Duchamp, whose radically playful senses of art stayed with Williams throughout his career.[4] His aversion to Eliot, on the other hand, was unnuanced and unchanging.

Williams assembled the manuscript of *Spring and All* in reaction to *The Waste Land*. The two works are now, of course, widely considered of the most signal importance to the history of American poetry. But at the time, in contrast to the impact of *The Waste Land*, the publication of *Spring* was a non-event: most of the three hundred copies printed in Dijon were destroyed by US customs (Mariani, 209). The single meeting between the two poets, in 1948, furnishes a fitting conclusion to Williams's inverse trajectory vis-à-vis Eliot. By this point, Eliot ruled poetry in English stylistically, critically, and, as senior editor at Faber and Faber, logistically; he would receive the Nobel Prize a month later. Williams's omission from Conrad Aiken's 1945 anthology of American poetry makes a suitable counter-emblem.[5] Eliot's one recorded remark was: "Williams, you've given us some good characters in your work, let's have more of them" (Mariani, 831 n.7). By pointedly praising the short stories (faintly, to be sure), Eliot was confirming Williams's status as a non-poet.

Eliot's triumph set the terms for Williams's critical reception during his lifetime and for decades afterward. To parse the battle schematically: on the victor's side there would be the major poem (*The Waste Land*, *The Cantos*), authoritative criticism, and established protocols of knowledge requiring the disseminative services of professional academics. Eventually, Williams could approximate these accomplishments: *Paterson* was crucial to his wider acceptance; Marjorie Perloff calls it his "major work, the poem that finally made him famous" (*The Poetics of Indeterminacy*, 148). To match the critical terms of Pound and Eliot there would be Williams's variable foot.[6] But where Eliot and Pound had spawned critical industries devoted to explication, Williams's work was always open to charges of confusion, even simple-mindedness. Randall Jarrell's rave review of the first book of *Paterson* had been most responsible for Williams's success; but when Williams concluded Book Two with eight pages of a Marcia Nardi letter, Jarrell's reaction was incredulousness: "What has been done to them to make it possible for us to respond to [Nardi's letters] as art and not as raw reality? . . . I can think of no answer except: *They have been copied out on the typewriter* [emphasis in original]" (Doyle, 239).[7] As for the variable foot, despite some smart and generous attempts to grapple with what Williams meant,[8] the term has always been vulnerable to commonsense dismissal. If the variable foot is taken as referring to syllables heard in real time, a skeptic would ask if the following units from one of Williams' stair-step lines were really intended to be similar in duration: (1) "even," and (2) "an initiation, since the spaces it opens are new places" (*WCW II*, 245).[9] The editor of the current *Oxford Anthology of American Poetry* writes, affectionately but dismissively, "One of the secrets of modern American poetry is that no one knows what 'the variable foot' really is" (Lehman, 277).

In a letter that Williams quotes in the Preface to *Kora*, Pound gives Williams the left-handed compliment of "opacity," which for Pound is due to Williams's mixed ancestry. It is not far from calling Williams dense: "And America? What the h—l do you a blooming foreigner know about the place. . . . You thank your bloomin gawd you've got enough Spanish blood to muddy up your mind. . . . The thing that saves your work is opacity, and don't forget it" (*IM*, 11). Pound's perception of Williams hardly changed: in 1930 he again praises Williams's "opacity"; *Kora*, for Pound, is "Rimbaud forty years late" (Pound, "Doctor Williams' Position," 392).[10] Such condescension carries through to Charles Olson, who complained to Robert Creeley that "Bill, with all due respect, don't know fr nothing abt what a city *is*."[11] In a private letter, he was harsher: "Bill's own lack of intellect is sabotaging . . . all our positions" (*Correspondence*, 84).

One might ascribe such swipes to the contentiousness of poetic rivals. But senses of Williams as an untutored bumpkin are not hard to come by: throughout his work, one finds moments of naïveté, pugnaciousness, clowning, crudity, foregrounded gaps, and mistakes—all manifestations of his aversion to authority and prestige. In *Kora* Williams quotes a letter from H.D. deploring his lack of seriousness, "the hey-ding-ding touch . . . as if you mocked at your own song," and then seems to prove her right by declaring, "There is nothing sacred about literature, it is damned from one end to the other" (*IM*, 13). While Book Five of *Paterson* (1958) contains much valedictory lyrical seriousness, the lines likeliest to lodge in memory are, "Paterson, / keep your pecker up, / whatever the detail!" (*P*, 231).

Such moments can't be separated out from what is most serious in his work. The foregrounded silliness of the opening of *Spring* and the brokenness of the prose throughout are not an avoidance of the challenge that Eliot's poetics posed: they are part of Williams's answer. However, Williams's turn away from cultured language does not always guarantee vivid liveliness. One of his most famous poems, "To Elsie,"[12] begins memorably: "The pure products of America / go crazy —" (*WCW I*, 217), but is soon full of cliché: "devil-may-care-men who have taken / to railroading / out of sheer lust of adventure." "The Black Winds" (poem V) in *Spring* begins with imagery that can only be called hackneyed: "Black winds from the north / enter black hearts. Barred from / / seclusion in lilies they strike / to destroy—" (*WCW I*, 189–90). Yet the poem ends with the crisp modernist credo: "How easy to slip / into the old mode, how hard to / cling firmly to the advance—" (191).

For all his own complaints about belatedness and all the accusations about his obtuseness, Williams has been frequently invoked at the beginning of literary initiatives as a talisman of the new. Donald Allen's introduction to *The New American Poetry* (1960) begins its list of notable modernist ancestors with Williams—Eliot is omitted. Robert Grenier's "On Speech" (1971) is often cited as a key opening articulation of the poetics of Language writing, attacking the presumed naturalism of everyday language. There, Williams is invoked as a prior limit to be superceded, with Grenier looking for "the progression from Williams"; but Williams is also used as the model for what is to come next. "*To me, all speeches say the same thing*, or: why not exaggerate, as Williams did, for our time proclaim an abhorrence of 'speech' designed as was his castigation of 'the sonnet.'"[13]

Charles Bernstein's polemic "The Academy in Peril" makes Williams's career emblematic of a century-long division between innovative and conservative writing: "Williams, more than almost any other American poet of his time, took an activist position . . .—his work is an intervention . . . against static forms of knowledge. . . . Official verse culture is no more hospitable to Williams's literary politics now [1983] than it was fifty years ago" (Bernstein, 243–51). Ten years later, Hank Lazer gives a succinct rundown of "the two Doctor Williamses," posing Bernstein's textual poet against Williams as "the poet of common objects, immediate description, and common life" (Lazer, 21).

This is where things stand in the twenty-first century; but the larger point is that Williams does not fit into such a binary struggle. To give a less abstract sense of what this means, I will turn back to "This Is Just To Say."

The poem's simple vocabulary, narrative economy, and realism—in the sense that Williams actually ate those plums and then scrawled those lines—make it suitable for eighth-grade pedagogy. However, referentiality was problematized by deconstructive critics in the 1970s. As Jonathan Culler put it: "A note left on a kitchen table which read 'This is just to say I have eaten the plums which were in the icebox and which you were probably saving for breakfast. Forgive me, they were delicious: so sweet and so cold' would be a nice gesture; but when it is set down on the page as a poem the convention of significance comes into play. . . . The value affirmed by the eating of the plums . . . transcends language and cannot be captured . . . except negatively (as apparent insignificance), which is why the poem must be so sparse and superficially banal" (Culler, 175–76).

Readers with more sensitivity to nuances of erotic relations have not found the poem to be (even superficially) banal. (In an interview in his old age, Williams himself called it "practically a rape of the icebox!" [Wagner, 17].) But first, note Culler's transcription: not his elimination of the lineation (which is his point), but his addition of normative punctuation. When Culler writes, "Forgive me, they were delicious: so sweet and so cold," the apology and the memory of the transgression are kept apart by punctuation; there is no punctuation in Williams's quatrain.

While the scribbling of the actual note may well have taken no more than one minute, it had taken Williams more than a decade to establish a form that was clearly syntactic but did not use punctuation. It does not appear in his work until the poems of *Spring*. In "To Elsie," while there are no periods, new sentences begin with capital letters:

while the imagination strains
after deer
going by fields of goldenrod in

the stifling heat of September
Somehow
it seems to destroy us

It is only in isolate flecks that
something
is given off

No one
to witness
and adjust, no one to drive the car
(*WCW I*, 218–19)

If we read the final quatrain from "This Is Just To Say" with this template in mind, we get the following: "Forgive me they were delicious so sweet and so cold." This run-on does not distinguish between atonement and vivid restatement of the crime; this in turn expresses a complex of possible emotions, from narcissism to sadism to intimacy. Readings of such a complex will vary widely: the fact that the poem is an artifact of address embedded in real life adds as much to the lability of poetic sense as any of the formal devices.

One more compositional element should be mentioned: the title, which is not a caption but the beginning of the poem. "This is just to say I have eaten": the title is both part of the poem and outside it. Williams was one of the first to use this specific form, though he does not use it all that often. But the aesthetic implications of being able to gesture both inside and outside the frame of the poem are important throughout his work, especially in *Paterson*. In regard to "This Is Just To Say," the effect is the opposite of the run-on, "Forgive me they were delicious": it bespeaks a detachment on the part of the author. This is not jejune confusion; it is a sophisticated registration of the vicissitudes of human relations.

There are two Williamses currently being used as emblems for opposing poetries: his own work, if cited judiciously, can prove him a textualist or a realist. But as we have seen repeatedly, Williams does not fit easily into such dichotomies. The interview with Mike Wallace in *Paterson* V shows the two approaches superimposed. Wallace, rather like our teacher in the opening anecdote, is upset by modern poetry, which is both obscure and too close to real life. He confronts Williams with an e. e. cummings poem as an example of obscurity:

(im)c-a-t(mo)
b,i;l:e

FallleA
ps!

The contemporary reader can strip away the typographic hijinks to produce the rather cute "I'm cat-mobile. Fall leaps!" But Williams admits to Wallace that he can make nothing of cummings's lines. Wallace stays on the attack, quoting some of Williams's own lines—"a Dungeness crab / 24 hours out / of the Pacific / and a live-frozen / trout / from Denmark"—and exclaiming, "Now, that sounds just like a fashionable grocery list!" At first Williams simply agrees, "It is a fashionable grocery list," but then continues, "Rhythmically it's organized as a sample of the American idiom. . . . [I]f you treat that rhythmically, ignoring the practical sense it forms a jagged pattern. It is, to my mind, poetry." But then, undoing the opposition he has just made between linguistic pattern and practical sense, he says that both are to be perceived: "In poetry, you're listening to two things . . . [ellipses in original] you're listening to the sense, the common sense of what it says. But it says more" (*P*, 222).

Williams, as the writer being interviewed (a character within the poem *Paterson*), offers a synthesis of reading for sense and music. But the author of *Paterson* is posing a still more complex framing. We are reading, as part of *Paterson*, a quoted interview, a conversation between a poet and a reader, and an example of a poem narrating its own reception—as Mike Wallace, reporter for the *New York Post*, expresses the public's incredulity. Williams is showing himself as much object of history as subject.

And there is one more layer: the "fashionable" excerpt comes from one of the most emotional poems Williams ever wrote, "Two Pendants: For the Ears," an account of Williams tending to his dying mother. One of the many strands of the poem involves coaxing the dying mother to eat. She has little appetite, but occasionally eats an eccentric assortment of items: oysters, a banana, ice cream. Thus when Williams lists what someone brought home from the market, "2 partridges / 2 Mallard ducks," it reads as a moving attempt on Williams's part to amuse his mother and to pique her desire for the particulars of the world she is about to quit (*WCW II*, 208).

When Williams admits to Wallace that "It is a fashionable grocery list," he is admitting to the problem that has plagued—and piqued—his readers. What he allows into his writing is too obviously real. But patterning, framing, and reframing make it art. This is like the paradox of the Duchamp ready-made, which is how Henry M. Sayer reads "The Red Wheelbarrow." But Sayre wants art to be uncontaminated: "It is crucial that Williams's material is banal, trivial: by placing this material in the poem, Williams underscores the distance the material has traveled, and the poem defines a radical split between the world of art and the world of barnyards" (Sayre, 12).

It is just such a split that Williams never accepted. For him, art could not begin without the artist's attention to, involvement with, and affection for everyday life. "Comedy Entombed," a short story centered around a woman having a slow-moving miscarriage, will furnish a final example. The quotidian details—discussions with the husband, interactions with the children—are not marshaled for narrative drama. Yet at the end, when the husband asks about the sex of the dead fetus and is told it would have been the girl he was hoping for, his sadness and his wife's odd callousness create a powerful tableau.

At one nondramatic juncture (and at 4:30 in the morning) the doctor has a revelation:

> The whole place had a curious excitement about it for me. . . . There was nothing properly recognizable, nothing straight . . . Tables, chairs, worn-out shoes piled in one corner. . . .—such a mass of unrelated parts . . . . That's it! I concluded to myself. An unrecognizable order! Actually—the new!
>
> And so good-natured and calm. So definitely the thing! And so compact. Excellent. And with such patina of use. Everything definitely "painty." Even the table, pushed off from the center of the room. (*FD*, 327)

One could call this a democratic readymade, if that term can encompass everyday use along with its commitment to perfected abstraction. Note how Williams's recognition of "the new!" does not end things: his aesthetic elation extends into effervescent commonalities: "So definitely the thing!" etc. The room looks like an exciting painting due to its "patina of use": the use adds to the newness. Williams is no demiurge: he didn't make this new order, he merely recognized it. This openness to the everyday is "the new" for the doctor in the story, new for Williams as he wrote the story, and new for readers today.

8
Stein as Explanation

I'm not a Woody Allen fan, but I did go to *Midnight in Paris* to see the modernists. To my knowledge-module, they were all a bit cringy, but a different part of me enjoyed the brute fact of seeing them in the public picture, projected on the big screen as interesting.

The cringiest moment was seeing Gertrude Stein as a no-nonsense professional writer, a hard-boiled pro dispensing tips on how to get published in magazines. It felt ridiculous, but then again, I had to admit that this delineation of her was part of the variegated impact she made. Stein did always address her writing to the public. When this you see, remember me. We do.

The oxymoronic notion of a democratic readymade applies as aptly to Stein as to Williams.[1] This is not to say Stein wrote readymades;[2] there are no readymades but Duchamp's, and those are the opposite of democratic (anyone can buy a snow shovel; only Duchamp could buy what became *In Advance of the Broken Arm*). But my oxymoronic term dramatizes an issue basic to Stein's work. The scandal of the readymade was to commandeer the common as a sign of the singular. Throughout her career Stein did this, deploying the commonest words and everyday objects for highly singular ends. She repeatedly created difference out of sameness and is today widely and casually identified with the trope of using the same word differently: "There is no there there" (*Everybody's Autobiography*, 298), or "Rose is a rose is a rose is a rose" (*GS I*, 395).[3]

But her provocation was more extensive. The scale and seriousness of her writing and the persistence with which she addressed her work (and herself) to the public produced complex aesthetic and social effects. Turning a snow shovel into *Broken Arm* was a gesture of separation, meant to shock the bourgeoisie; Stein's gestures were more pervasively unsettling: their singularity was obvious, but they were not in the service of separation. Stein commandeered the common with the aim of becoming part of the everyday world—an important part, an eminent one, but very much of that world. She may have written and acted as a singular genius who was ahead of her time, but hers was an avant-garde of the ordinary: both her early notoriety and her later popularity index this.

Stein's range was wide. Consider the stylistic distances between "Melanctha" (1909) and *Tender Buttons* (1914): the former with its tortuous syntax and rudimentary vocabulary opaquely narrating but never resolving complex emotional turmoil; the latter a playful, at times erotically charged venture into quasi-Cubist, polysyntactic portraiture of the everyday lifeworld. Another disparate pair, both written in 1932: the best-selling *Autobiography of Alice B. Toklas* and the uncompromisingly abstract *Stanzas in Meditation*. Her writing was various, but a foundational procedure throughout was the cohabitation of the ordinary and the different.

In "Composition as Explanation" (1926) Stein continually presents her own genius as almost indistinguishable from everyday modernity and at the same time as completely distinct. The play of sameness/difference begins with the opening clause: "There is singularly nothing that makes a difference a difference." Detractors found such language inane, but the two differences compactly demonstrate a word being either charged or empty: some differences don't make any difference. Stein then expands the point, contrasting war with genuine creativity. War is old-fashioned, "prepared" beforehand and thus academic. Bad writing and painting are similarly stultifying when produced by "those . . . who don't make it as it is made," as opposed to "the few who make it as it is made" (*GS I*, 520). We might translate Stein's praise as promoting artistic process over product; but she uses more elementary words ("make," "made") to keep this activity common but mysterious. Bad artists fail to unite make and made; Stein activates what is almost, but is not, a tautology.

A pleasantry in *The Autobiography of Alice B. Toklas* shows more of the imbrication of art and life. Toklas (that is, Stein writing as Toklas) tells us, "you cannot tell what a picture really is . . . until you dust it every day" (*GS I*, 776). The lightness and paradox are blatant—how quaint to put dusting above careful looking. But more is implicit here. Toklas is claiming special authority: it takes intimacy to know what pictures *really* are. Then, too, note how the quintessentially bourgeois activity of dusting becomes the prime aesthetic act. And, further, this bourgeois normativity presents, without disguise, the scandal of Stein and Toklas's unofficial, but very proper, lesbian marriage.[4]

"Scandal" will seem dated to many, though some have pushed for re-scandalization, with Stein's stance toward the Vichy regime the smoking gun.[5] There's not much smoke there, however. Stein's political and historical opinions, while part of the record of her celebrity, are epiphenomenal to her self-enabling egotism—in the main, they're patrician. More remarkable is the career that her behavior made possible. Her work remains an exciting exemplar for contemporary poets, with Bernadette Mayer, Joan Retallack, Juliana Spahr, Lee Ann Brown, and

Holly Melgard as notable examples. But her impact extends beyond the literary into the other arts.[6] Her work is influencing cultural matters in ways that aesthetic categories have not succeeded in containing. DJ Spooky's mash-up of the Wu-Tang Clan and "If I Told Him: A Completed Portrait of Picasso" makes a fit emblem of this incomplete, open-ended condition.

*

But Stein's writing does not voyage through history with autonomy intact. My point of departure saying this is "Reflection on the Atomic Bomb," but it is the entirety of Stein's work I am addressing via that one anomalous page.

"Reflection" stands outside the variousness of Stein's work, not so much for formal or stylistic reasons, but for the accidental fact that it was the last thing she wrote. And the piece itself, as we now have it, seems accidental, even un-Steinian—isn't *reflection* one of those secondary mental processes, such as memory, identity, and recognition, against which Stein defined her project? And in fact the title was not Stein's. The editors of the *Yale Poetry Review* added it when they published, as a stand-alone work, what seems, more than anything, to have been Stein's response to a query, if not a questionnaire.[7]

Responding to questions was not something Stein generally found interesting; when a student asked her about "Rose is a rose . . ." her impatience is palpable: "Now listen! I'm no fool. I know that in daily life we don't go around saying 'is a . . . is a . . . is a . . .'" (Mellow, 404). But in "Reflection" something external which she did not find interesting did in fact move her to write: "They asked me what I thought of the atomic bomb. I said I had not been able to take any interest in it" (*GS II*, 823).

She cannot have been in anything remotely like good health when she wrote "Reflection." Its brevity is most un-Steinian. And then there is this sequence of words: "so you see the atomic [bomb] is not at all interesting," where "bomb" is an editorial insertion.[8] Anomaly is a very un-Steinian notion, but "Reflection" is anomalous. As something Stein wrote, it is, theoretically and (mostly) in practice, an instance of the continuous present, but as something we read, it is the last thing she wrote. By the time it was published she had come to be a dead one, and history, which she had commanded, banished, toyed with, created, now throws its careless, iterative shadow across the page.

I would like to compare the pages of three books to examine the vicissitudes of the continuous present. First, the 1998 Library of America *Stein: Writings 1932–1946*. The paper is thin, strong, and bright, and is meant, as the colophon tells us, to stay that way: it "meets the minimum requirements of the American National Standard of Information Sciences—Permanence of Paper for Printed Library Materials." The font is legible but pushes toward the small as befits a classic author with much work to be presented. The book will last physically, and the edition will last institutionally. The continuous present will stay in print continuously, brightly legible, serious.

The paper of *Paris France* is thick and sturdy, a light cream color that has deepened over three-quarters of a century. There are four four-color plates (Gris, Picasso, Lascaux, and Francis Rose) and four black-and-white plates. Published in New York and London in April 1940, the edition is high end, displaying what Renaissance nobles would call *sprezzatura*, showing Stein as she said she always wanted to be: "a real lion a real celebrity" (Stein, *Autobiography*, 143). But the end of the book also shows the future not being kind to the continuous present. Stein's concluding words are remarkably unprophetic: "This book is dedicated to France and England who are to do what is the necessary thing to do, they are going to civilize the twentieth century and make it be a time when anybody can be free, free to be civilized and to be. . . . and this book is dedicated to them because I want them to do what they are going to do. Thank you" (*Paris France*, 120). France fell to the Germans two months later.

Wars I Have Seen makes quite a contrast. The paper is thin and graying, and the print is crowded. The printed words may reach a happy plateau with the arrival of the Americans (244); and for pages Stein resumes her quasi-imperial stature, asking for a general: "we met lots of officers and finally I met three majors in Aix-le-Bains. I said well it's all right, but now we have had everything from a second lieutenant to a full colonel and indeed several specimens of each now I want a general" (248). But the cheap paper and the huddling of the words on the page bespeak a more crimped situation. As the colophon states: "This is a Random House Wartime Book. It is manufactured under emergency conditions and complies with the government's request to conserve essential materials in every possible way." The writing is wartime writing: "Now in 1943 when there are armies and armies and they come humming in and the air at night, when the moon is bright is full of them going over to Italy to do their bombing . . . then you keep on thinking how quickly anybody can get killed, . . . more quickly than in any book, those up there flying and bombing and those down below, with houses tumbling, and burning" (22). This is unusual. For Stein, to write was to be active, certain of the ability to wield the materials; here the writing is reactive and anxious about the future.

War is the kind of large noun that had let Stein assert her prerogative of distance from conventional associations: "That is what makes politics and religion and propaganda and communism and individualism the saying yes and that is always the same and that is because it is the human mind and all the human mind can do is to say yes" (*GS II*, 417). War gives Stein a notable opportunity to display this distance: "and in the Boer war there were concentration camps where they had nothing to eat, and all that is natural enough. The concentration camps for the Boers excited us all" (*Wars*, 44). Oppositely, war is also boring: it "is prepared and to that degree it is like all academies it is not a thing made by being made it is a thing prepared" (*GS I*, 520). In the following paragraphs from "Lifting Belly" the word war does not occur, but what the word represents is shooed away:

> Dare I ask you to be satisfied.
> Dear me.
> Lifting belly is anxious.
> Not about Verdun.
> Oh dear no. . . .
> Lifting belly together.
> Do you like that there.
> There are no mistakes made.
> Not here at any rate
> (*GS 1*, 415)

The "here" of the last line is where the bliss of writing and living "Lifting Belly" happens. War—Verdun—is outside and is of no interest. Or, the war can be something the arts create: in *The Autobiography of Alice B. Toklas*, Picasso, when he first sees camouflaged cannon, exclaims, "it is we that have created that" (*GS I*, 753); in her lecture on *The Making of Americans*, Stein suggests a great power in writing capable of stopping time and, possibly, starting wars:

> It is like generations in the Bible, they really do not take very long. . . . Twenty-five years roll around so quickly and in writing they can do one of two things, they can either roll around more or they can roll around less quickly.
>
> In writing Making of Americans they rolled around less quickly, In writing a Long Gay Book, they did not roll around at all, and therefore it did not go on it led to Tender Buttons and many other things. It may even have led to war but that is of no importance.
> (*GS II*, 281)

But the prerogative of perfect freedom with regard to war is dashed by World War II: "this coincidental war this meaningless war, this war that put an end a real end an entire end to the nineteenth century" (*Wars*, 20). The writing of *Wars I Have Seen* does not triumph over the nineteenth century and enter the excitingly fresh air of the authentic composition. The words are not interesting—in fact, they're meaningless—and yet she writes them. The twentieth century no longer has any composition: "Anybody can understand that there is no point in being realistic about here and now, no use at all in any, and so it is not the nineteenth but the twentieth century, there is no realism now, life is not real it is not earnest, it is strange which is an entirely different matter" (44).

For years, I was not able to be interested in "Reflection." I first knew of it when it came out in the 1970s.[9] This was the period when my wife Francie, the brave one of us, was arrested protesting nuclear weapons development at Lawrence Livermore Lab (I provided childcare). In such circumstances, I didn't make it past the first paragraph: "They asked me what I thought of the atomic bomb. I said I had not been able to take any interest in it." For years, I read no further.

The continuous present: did it have a birth, a moment of coming into being? If the continuous present is beginning again and again, can it also have begun being continuous for the first time? If it is born in a time and setting, does it have the characteristics of that time and setting?

Is the continuous present prewar? (Pre–World War II, that is.)

Stein places the emergence of the continuous present during the writing of *The Making of Americans*: "there was a groping for a continuous present. . . . In this beginning naturally since I at once went on and on very soon there were pages and pages and pages more and more elaborated creating a more and more continuous present including more and more using of everything and continuing more and more beginning and beginning and beginning. I went on and on and on to a thousand pages of it" (*GS I*, 525).

The continuous present emerged in print in the August 1912 special number of *Camera Work*, where Stein's portraits of Matisse and Picasso appeared in the issue devoted to the two painters.[10] It was not her initial appearance in print, but it did mark an unmistakably major entry in the burgeoning dictionary of new art.

One hundred years later, the portraits are now staples on introductory syllabi and the phrase "one whom some were certainly following was completely charming" (*GS I*, 282) is, doubtless, well known to those who introduce Stein in and out of classrooms. Nevertheless, it's worthwhile to suspend our familiarity and to register Stein's present-tense credentials at that moment (1912). She is writing what amounts to the catalogue essay for the first publication/presentation of Matisse and Picasso by their US conduit, Stieglitz; she is demonstrating an apt sense of Cubist practice; she is showing herself to be one "creating the modern composition authentically" (*GS I*, 521). In the perfect timing of Stein's portraits, activity and knowledge are one. She is entering the present as its equal.

The writing continually manifests its activity, untrammeled by time. It happens at the moment it happens, with moments differing as moments continually do. "One whom some were certainly following was one who was completely charming" (521).

How could the Men of 1914 (as Wyndham Lewis referred to himself, Pound,

Joyce, and Eliot) have been so unperceptively scandalized by such a demonstration of critical acuity and artistic power? Didn't Pound laud poetic invention? But the Men of 1914 held their noses. Lewis accused her of "counterfeit," childishness, and "deadness"; her "prose-song," he wrote, is "a cold, black suet-pudding . . . of fabulously reptilian length" (Lewis, 77). Eliot tut-tutted: "it is not improving, it is not amusing, it is not interesting, it is not good for one's mind. But its rhythms have a peculiar hypnotic power not met with before. It has a kinship with the saxophone" (Eliot, *Selected Prose*, 595). Perhaps it was that Stein, while rigorously addressing the ear and mind, was quite hard on the eye. It takes a lot of energy to read her; it's not recommended for the treadmill or elliptical trainer. She certainly was impeccable in directing the reader's attention only to a legible surface, nothing else. There was no time for depths. "One whom some were following was one who was charming (*GS I*, 521).

This is "abstract" writing in that it is not emotional: the limbic system is not being addressed. But abstraction does not entail deprivation—far from it. It is of the greatest interest for our own world: the charm of Picasso's art (its play and its power, both) is a good and very real thing that Stein feels and shows as a new worldly fact. Stein is describing something exciting: Picasso and his art. Simultaneously, she is evaluating: sometimes what Picasso is doing is completely charming and sometimes not. She is writing an intimate, uncowed homage, giving a knowing demonstration of Cubism, and inventing a mode of poetic address.

Thus far, I've been assuming a contrast between Stein's impeccable display of the continuous present (different kinds of writing, always continuously present) and the accidental, contingent "Reflection on the Atomic Bomb." But recently I read it quite differently: it was the heroically present Stein. The other facts remained: she was old and ill, and the continuous present was always a performance. She could call her writing a daily miracle, yes, but it took strenuous attention. It takes energy to read Stein, as I said; what "Reflection" and the other reactive moments show us is how much energy it took to be Stein. She did not always succeed at it as she aged. Her human mind, memoryless, history-proof, continuously present, was, it turned out, predicated on her historical situation. Still, I suddenly realized that to write, in 1946, that the atomic bomb was not interesting was to perform a powerfully insouciant refusal of military-industrial language. What a heroic, instructive, *lively* gesture. "That it has to be secret makes it dull and meaningless" (*GS I*, 823): only what can be publicly known has meaning. What a sane politics and poetics can start there.

9
Taste Test

It's tempting to use complexity as shorthand for poetic value.[1] In some ways, it would be true enough: many examples of complicated poems spring to mind, things I always like reading. It is often complexity that catches my eye. But complexity in that kind of shorthand can also feel exactly wrong. It's the hook of a thousand commodities: say, a *New York Times* spread on cocoa, where only a few (expensive) brands impart the necessary complexity.

Why is that a sacrilegious comparison? Complexity that you taste immediately but that provides a continuing articulation of thoughtful pleasure, making you want to repeat it, share it, tell people just how it's good—isn't that a provisionally acceptable analogy for a useful poetics?

Well, maybe, but poetry, I would answer, can be more complex than the most exquisitely crafted hot chocolate. In both cases, body tastes world; but drinking hot chocolate is a private experience. When poems are interesting, body tastes writing, a process where a known language displays some of what is not known, other people and histories, revealing a not exactly comfortable public arena where, it turns out, one's body, among all bodies, actually has lived, lives, and may continue to live.

I do admire (and like) good cooking; but taste in poetry is more paradoxical, working in longer interpersonal circuits. Interesting poems (by definition undefinable beforehand) offend good taste in the most complex ways. The present does not always taste good to any one palate, but it is the crucial poetic ingredient.

Every manner of poem is complex in manifold ways. But complexity without immediacy is not enough. There are self-contained complexities that stay on the page, awaiting (belle-lettristically) appreciation or (academically) explication or (iconoclastically) revolution, predefining their proper reading contexts without making much contact with the present. Poems can aim for wider contexts. The situation of poets and readers in America in the twenty-first century is of such complexity that individual poems are hard pressed to register anything like an interesting amount of the present, of new and old history, of globalized flux and reflux, technology, fashion, emerging body stances, weather patterns, street codes, Web rhetoric.

Immediacy is just as opaque as complexity. Both have to be written and at the same time are results of reading experiences, and reading experiences change.

My high school poetry initiation, self-authored, accidental, posed the complex (Eliot) against the immediate (Whitman): I went for *The Waste Land* because it was hard in that dumb sense that appeals to some teenagers, and I went for Whitman because it was compellingly obvious. In *The Waste Land* I couldn't understand the chopped-up literary parts, the foreign phrases, I couldn't understand the bar talk, the typist's seduction. And of course "shantih"—how weird was that? But through those closed doors, a vivid seriousness called to me. And on the outside there was sex (good), dogs digging up corpses (good), and other vague gothic religious stuff (pretty good then, not so good now). *The Waste Land*, with its hints of crucial adult problems, made me want to read and, later, write poetry: perhaps the world would be like this when it and I got interesting.

Whitman was the opposite: the world was inescapably great, life was great, self-expression was great. Just say it. Great and easy—anyone could do it—in fact, anyone and everyone *had* to do it: "The pure contralto sings in the organ loft, / The carpenter dresses his plank—the tongue of his foreplane whistles its wild ascending lisp" (Whitman, 200). I absolutely agreed.

What was I agreeing to? These two lines now seem wonderfully complex: the woman with low voice (it took me about forty years to realize contralto meant low) singing from the high loft; below, on the street, the sound of the foreplane leaping upward. One of Louis Zukofsky's oft-quoted definitions situates poetry above speech and below music: "Lower limit speech, / Upper limit music" (*A*, 138). Here, in Whitman, as part of a much larger catalog, there is a human voice making music in one line and metal and wood producing speech in the next, the music coming down to its hearers, the wood/plane lisp wildly ascending.

This is the most straightforward eloquence, immediate in its descriptive rush, but thoroughly surprising (complex) from word to word. A metal tongue produces both a thin curl of wood and a language with no mistakes; and the lisp is the perfect pronunciation.

A hundred years ago Paul Laurence Dunbar's dialect poems were read (by whites) as simple, "childlike" entertainment; Dunbar himself labeled them "Minor" as opposed to his "Major" poems in standard English. But his 1895 "Ante-Bellum Sermon" is nothing if not complex, preaching resistance under cover of piety:

An' yo' enemies may 'sail you
    In de back an' in de front . . .

But de Lawd will sen' some Moses
    Fu' to set his chillun free. . . .

But fu' feah some one mistakes me,
    I will pause right hyeah to say,
Dat I'm still a-preachin' ancient,
    I ain't talkin' 'bout to-day. (Dunbar, 13–15)

Of course Dunbar, through the mask of the antebellum preacher, is talking about "today"—about 1845 and 1895 for him; about 1845, 1895, and the twenty-first century for us. Such history is part of what I keep calling the present.

More complex immediacy: Melvin B. Tolson's (once-invisible) *Harlem Gallery*:

"A black stevedore bulked his butt
in a high-hat restaurant
not far from the bronze equestrian statue
of Andrew Jackson.
The ofay waitress hi-fied,
'What can I do for you, Mister?'
Imagine, if you can, Harlem nitwits,
a black man mistered by a white dame
in the Bible Belt of the pale phallus and the chalk clitoris!
The South quaked.
Gabriel hadn't high-Ced his horn,
nor the Africans invaded from Mars.
It was only the end-man's bones of Jeff Davis
rattling the Dies Irae
in the Hollywood Cemetery!"
(Tolson, 275)

The quotes around this stanza indicate that the tragic hipster Hideho Heights is speaking. That's one element of Tolson's complex narrative framing: we're in the Zulu Club in Harlem where the poem's narrator has been taken by the Curator to hear inspired social historians (bards, rhapsodes, griots) spout poetry.

Allegiance to orality does not preclude complexity. Tolson can easily match Zukofsky in density of meaning within a word. Take the phrase "olivets and pearls" (Tolson, 230); from my default mode as white reader I took this as a contrast of two objects, olives (of some sort) and pearls. But no. Looking up "olivet," I see the OED illustrates it with a usage straight out of darkest colonialism: "a kind of mock pearl or white bugle made for the African trade and prized by the Negroes of Senegal, *Simmonds Dictionary of Trade*, 1858." Olivet/pearl is illustrating, with the bitterest humor, the play of ersatz/real, false marketing/just price in a strongly dissonant chord.

Immediacy is a necessary component of complexity. Tolson, in 1965, was not just writing "clitoris" but racializing it in the service of a critique of racialized feeling. Imagine writing "the pale phallus and the chalk clitoris" in the early 1960s.

This is more or less the same time that Muriel Rukeyser was writing, "Whoever despises the clitoris despises the penis" (Rukeyser, 133).

I do not know if Rukeyser and Tolson read one another's work. But it is my sense that these two clitorises took awhile to circulate. Shelley may in fact still be right in his claim that poets are the mirrors of the gigantic shadows which futurity casts upon the present, but Tolson and Rukeyser remind us that sometimes poems move like messages in some whispering gallery held back by a particularly dense medium.

What is obvious can be quite complicated, as in Harryette Mullen's early poem:

Father (Part 1)

My mother told me that after he left us
and we moved back to Texas,
for weeks whenever she'd take me out
I'd run and grab the pantleg
of any man I saw
(no matter if he was black or white)
shouting, "Daddy, Daddy!"

She said the white men
backed away redfaced and stiff.
The black men only laughed. (Mullen, 18)

The longing of the grabbing, shouting child (indiscriminate racially, but specific about gender) jumps out at us; the mother's wry grasp of the white men's embarrassment, coupled with the black men's knowing acknowledgment of the hopelessness of the child's grabs, appears more slowly; and what the poem makes clear is the tremendous historical complexity that reaches from the child's longing for her father into the ethical miasmas of miscegenation which are so palpable to the black and white men, and then to the mother, and then to the poet, and then, thanks to the poet, to us.

One last example to testify that complexity can thread itself through the simplest ditty and that a childlike rhythm can encode the thorniest theological cruxes. Heine, translated by—quite a bit of historical complexity here—Pound:

I dreamt that I was God Himself
        Whom heavenly joy immerses,
        And all the angels sat around
And praised my verses. (*P/T*, 162)

Are God's poems complex enough, immediate enough? Possibly not. Even immersed in a heavenly bathtub of joy, he is anxious. In this, he is not unlike any other Not Necessarily Great poet. Therefore he needs angelic approval no matter how bureaucratically enforced.[2] It's better, and more bitter, out here in the world for us writers and readers, offering, withholding, refusing, accepting our varying presents, never at rest with the taste.

10
The Pound Cage

My wife, Francie Shaw, asked me recently why I'm still working on Pound. You were working on Pound when we got together and, forty-four years later, you're still working on Pound. Why? It's a good question.

There are circumstantial answers. I am a teacher of poetics and poetry and you cannot teach either without dealing with Pound. *Poetry* magazine might have gone under after a few years if Harriet Monroe hadn't met Pound. Eliot may well have stopped writing after "Prufrock." Certainly *The Waste Land* wouldn't be what we read today. Williams would have been a doctor, perhaps continuing to write Keatsian sonnets in his free time. *Ulysses* may not have been written. Certainly no Zukofsky, no Olson, no Creeley. No Objectivists and no Projective Verse. No New American Poetry. No Language writing. Without *The Cantos* no investigative poetics. Although, in fairness, it should be said that in this alternate, Poundless universe Gertrude Stein would have been just fine, idem the same, to quote one of her titles.

I'm a Pound scholar, and thus I'm part of the ever-more unsettled critical conversation on Pound, who remains an intriguingly overdetermined object of literary scholarship; even the text, as Ronald Bush has demonstrated, won't stay still (Bush, "The Composition of *The Pisan Cantos*"). It's not just the upside-down Chinese characters and backwards Greek accents; over my four-plus decades of reading Pound, *The Cantos* have gone from a poetic monument that seemed massively structured a la *Ulysses* to something quite contingent. As an emblem of this latter condition, take the frontispiece of the contemporary scholarly edition of *The Pisan Cantos*: a facsimile of the sheets of toilet paper on which Pound wrote what are now the opening ten lines of the poems. These lines, mourning Mussolini and comparing him obliquely to Dionysus and Christ, frame *The Pisan Cantos* as an elegy for Mussolini and Italian Fascism. If we remember how central Pound's hatred of impurity was to his politics, the fact that toilet paper was the original medium of this statement of allegiance is one of poetic history's blunter ironies.

Little can be said about Pound that will not lead into intractable discussion. Contradiction is his salient defining feature: no poet in the twentieth century did more to enliven English-language poetry; but for long stretches he hardly uses the English language at all. No poet insisted more on the circulation of crucial fact; none was more secretive and eccentric. None was more generous; none more possessed by hate. The enemy of all beaneries (Pound's mocking term for the university as center of pedantry); the provost of the Ezuversity. Modernist; belated pre-Raphaelite medievalist. Inventor of the modernist long poem; or, in his late sardonic self-description, "minor satirist." Polymath; bluffer. Pedagogue; solipsist.

Why Pound? has an inescapable biographical answer for me. When I was 16 in the summer of 1964 at Interlochen Music Camp I found his *ABC of Reading* at the bookstore, and immediately woke up to a life in poetry. I was already an adolescent notebook-poet, but Pound's invitation to the big world was immediate and the attractiveness was lifelong. Pound offered a dynamic sense that living knowledge was what mattered, only that.

The miscellany of *Guide to Kulchur* wasn't particularly important; what I took to heart was the invitation to be single-minded about what was interesting in writing:

> [O]nce the process is understood it is quite likely that the knowledge will stay by a man, weightless, held without effort.
>
> About thirty years ago, seated on one of the very hard, very slippery, thoroughly uncomfortable chairs of the British Museum main reading room . . . I lifted my eyes to the tiers of volumes and false doors covered with imitation bookbacks which surround that focus of learning. Calculating the eye-strain and the number of pages per day that a man could read, with deduction for say at least 5% of one man's time for reflection, I decided against it. (*GK*, 53)

Here was that weightless feeling of certainty; it was a live voice confidently dismissing the mass of deadening verbal product, false doors, and imitation bookbacks. Like many moments in Pound, it offered a glimpse of the Ezuversity, where learning is anti-systematic and energizing and knowledge is instantaneous recognition. I enrolled immediately. Decades later, the question is: what did I learn to recognize? Which brings me back to Francie's question.

*

The cover of the contemporary scholarly edition of *The Pisan Cantos* shows a row of cages at the Disciplinary Training Center in Pisa, where Pound was first held by American forces in 1945, though it doesn't show the particular cage Pound was put in. This is an excellent emblem of the problem that Pound leaves to the contemporary poetry world. Pound himself was constantly imploring his readers to discriminate, to weed the muses' garden. It would be a relief if we could weed out Pound's phobia, idiocy, and solipsism and keep the vivid, attractive energy of his poetic desire. It is tempting to split his career chronologically: in the first half a charming and heroic figure (cosmopolitan, aggressive, macho-lyrical, generous, a legendary networker, a passionate visionary of a new poetics); in the second half the fascist, conspiratorial, closed, mad poet. But the Pisan cantos, which clearly belong to the second half, are the most important thing Pound wrote: they can't be weeded out.

Pound's effect on poetic history is more overdetermined than any binary scheme allows for, and thus I will now propose an overdetermined reading of the cage itself. I will use a kind of inversion of Pound's ideogrammic method. He wanted uncontaminated meanings to arise from the juxtaposition of pure, unambiguous things—the naturalness of rose, cherry, rust, and flamingo making up the ideogram for red (*ABC*, 22). My reading of the cage will juxtapose an incommensurate group of baggy metaphors or allegories.

First, I want to consider the cage, not as a violent mark of separation, but as one of a series of exotic enclosures within which his poetics functioned throughout his career. The series will run like so: the *fantastikon*, Eleusis, the cage, the hospital for the incurably insane at St. Elizabeths, and "the great ball of crystal" at the end of *The Cantos*. The half-revealed, half-hidden quality of what he was insisting on was a great source of charisma.

The *fantastikon* is a term Pound tried out first in a 1912 essay, "Psychology and Troubadours," where he writes, "[T]he consciousness of some seems to rest, or to have its center more properly, in what the Greek psychologists called the *phantastikon*. Their minds are, that is, circumvolved about them and are like soap-bubbles reflecting sundry patches of the macrocosmos." This sounds Shelleyan, but Pound goes to celebrate the more poetic of these visionaries as "germinal": "Their thoughts are in them as the thought of the tree is in the seed, or in the grass, or the grain, or the blossom" (Pound, *The Spirit of Romance*, 92). Pound then moves from Whitmanian pantheism to something more polemical in a note to Harriet Monroe. The *fantastikon*, he tells her, signifies "what Imagination really meant before the term was debased—presumably by the Miltonists, tho' probably before them. It has to do with the seeing of visions" (Liebregts, 44). Here, already, we have the visionary crying in the wilderness, ready to do battle with Miltonists. Later, other groups would take their place. Jews, of course, but not only them. Buddhists and Taoists—seemingly any group would do depending on the occasion, as seen for instance in Pound's dig at Charles Olson near the end of their encounters at St. Elizabeths: "Wot Olson don't know

IZ, I hate Swedes as much as I do Jewz" (Olson and Creeley, *Complete Correspondence, Vol. 1*, 147).

"The Condolence" from *Lustra* (1916) is not one of Pound's notable poems, but it is worth quoting here for its oxymoronic blend of *fantastikon* and aggressive rhetoric. Just to be clear, the "fellow sufferers" addressed in the poem are the prior poems of Pound's:

> The Condolence
>
> O my fellow sufferers, songs of my youth,
> A lot of asses praise you because you are "virile,"
> We, you, I! We are "Red Bloods"!
> Imagine it, my fellow sufferers —
> Our maleness lifts us out of the ruck,
> Who'd have foreseen it?
>
> O my fellow sufferers, we went out under the trees,
> We were in especial bored with male stupidity.
> We went forth gathering delicate thoughts,
> Our "*fantastikon*" delighted to serve us.
> We were not exasperated with women,
> for the female is ductile.
>
> And now you hear what is said to us:
> We are compared to that sort of person
> Who wanders about announcing his sex.
> As if he had just discovered it.
> Let us leave this matter, my songs,
> and return to that which concerns us. (*P/T*, 263–64)

Here the *fantastikon* suggests qualities of isolation, a feminized withdrawal into delicate thoughts, or perhaps just narcissism; but the rhetoric of the poem, on the other hand, is a display of Renaissance machismo and up-to-date cosmopolitan cultural capital.

I will but briefly touch on the next enclosure, Eleusis.[1] What Pound intends by this has been widely commented on by scholars. Here I will just quote a key passage:

> The Duce and Kung fu Tseu equally perceive that their people need poetry; that prose is NOT education but the outer courts of the same. Beyond its doors are the mysteries. Eleusis. Things not to be spoken save in secret.

> The mysteries self-defended, the mysteries that *can* not be revealed. Fools can only profane them. (*GK*, 144–145)

This mixture of secrecy and authoritarianism is not news to Pound scholars; nevertheless, to a non-expert ear such pronouncements must seem remarkable. Calling Mussolini by a nickname and naming Confucius via estranging scholarly syllables—both are the gestures of an insider. Or take these two lines from *The Pisan Cantos*: "nor Charlie Sung's money on loan from anonimo / that is, we suppose Charlie had some" (74/35).[2] Whether alluding to sacred mysteries, hobnobbing with the powerful, or hinting at world conspiracies while locked in punitive enclosures, Pound always spoke from the position of insider.

*

This brings us to the physical cage at Pisa. Pound's treatment there has been deplored for obvious reasons. To put a 60-year-old broadcaster of eccentric rants in a specially reinforced steel cage with spotlights shining on it around the clock is hardly to be excused by the bureaucratic uncertainties of the US army. But another dimension to Pound's situation is now visible in hindsight: a hypermasculinization.

Robert Allen's description of his encounter with Pound has a Hemingway-like patina: "We saw flakes of blue light coming from the stockade at the Disciplinary Training Center one night in May of 1945. Acetylene torches, someone said; later we heard that they were reinforcing a cage to hold Ezra Pound." The prisoners, "rapists, murderers, and traitors . . . could 'soldier out,'" Allen tells us:

> By following a fantastic routine, accepting cruelty in the extreme, and by turning himself into a "G.I." automaton, a trainee could have his federal prison term canceled and be returned to duty. This took a lot of guts or a lot of hate and not all men could do it. Some of them tried to run away one afternoon, but businesslike short bursts from an automatic rifle in a guard tower chopped them down. (I rode to the hospital with two of them while they bled to death.) (O'Conner and Stone, 33)

Except for the last detail, this makes the Disciplinary Training Center (DTC) seem like a hyper-tough version of a National Football League training camp. *The Pisan Cantos* only registers this occasionally: "niggers scaling the obstacle course" (74/315). More often, Pound looks through a classical lens, as when he compares himself to Odysseus and the other prisoners to swine: "ac ego in harum / so lay men in Circe's swine-sty; / ivi in harum *ego* ac vidi cadavers animae" (74/403–5). In the preceding lines we read, "and the guards op/ of the . . . /

was lower that that of the prisoners / 'all them g.d m.f. generals c.s all of 'em fascists'" (74/400). Here, incidentally, is the beginning of Pound's postwar political wobble. Do we hear "fascists" there as an insult that Pound is quoting ironically, or is he participating in the language that he quotes? While the record overall shows Pound not recanting his fascism (his fascist salute when he gets off the boat in Italy in 1958 is Exhibit A), there are opposed moments, such as when he shouts out in the courtroom in Washington that he was never a fascist.

But let me return to the cage as chrysalis of the heroic male. The topography of the DTC in Allen's description can be analogized to that of the *Inferno*:

> Inside the stockade there was a secondary enclosure for the Medical and Dental sections, two mess halls, several areas where the trainees pitched their pup tents, and solitary confinement and death cells. The solitary cells, "boxes," were seven-foot concrete cubes with peepholes in their steel doors. To be "boxed" meant two weeks on bread and water with a blanket and a bucket. The death cells were wire cages about ten feet square at the base and seven feet high. Condemned prisoners, later to be hanged at Aversa, paced the cages. (O'Conner and Stone, 33–34).

Translating this into Dantescan terms gives a version of the topography of hell, with the death cells at the center. Pound's specific death cell was, as the 24/7 illumination shows, felt to be the locus of most extreme danger. The US government was, in this mythic-topographic reading, placing Pound in Satan's situation, the center of hell—thus adding to Pound's machismo.

There is another strand to be drawn from the Dantescan scenario: remember that as Dante starts climbing down Satan's body he finds himself climbing upward, first toward Purgatory and eventually toward Paradise. We can apply this in a loose analogy to Pound's own progress, with the cage marking the point where his temporal orientation starts going backward. His life continues chronologically forward, but he is no longer the heroic quester for the new, charismatically ahead; he is now facing backward, lamenting his lost Italian "paradiso perduto" (*PC*, xliii), the diamond which survives only metaphysically, elegiacally (74/194–95).

David Rattray's "Weekend with Ezra Pound," from the mid-1950s, is a chilling document. The conspiratorial creeps Pound is hanging out with are a depressing lot and his behavior as charismatic teacher in that context is a deeply pathetic display, which I will not quote here. But one moment strikes me as sharply emblematic of the pivot from Pound as heroic quester for the new to Pound as relic. First, Rattray asks Pound about Provençal music and we get some of Pound's expertise:

> Oh, yes, it seems to me that one of those old fellows—could it have been Pellizzi?—one of them told me something about a facsimile edition being printed in Barcelona. Of course you know that most of those old manuscripts are just *motz* without *sons*. I've seen 'em with the staves carefully drawn on, but no *sons*, just the verses underneath, an entirely understandable bit of laziness: the fellow just knows how it went, a perfectly simple tune, why waste time writing it all out? And as you know, transcribing those songs from the original to the modern notation is a job for a musicologist. Maybe that's why so few have been published. But you know, that old notation, it's just a kind of musical shorthand, an aid to memory, to be used only by someone who had already heard the tune at least once. (O'Conner and Stone, 111–12)

This seems to be the same Pound from Canto 20 who visited "old Levy" in Freiburg. But when Rattray, enthused by Pound's enthusiasm, contributes his own information, Pound is totally uninterested: "I told him about the record of Provencal songs made by Yves Tessier, who in addition to being a musicologist was an excellent singer. [Pound] waved his hand impatiently. Don't expect Grandpa to know anything about Provencal after 1920. That's all after my time. You have my *Spirit of Romance*? You do? All right, I cover all that in there" (112).

Once Pound's retrograde stance in time is admitted, many examples come to mind. Bush writes: "The goddesses of *The Pisan Cantos* are disconcertingly slight in relation to the depth of experience we find in Pound's more genuine moments. They are also oddly disengaged from it: they tend to appear in histrionic, even sentimental passages that speak of ecstasy, whereas the poem's great moments invoke human sympathy" (Bush, 76). This retrograde quality has its political counterparts. When Olson met Pound at St. Elizabeths he grumbled, "Pound can talk all he likes about the *cultural lag* in America (he was at it again yesterday as of the Vanguard Press announcements, the 20 year lag) but he's got a 200 year *political lag* in himself" (Olson, *Encounter at St. Elizabeths*, 53). One can place Pound's political imagination in a number of retro niches: in the late 1940s Olson makes him a Federalist; in the 1920s, Wyndham Lewis called Pound medieval; in the twenty-first century I find it increasingly hard to ignore the nineteenth-century cast of much of his stance. His heroic Renaissance comes from Burckhardt; his sense of science from Agassiz; when he writes out his visionary moments (rather than simply referring to them) the machinery involves the ecstasies of Edwardian Greek gods. What Pound used for leaven to break out of his own poetic time lag was masculinity and violent assertion. Two Edwardian figures of violent splitting are apropos here: Dorian Gray and Mr. Hyde. These are two more components of my cage anti-ideogram.

Pound as Mr. Hyde works as follows. In *The Pisan Cantos*, Pound displays a mix of attitudes toward the mostly black prisoners he is with: condescension, respect, and racist objectification. Along with this, there is a jocular appreciation of male sexual aggression: e.g., when he quotes an obscene song: "'Just like Jack Dempsey's mitts' sang Mr Wilson / / so that you cd/ crack a flea on eider wan / ov her breasts / sd/ the old Dublin pilot" (77/489). The full lyrics, the notes tell us, are "My gals got great big tits / Just like Jack Dempsey's mitts." Unashamed sexuality, with Irish and African-American accents—like Eliot's Sweeney. Or take the lighthearted tone of the following lines: "and Till was hung yesterday / for murder and rape with trimmings plus Cholkis / plus mythology, thought he was Zeus ram or another one" (74/171–72). This tone recalls an earlier moment from Canto 9, describing one of Malatesta's rapes: "And there was the row about the German-Burgundian female" (*C*, 36). Pound's celebration of masculinity can mix the hieratic with the jocular, as in the following passage, which uses Latin to solemnize Malatesta (*olim de Malatestis*, meaning "once Malatesta's"), following it up with a bouquet of machismo ("mountain oysters," i.e., bull testicles):

Olim de Malatestis
        "64 countries and down a boilin' volcano"
                says the sargent
ex rum-runner (the rum being vino rosso)
        "runnin whisky" sez he; mountain oysters? (76/313–17)

At times it may seem like Pound is undergoing a Wordsworthian immersion course in the "real language" of the DTC prisoners, but not quite. Wordsworth may have admitted rustic speakers into his poems only conditionally, but the point of his polemical "real language of men" was its standard orthography—unelevated diction using the same spelling as the real language of serious poetry. In the excerpt above, Pound admits Italian into his real language (vino rosso is not italicized), but switches to eye dialect (runnin, sez) for American speech. It is Edwardian anthropology: an exoticism.

*

Recalling how Shelley and Blake read Satan as the hero of *Paradise Lost*, the cage makes an excellent hatching-spot for the Romantic hero, which is how Pound was taken after the war by Charles Olson and Robert Creeley at the beginning of their careers. Here is Creeley's registration of Pound's charisma, writing to Olson in 1951: "I think I wd honestly faint dead-away, face to face with him"; imagining himself at St. Elizabeths, Creeley writes, "Myself, I never wd have got over the lawn; they cd have buried me, where I fell, etc." (Creeley and Olson, *Complete Correspondence, Vol. 8*, 59). In *For Love*, Creeley shows himself as the proper instantiation of the Poundian jongleur. Compare Pound's translation of Arnaut Daniel:

> What curse
> I strive to shake!
> Me hath she cast from high,
> In fell disease
> I lie, and deathly fearing. (*P/T*, 489)

with Creeley's "The Gift":

> This
> is the present
> of the ages, all
> rewards
> in itself
>
> But the lady —
> she, disdain-
> ful, all
> in white for
>
> this occasion — cries
> out petulantly, is
> that all, is
> that all. (*Collected Poems*, 236)

Although Creeley was never much interested in *The Cantos*,[3] nevertheless he was the freshest, best incarnation of *early* Pound, the troubadour, the outlaw Don Juan—hard-boiled but chivalrous, alert to the demands of amatory excellence, which were close enough to the demands of poetic excellence. You need a strong emotional-social motor to carve contemporary speech into such sharp-etched syllables.[4]

To recapitulate: thus far, I have presented the cage as *fantastikon* or sacred enclosure; as proving ground for the alpha male; as site of Pound's transformation from the good Dr. Jekyll into Mr. Hyde; as the setting for Satan's—or is it Prometheus's?—punishment; and as an emblem of time turning back, avant-garde blueprint switching to elegiac vision.

The cage is also like a cloud chamber—to use an image from the atomic age—

where we can see poetry splitting off from politics, as the New Critics would have it. Or, in the postmodern instantiation, the fissioning of words into research material, musical notes, procedural matter—going off to the left, let's say, while off to the right trails the cloud-track of meaning. Here, we can apply the parable of Dorian Gray (loosely, as is my non-Poundian practice throughout). Like the hideous corpse at the end of Wilde's tale, Pound the insane, traitorous fascist is a loathsome object best consigned to the Out Basket, while the patterned energy of the lines, the beauty and surprise of the syllables, the projective panache of the line-by-line motion—this would be like the attractiveness of Dorian's portrait.

What is Pound saying when we read, to pick one line from thousands, "and I hear that G. P. has salmoned thru all of it" (79/26)? To read that line—beyond appreciating the vividness of "salmoned"—we turn to Richard Sieburth's notes, where we learn that "G. P." was "Giorgio Paresce (1900–82), Pound's supervisor at the Italian Ministry of Popular Culture" (*PC*, 143). In my copy of *The Pisan Cantos*, the notes are, I have to admit, as well thumbed as the poems are. Does this mean I'm still in the Ezuversity? Or are the notes a way out, some degree of objectification? Is being in the Ezuversity putting oneself in a cage of sorts?

*

As it turns out, I was one of the later matriculants. Olson had been enrolled since the 1940s. Zukofsky, with his characteristic luck, got in as a very young man. He never got a degree. But then again, nobody gets a degree at the Ezuversity.

When I was discovering Pound in 1964 I was, without knowing it, entering a current of anti-academic, counter-cultural poetics that had been gathering since the end of World War II. Charles Olson is often thought to be the poetic anchor of Donald Allen's *New American Poetry* in 1960; but Pound, along with Williams, furnishes the bedrock for that anchor. Allen begins his introduction by establishing a counter-history: "American poetry has entered upon a singularly rich period," he writes, beginning his honor roll with *Paterson*, *The Desert Music*, and *Journey to Love*; and with *The Pisan Cantos*, *Section: Rock-Drill*, and *Thrones* (xi). After praising the first-generation modernists (polemically omitting Eliot), he proposes his—quite eccentric to us—second generation: Elizabeth Bishop, Edwin Denby, Robert Lowell, Kenneth Rexroth, and Louis Zukofsky. The third generation in his history is the stuff of the anthology: Black Mountain, the Beats, the New York School, miscellaneous others. What unites these different poets is "a total rejection of all those qualities typical of academic verse. Following the practice and precepts of Ezra Pound and William Carlos Williams" (xi).

I will stop quoting Allen there and consider the practice—the precepts not so much—of Pound, both as I have felt it as a writer over the past half century and how it seems to be faring more generally in the poetic, cultural, and academic multiplex of our present. Some kind of parallax has taken and continues to take place. My understanding is that parallax is what happens when the position of a star observed in March changes when seen again in October, due to the earth's swing around the sun. In other words, the fixed stars (the near ones anyway) move. In poetic terms, this means that foundational values alter. Of course this would be Pound's worst nightmare—changing the currency is the evil of evils for him. Poetry is the best of goods because its value never changes: literature is news that stays news. Pound, especially in the later stage of his career, is focused on fixed stars of one kind or another: "Agassiz with the fixed stars, Kung to the crystalline" (*PC*, 93/645).

"Crystalline," according to Plotinus—and Aristotle and Plato after him—was the description of the final perfect sphere in our concentric universe (dark central matter; earth's surface; heavenly bodies; stars; lastly and outermost, the crystal empyrean). It now has an Edwardian ring. The passing of time has played havoc with the singularity of Pound's poetic desiderata, his unambiguous meaning, natural authority, unwobbling pivot. Pound provided an endless bonfire of virtuous names, historical glimpses of the good in action—Kung, Agassiz, Gaudier, Martin van Buren; but the result has not been as Pound intended. What he wanted to be a ball of light has become instead a smoky territory best ventured into by specialists.

I learned that one can learn 'Pound'—as in learning a language and its culture. To do this one studies Pound's vocabulary, reads some of what he read, and creates synopses of his references (Jefferson, Erigena, periplum). Pound speaks of his own learning as weightless and permanent and, truly, *The Pisan Cantos* gives strong evidence of the staying power of Pound's touchstones. But for myself, at least, it is increasingly hard to call such learning weightless.

After forty years of learning the specific language in which Pound writes and teaches, it has become more difficult to say what it is that Pound is affirming with such energized vehemence. Consider the beginning of "Time-lag" in *Guide to Kulchur*:

> Here again is the time-lag. Van Buren's autobiography was written in 1861, and unpublished till 1920. Are we to assume that Radloff buried a very few lively poems in a mass of dullness? Are we to assume general incuriosity, while faddists and university infants carded out again the overcombed wool of a limited set of "classics." Did Pere Lacharme's latin arouse NO curiosity whatsoever. We must assume Lacharme's latin as a basis. Who saw it before Mohl? and after Mohl's edition where did it lie doggo for 107 years? (*GK*, 214)

This, like much of Pound's poetic news, has become antiquarianism. As I noted before, his positive values (Eleusis, light, excellence of bodily perception) seem ever more Edwardian. His hatreds, unfortunately, have a much longer shelf life: for instance, in William McNaughton's "The Secret History of St. Elizabeth," we see Pound's foundational status for what McNaughton refers to as "the men of 1994" (Dick Armey and Newt Gingrich) (Dennis, 272). McNaughton compares Pound's "It may depend on one man" (*C*, 583) to Dick Armey's celebration of "Individuals—not vague historical forces" (Dennis, 263). Then there's the Casa Pound, the violent neo-fascist organization in Italy.

To go back to Francie's question: what am I still learning from Pound?

Part of it, I suppose, is negative. The excellence of the rhythm of Pound's attention, to be appreciated without cringing, requires that any irritable reaching after content be dropped,[5] and the rhythmic panache alone be received. It is something like what von Sternberg said of his movies, that they should be seen upside down to make the narrative irrelevant. Here is "My Pound Decoder Ring," which imitates the syntax while changing the content of the Pound passage:

My Pound Decoder Ring

Le Paradis n'est pas artificiel
but is jagged,
For a flash,
for an hour,
Then agony,
then an hour,
then agony,
Hilary stumbles, but the Divine Mind is abundant
unceasing
improvisatore
Omniformis
unstill
and that the lice turned from the manifest;
overlooking the detail
and their filth now observes mere dynamic;
That the Pontifex ceased to be holy
– that was in Caesar's time –
who was buggar'd
and the coin ceased to be holy,
and, of course,
they worshiped the emperor. (Pound, *Cantos*, 634)

*****

Poetry isn't an art facial,
                                        but is jagged,
flushes,
            stays hot,
then crumples,
                stays hot,
                                        crumples into
old jokes, but the Reading Horizon is agile
                undulating
not what you thought
over the top
                unrepeatable
so that: the meter readers turned to their manuals,
                cementing the detachments
and the institutes now dish up mere panorama;
so that: the Present ceased to be legible
        – that was in the Stein Era –
            who had great sex
and new sense started making sense,
        but, of course,
                they re-ordered the anthologies. (Perelman, *Iflife*, 107)

My procedure here is contrary to Pound's great translation practice, in which he aimed for the spirit of the original while using the letter for surprising pivots toward that spirit. Mine is faithful to the letter (the specific phrase-shapes).

It is only Pound's practice as translator that enabled me to write this.

The Pisan Cantos are the crux of Pound's career. If he had died coming back to Rapallo from America in 1939 and if, therefore, his epic had ended with the Adams Cantos, it is likely *The Cantos* would now be consigned to high-density storage. *The Pisan Cantos* are the affirmation that poetry can only exist in the present, and in the case of live poetry, that present has a past and a future:

and I hear that G. P. has salmoned thru all of it.
Ou sont? and who will come to the surface?
And Petain not to be murdered 14 to 13
        after six hours' discussion
Indubitably, indubitably re/ Scott
                I like a certain number of shades in my landscape
as per / "doan' tell no one I made you that table"

or Whiteside:
"ah certainly dew lak dawgs,
ah goin' tuh wash you"
(no, not to the author, to the canine unwilling in question)
with 8 birds on a wire
or rather on 3 wires, Mr Allingham
The new Bechstein is electric
and the lark squawk has passed out of season
whereas the sight of a good nigger is cheering
the bad 'uns wont look you straight
Guard's cap quattrocento passes *a cavalloi* (*PC*, 79/26–43)

This is a poetic rhetoric—even, to use that despised term, a poetic voice—that is quite out of the reach of Pound's familiar poetic terms and ideograms: the don'ts, the phanopoiea, melopoiea, and locopoiea. Widely cited as these are, these terms cast little light on his own writing in *The Pisan Cantos*, on the actual variety of paces, textures, social rhythms of interjection, interruptions, oblique continuities, and pastiche effects. However, I do find one of his more dubious constructions useful: "Apart from the social aspect he was of interest, technically, to serious writers. He never wrote a sentence that has any interest in itself, but he evolved almost a new medium, a sort of expression half way between writing and action" (*SP*, 217). Pound wrote this in 1928 discussing Lenin, but since Pound knew no Russian, it seems better to apply it to the generalized Poundian hero who changes the language, the political landscape, and the culture in a single act.

At Pisa, the context of address became, perforce, that of his captors. The cage is the site of Pound's "new medium, half way between writing [epideictic poetic speech] and action [balked politics]":

no sooner out of Troas
than the damn fools attacked Ismarus of the Cicones
4 birds on 3 wires, one bird on one
the imprint of the intaglio depends
in part on what is pressed under it
the mould must hold what is poured into it
in
discourse
what matters is
to get it across e poi basta
5 of 'em now on 2;
on 3; 7 on 4

thus what's his name
and the change in writing the song books (*C*, 79/64–77)[6]

Pound, too, is a "what's his name," responsible for many recent changes in our "song books." *The Pisan Cantos* are, as Burton Hatlen pointed out, the model for Olson's projective verse, as well as for poems like Ginsberg's "Wichita Vortex Sutra."[7] It is similarly easy to find a prototype of O'Hara's personism in the ubiquitous mixing of personal and public throughout *The Pisan Cantos*—in the famous line "yet say this to the Possum: a bang, not a whimper" (74/9).[8] Or later: "but Eileen's trick sunlight softens London's November / progress, b . . . . h yr / progress" (76/54–55).[9]

The legacy of Pound's inventiveness reaches beyond the Allen anthology to the Noigandres group, to conceptual writing, to Young-Hae Chang's "Dakota," et al.—but such a list suggests a kind of happy ending that I want to resist.

There is a temptation to identify the time of Pound's writing with one's own. There are strong forces pushing toward a read-writing identification. There is the lively motion of the writing—a stuttering, stroboscopic series of attempts at poetic fixity, a kind of light show flashing amid the dark dioramas of Pound's retrograde histories. There is the charisma of half-revealed knowledge, shading over into the anxiety generated by the Ezuversity. The varied rhythm of the gaps has its own compelling legibility.

But at the end of the day I think it is best to borrow Agassiz's advice and "look at the fish" (*ABC*, 18). Here, this means naming the different times on display in the sets of lines I have quoted from Canto 79. There is the powerfully close approach to the present: the various configuration of birds on wires, as if Pound were inventing the live cam. There is, typical of Pound, the freshness of local contradiction, when saying something instantly makes the mind see it the other way: in this case, the terse advice to "get it across e poi basta [and then stop]" is belied by the ever-varying disposition of the birds. There is the Renaissance ("Guard's cap quattrocento"); there is straight-from-the-plantation-veranda racism (good niggers and the bad'uns); there is the fascist reading the latest political news (G. P. has salmoned thru; Petain, by a 14/13 vote, was not "murdered").

What Pound is saying—his matter, if you will— is still toxic. The movement of his writing remains vivid and poetically generative. This is not a unique paradigm: consider *The Birth of a Nation*. Insofar as technique, procedure, and system are made focal, the New Critical, post-Bollingen peace pact is still in effect: Cage and Mac Low writing through *The Cantos*, for instance. Form trumps; content is for the naive. Okay, but it is a fragile truce.

Pound sparked a utopian enthusiasm in poetry, for me as for many others. He himself confused news with poetry. He remains in the cage.

11

In One Language and Out the Other

Harryette Mullen and Ezra Pound

Harryette Mullen and Ezra Pound are a far from obvious pairing. For those who know Mullen's work, the expected modernist association would be Gertrude Stein, who was a primary influence on Mullen's second and third books, *Trimmings* and *S*PeRM**K*T* (*CB*, 26).[1] Pound, on the other hand, has not influenced Mullen's writing, and Mullen has not engaged with him in her critical work. In verbal surface, politics, position in the literary field, and audience, the two are simply distant.

My bringing them together here is sparked by Pound's line, "It can't all be in one language" (*C*, 576), which strikes me as exactly wrong for Mullen's work, especially *Muse & Drudge*, where the proposition seems more: All this, full of difference as it is, *is* one language.

In what follows, I will be reading *Muse & Drudge* against Pound's *Cantos*, contrasting her boundary-crossing inclusivity with his vigilance toward linguistic boundaries. It is a fundamental difference, but the two poets share an equally fundamental feature: both are insistently pedagogic, and it will be interesting to see that common aim working in the two very different cases.

"In one language" is an open-ended notion; as my joke-without-a-punchline title suggests, my aim is to keep it open. To start to explore its variety, I'll turn to a nonliterary context.

In the wake of the 2013 acquittal of George Zimmerman for shooting Trayvon Martin, there was an article on the linguistics blog Language Log deploring the decision and, at one point, discussing how well the jurors might have understood defense witness Rachel Jeantel. In the commentary, this morphed into a general discussion of how well speakers of Standard English (SE) understand African American Vernacular English (AAVE). Many commentators offered examples of how understanding a language can vary. Here are three:

> I used to work for an American company, and often spoke on the phone with our office in Houston, Texas. I had difficulty understanding one person. So. I asked someone where he came from. Bombay. As soon as I knew

that I could understand him. It was a normal Asian accent but I had expected him to be some kind of American and so misheard what he said. Once I knew where he was from I could follow his speech.

. . . in New Zealand, when I asked some people from India what language they were speaking. They replied: "English."

. . . you are talking about AAVE as though it were a single dialect. It isn't. Oakland AAVE ("ebonics") is different from east coast AAVE ("jive") is different from Kansas City AAVE ("black talk") is different from New Orleans AAVE. . . . I don't recall having difficulty learning to understand them, but a new learning experience (at least a few hours) was required each time before I could rely on getting it right. . . . "AAVE" appearing in movies, etc, is mostly written by white guys who don't necessarily speak it very well themselves, and besides are writing for white audiences to understand.[2]

These examples differ: in the first, a single shift in attention makes for excellent reception; in the second, misapprehension (on the writer's side) is nearly total; in the third, beyond the writer's impatient expertise, we get a sense of the difficulty of hearing, at speed, the nuances of different AAVEs. But in each case, can't we say that the language as a whole—Standard English, Bombay-inflected English, Oakland AAVE, whichever language—is the primary fact? That comprehension, across the scale from rudimentary to fine-grained, depends first on gestalt and then on detail? That as we focus on the words, we are already hearing what language they're in?

Three anecdotes will not resolve the intractable relations of part and whole in language, but I want them to suggest that we hear language before words. In place of that familiar modernist praise, "the word as such" (Kruchenykh and Khlebnikov), I want to draw our focus to language as a shared social membrane: both in the sense of skin dividing outside from inside, and as a semipermeable screen allowing some exchange between inside and out. Not words, then, but language-as-gestalt, involving complicated mixes of empathy, distance, historical resonance, sonic expectation. I am intending no linguistic, philosophic, or poetic rigor here—quite the opposite: I want senses of language to stretch from the rudimentary level of comprehension (I don't know Hungarian) to highly focused aesthetic reception (but I know 'Pound'—the language, 'Pound,' that is).

To start at a literal level ("is that French or Hungarian?"), take this quatrain from *Muse & Drudge*:

spaginzy spagades
splibby splabibs

choice voice noise
gets dress and breath
(*R*, 165)

Is this written in one language, or are the first two lines in a different language than the last two? I would answer that all the lines are in English, since the first two are African-American slang, as we learn from one of Mullen's sources for her poem's vocabulary, *Juba to Jive: A Dictionary of African-American Slang.*[3] That *spagades, choice, voice,* and *breath* belong to the same language is a polemical/pedagogical claim: *Muse & Drudge* is written in one conglomerate language. This is not to say Mullen is not code switching; but she is crossing more boundaries than simply between black and white speech.[4] She is mixing learning (both Eurocentric and Afrocentric) and vernacular; present and past. She is not writing in the American language in any singularizing, standardizing sense, but what she's writing is in American.

Mullen says that *Muse & Drudge* "was written specifically to . . . bring different audiences together" (*CB*, 229). At the same time, she is equally explicit that she is writing in one language: "My poetic idiom is the product of American English and its vernaculars, including those associated with black speakers of American English" (*CB*, 5). She insists on democratic access and commonalty: "The idea that there is a black language that is a nonstandard English, that Standard English is therefore white, is very problematic" (235). Her language is mixed, mongrel, miscegenated, and, at the same time, imperial, global, late-stage US hegemonic. Consider these two quotes: "American culture is a miscegenated culture. . . . [M]y text is deliberately a multi-voiced text, a text that tries to express the actual diversity of my own experience living here. . . . *Mongrel* comes from 'among.' . . . We are all mongrels" (186); and this one: "Although I happen to be working in what is currently the global language of international capitalism, or what some call 'Imperial English,' the quirks, contradictions, even the inanities, in the language of the declining Anglo-American empire are what interest me most" (7). The complexity of what language involves for her becomes more and more evident as her description of *Muse & Drudge* gathers steam. It is, she writes, "an attempt . . . to return to a more-or-less recognizably 'colored,' 'negro,' 'black,' or 'African American' base of folk-street-blues-based riffs, rap, and rhetoric without returning to the specifically located subjectivity of my earlier work." Her practice "has been something of a traditional, eclectic, folksy, trashy, classical, avant-garde, worldly, naive, unorthodox, spiritual, polymorphously perverse, mammy-made, jig-rig, and Rube Goldberg operation" (19).

There is code switching here: "classical, avant-garde" in the same verbal rush as "mammy-made, jig-rig." But if code switching is thought of as addressing two or more audiences each in its own tongue, then what is happening here is the opposite: code amalgamating, perhaps. Mullen is addressing different subsets of listeners as part of the same audience.

In the following lines from *The Pisan Cantos*, how many languages are there?

"all them g.d. m.f. generals c.s. all of 'em fascists"
"fer a bag o' Dukes"
"the things I saye an' dooo"
ac ego in harum
so lay men in Circe's wine-sty;
ivi in harum *ego* ac vidi cadavers animae
"c'mon small fry" sd/ the little coon to the big black;
of the slaver as seen between decks
and all the presidents
Washington Adams Monroe Polk Tyler (74, 400–409)

Pound stretches English in many ways here: GI slang abbreviated (g.d. m.f.); song lyrics and speech presented as sound (saye an' dooo); archaicism (so lay men, wine-sty); bigotry (coon) juxtaposed with empathy (the slaver as seen between decks); but "ivi in harum *ego* ac vidi cadavers animae" is Latin, not English.

In the previous chapter,[5] I presented my view of the charged contradictoriness of 'Pound,' the language, its opposed senses of charismatic authority (Pound the insider) and confinement (Pound in the cage at Pisa). But here I need to acknowledge one commonsense meaning of what Pound is saying with "It can't all be in one language." He is making the point that there are many languages—Latin, French, Greek, etc.—in *The Cantos*.

This is part of the legacy of the epicurean Pound: cosmopolite, life-affirming globalist, extoller of the arts as refinements of the senses. The subtlety of Flaubert's French is an exquisite specific that one would be the poorer for missing. Sharpening one's senses simultaneously sharpens one's senses of words: sensory education of all kinds leads to poetic excellence and political and ethical well-being.[6] Even in the cage at Pisa, when what we now know as *The Pisan Cantos* may have felt like a Villon-esque final testament rather than the next installment of his ongoing epic, Pound was citing good food as part of what he was fighting for:

but coffee came to Assisi much later
that is, so one cd/ drink it
when it was lost in Orleans and France semi-ruin'd
thus the coffee-house facts of Vienna
whereas Mr Carver merits mention for the

cultivation of peanuts,
arachidi, and the soja has yet to save Europe
                    and the wops do not use maple syrup
the useful operations of commerce
            stone after stone of beauty cast down
and authenticities disputed by parasites
(74, 805–15)

But as the anti-Semitic code word "parasites" reminds us, the Manichaean Pound coexists with the urbane epicurean. "It can't all be in one language" can also be taken in the harsh, phobic sense that affirms essential, unbridgeable difference between languages. This echoes the thought of one of Pound's masters, Agassiz, who fought Darwin in the name of polygenesis—the doctrine that humans are not one species, but come from different stocks.

The Pound who knows many languages but also knows he is addressing a mostly monolingual audience is an attractive figure. "For *those who read only English*, I have done what I can" (*ABC*, 58). His insistence that poetry is more vibrant when its makers and readers know a few languages was lifelong, and much of Pound's enduring poetic achievement was performed in his role as linguistic facilitator, expanding the resources of English by forcing suggestions of other languages into it: the quasi–Anglo Saxon of Canto 1, the quasi-Chinese of *Cathay* and Canto 49, the quasi-Latin of "Homage to Sextus Propertius," among many examples.

But these expansive impulses are increasingly countered by his sense of language boundaries as natural, sacred, biological barriers not to be transgressed. This is the phobic Pound who declares that poetry is an Eleusinian mystery;[7] or, more plainly, "Not a jot or tittle of the hebraic alphabet can pass into the text without danger of contaminating it" (*SP*, 320).

It is this vision of language as a site of enclosure and containment that I am writing against here: Pound's hypertrophied sense of language as having an inside and an outside, with purity inside and disease outside. The early Pound, the generous dandy-pedant-revolutionary, and the various later Pounds, phobic, fascist, elegiac, post-fascist, all share a rhetorical stance: the figure of the insider frames many of Pound's gestures, early and late, admirable and execrable. (The early Pound was more open-handed with his insider knowledge.) Throughout his career, though, a structure of initiation, with knowledge held away from the vulgar and the merely curious, is the governing frame, from the fourth doctrine of Imagism (the secret that drew Amy Lowell across the Atlantic) to *The Cantos*'s final self-description: the great ball of crystal.

Mullen's sense of enclosure is radically different: escaping from historical bonds is part of what she models in *Muse & Drudge*. Discussing the book in an interview with Cynthia Hogue, Mullen says:

> I wanted things to be in flux . . . If you stand still too long they will put chains on you, so you want to keep moving. This is one of the things that is most fascinating to me about . . . slave narratives. . . . The true freedom in the slave narrative is at the point of deciding to escape and the journey north. Once they get to the North, they are, again, part of a hierarchy, and they are still at the bottom. . . . The freedom people experience is actually when they are on the road, in flight. I associate that with writing. . . . The poem is running; the poem is flying. (CB, 248–49)

This poetics of freedom and flying is not an avoidance of identity; quite the opposite, as the place of *Muse & Drudge* in the narrative of Mullen's writing makes clear. Mullen testifies that labeling has been a major fact in her reception. Her first book, *Tree Tall Woman*, allowed her "to be placed rather neatly within the category of 'representative blackness' (as well as the categories of 'feminist' and 'regional' poet)" (*CB*, 10). There, Mullen used black language—"I'm your momma, and I could always tell when / you're doin something you aint got no business" (*TTW*, 4)—but also wrote in Standard English.[8] Her next two books, *Trimmings* and *S*PeRM**K*T*, are sequences of prose poems clearly signifying on Stein.[9] Here is one piece in its entirety: "A little tight, something spiked, tries on a scandal. One of a pair vamps it up with a heel. If the shoe fits, another mule kicking, a fallen, arch angel loses sole support" (*R*, 9). Besides the other things they are doing, each phrase here puns on shoes: tight, spiked, one of a pair, a heel, fallen arch, sole, scandal (sandal). In this, the semantic focus is tighter than in *Tender Buttons*. But *Trimmings* is Steinlike in form (prose, commas, periods, variety of sentence-shape), density of semantic play, and absence of narrative or setting, and, to an extent, in its subject matter of clothes. If a reader did not know Mullen was black, this piece would not necessarily make that clear; if a reader did know, "another mule kicking" would stand out as a quote from the blues. But in fact such glancing quotes were not enough to span the gap between avant-garde and African-American audiences.

As I said earlier, Mullen wrote *Muse & Drudge* to make her identity as a black poet obvious. She points out that at times you can, if not judge a book by its cover, then at least begin to read it from the outside: "You can tell a black book fifteen feet away. . . . The color is usually much brighter . . . with maybe a kente pattern in the design" (*CB*, 229). The cover of her own *Muse & Drudge*, in its original Singing Horse Press publication, uses different means to show that it is a black book: a border of deep blue—sapphire, to anticipate the poem's open-

Cover of original edition of *Muse & Drudge* (Singing Horse Press 1995)

ing word—surrounding a severely xeroxed black-and-white image of a black woman in ecstatic song.

Although I will quote from the currently more available edition, this image from the older cover (offered here in black and white, alas) furnishes a vivid emblem of Mullen's procedure in the poem and of her position in the poetic field. The woman herself is not Mullen, but we are seeing Mullen's design, both in the colors and in the handling of the image. The colors are intentional, signaling the fact that *Muse & Drudge* is a black poem with an unambiguous bond with the blues. "It had to be a black and blue cover," Mullen tells an interviewer (*CB*, 228).

The cover image began as a photograph Mullen got from publisher Gil Ott. In Mullen's description, the woman "is not a performer; she is a woman who attended a public hearing about access for people with disabilities . . . and she is actually in a wheelchair, but you can't see that in the picture. She was participating in a public protest. . . . [I]t looks like she could be praying, singing, or clapping. . . . It is an ambiguous image, which I liked. She looked very soulful. . . . She definitely looked like a black woman" (224).

Mullen then describes how she "put the photo on the Xerox machine and made it bigger, used black marker to crop it, and blacked out everything around her. She kind of shines out of the black background. She seemed just right" (224). Besides suggesting some of the painful history and serious ecstasy to be encountered in the poem, this image reflects how the writing works in the poem. Like the language, the cover image is inescapably recognizable yet impossible to pin down. It is abstracted, denarrativized, unmoored. The setting (wheelchair, disability hearing, protest) is erased; the activity is powerful but undefined ("she could be praying, singing, or clapping"); its high contrast makes it seem simplified, as if photocopied many times. But it is not ambiguous: "She definitely looked like a black woman."

Like the cover image, the materials Mullen uses—words, phrases, sayings, blues lines—are identifiable: *Muse & Drudge* is definitely written by a black woman and is about black women. But Mullen's language shares in the cover image's unmoored quality: it has been around, immersed in use, misuse and reuse, and it is being used now with tremendous specificity and mobility.

My photocopy simile has its limits, since it too easily suggests a progress toward total effacement of particulars. The information in a photocopied photocopy eventually degrades; but Mullen's constant working with words, phrases, blues lines, makes something new and vivid; its social mobility adds information.

This "just right" language of Mullen's presents a compelling alternative to a Poundian poetics of precision, his celebration of "le mot juste" (Pound, "Doctor Williams' Position," 373). Pound's insistence on getting the words right remains crucial. But in practice—Pound's practice as much as anybody's—the mot juste can authorize a search for singularity and a flight from the common, often producing results that can be described by another French phrase: cul-de-sac.

Muse & Drudge is eighty pages of non-narrative quatrains, though non-narrative should not imply nonhistorical. The texture of the language continually evokes and critiques ranges of history throughout. Sampling across disparate quarters is densely audible. The poem begins:

> Sapphire's lyre styles
> plucked eyebrows
> bow lips and legs
> whose lives are lonely too
>
> my last nerve's lucid music
> sure chewed up the juicy fruit

you must don't like my peaches
there's some left on the tree

you've had my thrills
a reefer a tub of gin
don't mess with me I'm evil
I'm in your sin (*R*, 99)

Like the beginnings of Kamau Brathwaite's *X/Self* and Derek Walcott's *Omeros*, the opening line here invokes the Western classical world while making its own distance audible. "Sapphire's lyre" plays both the blues and Sappho's lyrics; "lyre styles" indicates a library of music styles. If we hear the lines as enjambed, a complete sentence emerges: "Sapphire's lyre styles plucked eyebrows"—where the classical/blues lyre articulates the fashion sense that shapes eyebrows. But the "plucked" of "plucked eyebrows" goes back to the lyre and activates ancient Greek music more than a contemporary beauty shop. "Bow" continues this sense, suggesting violin bow, but if it is connected to "lips and legs," as the lineation suggests, then we're back to the blues and bow-legged women.

We are being addressed as subjects who have been saturated by phrases. Are they clichés? The sediment of history? We are simultaneously invited to recognize what we already know and to use it in decoding tangled twists of cultural code that we might not yet know. The speaker does not remain in one place. A black woman of the blues says "you must don't like my peaches / there's some left on the tree," complaining that we aren't passionate enough about her. The next lines turn that same subject position inside out. It's not Bessie Smith singing, "I've had my thrills" and "I'm in my sin." A critical intelligence is telling the aggrandizing man that *he's* been the consumer of *her* thrills, and that *he* has put her at the center of his conception of sinfulness, not that she considers herself sinful. These are some details of what I hear; there's more.[10]

A quatrain from the middle:

massa had a yeller
macaroon a fetter
in his claptrap
of couth that shrub rat (156)

and Mullen's comments:

> Some [of the puns] are subliminal, some so conspicuous I'm sure people are groaning as they hear them. . . . In [that quatrain] there's "Yankee doodle went to town" [the second line echoes "stuck a *feather* in his cap and called it *macaroni*"]. There's also "Massa had a yellow gal," an old folk

> song from the South. . . . And there's "macaroon": you know, they fractioned people's blood—quadroons, octoons, and so on. There were people who escaped from slavery, the Maroons. There's the African country, Cameroon. And "of couth that shrub rat" is an anagram of "that touch of tar brush." I was trying to think of all that. No one would necessarily hear it all. (Mullen, "Harryette Mullen in Calgary, Alberta")

Mullen is using sound to reflect diasporic history. Neither origin nor dispersal is privileged; the sound play contains sinuous sets of possible constructions. We can hear the lines as separate: Massa had a yeller and macaroon had a fetter. This would pose massa against macaroon in a kind of grammatical agon; the objects yeller and fetter would also be counterposed, allowing a suggestion that massa was fettered by his sexual attachment to slavery: as macaroon had a fetter, so massa had a yeller. But reading the quatrain as a connected statement gives a different sense. Massa had two things: a yeller macaroon and a fetter, which he kept in his "trap"—his wagon, or his mouth, or his claptrap of couth—his ideological language. In all cases, he's a shrub rat. He's been touched by the anagrammatic tarbrush; as he was from the beginning of the quatrain by his association with his yeller.

One of the great strengths of *Muse & Drudge* is how easily the oral and the written coexist. There are places where lines that are clearly constructed by writing are suddenly caught up in the utter self-evidence of orality:

> bigger than a big man
> cirrus as a heart attracts
> more power than a loco motive
> think your shit don't stink (*R*, 103)

"[C]irrus as a heart attracts" might well read as sublime cloud-watching, but is probably more easily heard as a wrenching of the phrase "serious as a heart attack; "more power than a loco motive" might need to be read aloud before it reveals itself as a groan-inducing pun on the old Superman intro ("more powerful than a locomotive"); but the next line is instantly audible-oral: "think your shit don't stink"—the unwritten question mark is audible. It's a question asked of every reader.

Whole quatrains avoid any clever layerings:

> keep your powder dry
> your knees together
> your dress down
> your drawers shut (115)

A little gender and cultural variety is provided in the first line, perhaps, as Daniel Boone is the type who needs to keep his powder dry, but not his dress down. The following quatrain seems even more committed to avoiding variety:

mutter patter simper blubber
murmur prattle smatter blather
mumble chatter whisper bubble
mumbo-jumbo palaver gibber blunder (155)

Almost all these words are descriptions of speech; some of them, though not all, verge on being slurs. From a Vachel Lindsay perspective, this is all mumbo jumbo, jungle chatter—there are even some gibbons visible if not audible in "gibber." But in a different frame each line enumerates a nuclear family: mother father sister brother → mutter patter simper blubber. Can this be construed to mean that, with difficulty and under disguise, family structures survived the racism that saw Africa as containing nothing more than mumbo jumbo? Maybe. But the family pattern gets harder to hear as the lines play telephone with one another: murmur prattle smatter blather → mumble chatter whisper bubble → mumbo-jumbo palaver gibber blunder. This scattering is heightened because Mullen does not feel compelled to keep the rhythm steady. The blues rhythms she occasionally quotes are never allowed to build up. Critique is onstage as often as rhythmic presence.

Do the following lines refer to one woman? Is she blonde (rubia) or black, or both?

go on sister sing your song
lady redbone señora rubia
took all day long
shampooing her nubia (149)

And what is being washed in the fourth line? *Juba to Jive* does not tell us. Is "nubia" the site of pride, shame, colonization, sexuality? Is it wonderfully clean after such a long washing—was it especially dirty?[11]

members don't get weary
add some practice to your theory
she wants to know is it a men thing
or a him thing (149)

Is this writing sociological or individual? Is it a black thing? A woman thing? A black woman thing? A Harryette Mullen thing? A poetry thing?

Orality can be taken as conservative in a diasporic context: the stories are handed down in songs, fragments, phrases. Mullen avails herself of this power:

cram all you can
into jelly jam
preserve a feeling
keep it sweet (178)

But the next two quatrains, the last two of the book, are wry odes to the future, to the possibility of re-signifying on a tradition of signifying:

so beautiful it was
presumptuous to alter
the shape of my pleasure
in doing or making

proceed with abandon
finding yourself where you are
and who you're playing for
what stray companion (178)

In some ways Mullen and Pound are attempting similar things. *Muse & Drudge* and *The Pisan Cantos* are both mostly paratactic, with clusters of autonomous lines each sounding out very specific language, the sound always pedagogic. Both poets want to provide a sense of a whole language (and a whole world) via the sounds of each line.

one tanka entitled the shadow
babao, or the hawk's wing
    of no fortune and with a name to come
Is downright iniquity said J. Adams
        at 35 instead of 21.65
(*C*, 453)

Mullen's pedagogy includes its own autodidacticism much more straightforwardly. She tells of a crucial learning moment, where she was the one black person in a large undergraduate class on Afro-American folklore taught by a white male (*CB*, 203). The acronym "HNIC" came up and the professor, not intending any hostility, asked her to tell the class what the letters stood for. The one black woman telling the class that HNIC stood for "head nigger in charge" would have had a certain didactic force. She would have been, at least momentarily, in charge as a black woman. She would have been modelling the historical transformation from being an object of a brutal history to being an articulate subject. But Mullen did not know the phrase; and, in hindsight, why should she have? In addition to being a black woman, she had an individual linguistic history. The teacher's pedagogic gamble relied on the entire dictionary of racism being extant within every black body, like a kind of natural-historic DNA. Mullen's account continues, "It was a crisis for me. Here I am, the one black person in the room, in the Afro-American folklore class being taught by the white male authority figure, who then selects me as a native informant and I'm unable to perform as a native informant, because I had to be there in the class in the first place to learn what my oral tradition is" (*CB*, 203).

This moment was not simply a trauma. Mullen's account concludes with her insisting on learning, "from books, from media . . . from an actual oral tradition." In writing *Muse & Drudge* she used Major's dictionary along with old phrases from her mother and grandmother that she understood only years later.[12] Such cultural research she called "collecting virtual index cards," and said she had been collecting them "for a long time. Not wanting to be that person who does not know her own culture and must learn it from the white male authority figure, although I figure that once I get it, it's mine. . . . It's a very hard-won knowledge that I treasure" (*CB*, 203).

Part of the learning came from the same professor who had asked her that traumatic, transformative question. Mullen writes that her "understanding of African-American culture really had a lot to do with taking courses with Roger Abrahams in black folklore." Abrahams first introduced her to the Afro-American folklore

> that he had collected from black men on street corners in Philadelphia. He went from there to collecting in prisons because he could get a higher concentration of black men from different parts of the country. He would go to federal prisons and collect twenty different versions of "The Signifying Monkey" . . . I would never have heard such stuff, because my family's version of black culture consisted of our household, our church, and our school. It was the street corner and it definitely was not the prison. (*CB*, 236)

(As I wrote in the previous chapter, one of the most vivid strands in Pound's language in the *The Pisan Cantos* comes from the fact that he is in prison.)

"I shall have to learn a little greek to keep up with this, / but so will you, drratt you," wrote Pound in Canto 105 (*C*, 764). Greek, for Pound, was not the language of a historical community. It was one of the facets of the anti-diasporic language that he hoped to create in *The Cantos*: a compound of the classics, Chinese, Provençal, Anglo-Saxon, etc., meant to radiate eternal value at all points, and to "cohere," to be "an unwobbling pivot."[13]

Learning wobbles and changes in circumstance. But it is always a start. Mullen is a diasporic poet, somewhat at home in contemporary multicultural American English. In *Muse & Drudge*, she writes in American English and wants to change it. As a black woman, she does not automatically embody these changes; she went to the dictionary, to her mother's and her grandmother's conversation, to the blues, to Sappho. She had to learn a little of the African diaspora to write *Muse & Drudge*. To read it, we will have to learn a little, too.

12

A Span for Burton Hatlen

From Pound to Flarf

1. Large, shy, a force for the good of poetry

2. There have been two major rearticulations of Ezra Pound since the end of World War II and both have been excellent for the subsequent vitality of the poetic field. I want to juxtapose emblems of these two Pounds, not so much for the contrast—which will be obvious from the following quotations—but to suggest the scope of poetic territory Burton Hatlen was able to span.

3. For the first Pound, let us cite a foundational claim from the introduction to Carroll F. Terrell's *Companion to The Cantos of Ezra Pound*: "To me, *The Cantos* is a great religious poem" (viii). And for Pound 2.0, this from Benjamin Friedlander's *One Hundred Etudes*:

Please Help
Us in Texas
Two years ago

My high school
Sophomore got on
An Ezra Pound

Listserv to get
Help on his
Research paper. We

Have tried following
The procedure exactly
At least 15

Times to get
Off. We've been
Nice. We've been

Mean. We've written
To the school
Numerous times. PLEASE

PLEASE get us
Off? My gosh,
The child is

Graduated now and
Not even home
And you still

Keep us on
The list. Poets
Are great, but

Quite frankly, we
HATE Ezra Pound.
Can you help? (161–64)

4. While I'm on record deploring the consequences of Pound's absolutism, that's not my point here. I'm not setting these two moments in opposition, with Friedlander's poem representing progress, escape out of mystification to critique, sublation, revolution, etc. I do not intend to evoke the Ozymandias scenario where Pound-as-idol has been pulled down. As Shelley's last line suggests ("The lone and level sands stretched far away"), Ozymandian panoramas remain sublime, and, placed in those sands, the deposed "sneer of cold command" often remains surprisingly charismatic (Shelley, 589). The dimensions in which Hatlen acted were not sublime, quite the contrary. They were specific, bureaucratic, inertial: success in navigating them was not an epic given. This makes the contiguity and transformation he effected at the University of Maine, in Pound studies and in poetry more largely, all the more remarkable. As the National Poetry Foundation website has it: "Established in 1971 by Carroll F. Terrell (1917–2003) as a center for Pound scholarship, our mission was expanded by Burton Hatlen (director from 1990 until his death in 2008) to include the entire tradition of innovative poetry from modernism to the present day."

5. My thoughts are from a middle distance: we had little correspondence, not many conversations. My knowledge came by reading and, primarily, via NPF conferences. Hatlen was the guiding force of these, but there was no hint of rank in his bearing as he took part, one voice among others, large, shy, deeply informed. It is only from my present vantage that I begin to sense the scale of what he must have done in shaping the NPF (the publishing, the conferences, et al.) and bringing Ben Friedlander, Steve Evans, Jennifer Moxley, and Carla Billitteri to the English department in Orono, with the aim—Poundian in the best sense—of creating multifactual, ongoing situations for poetry.

6. I think it is accurate to say it was Hatlen's insistence that brought two hires to Orono from one job offer. I'm told that he proposed to cut his own teaching pay to make sure that Evans and Friedlander, and their partners Moxley and Billitteri, got to Orono. This is as far as my details go, but the bare outlines suggest an exemplary, polemic generosity, insisting that poetry is worth it.

7. Poetic vitality takes different forms at different times—wasn't that one of the wiser things Pound taught?

8. Re: those "two major rearticulations of Ezra Pound": "rearticulation" is critics' latin for work. Think of how poisonous Pound was after World War II: broadcaster for Mussolini, winner of the prize that broke the Bollingen, host of Thursdays at St. Elizabeths with John Kaspar. It takes work to make such a figure worthy of sustained attention, an example for poets, possible matter for teachers at various levels. Different things have to happen: there must be poets (Olson and others) to reconfigure the charisma and make the long-term value of the tarnished figure obvious; critics such as Kenner are needed to fashion established critical terms into new modes of legibility, to clarify intriguing examples, and to write anecdotes tellingly; and it's fortunate to have guidebooks (Terrell) to initiate standards of scholarship.

9. The effects are multiple, and the histories remain unsynchronized. Nevertheless, labor effects change—work works, as they say. By the beginning and middle of Hatlen's career the bulk of Pound's writings were in print, sayings and anecdotes were circulating, and textual riddles were being glossed, with Orono central to this activity. But the import of all these particulars remained elusive: what to make of Pound? The questions he posed (both as writer and as figure) remained sharply relevant, but his own history-bound answers were becoming ever more eccentric by the decade. Mussolini couldn't read *The Cantos* better than the aesthetes; Agassiz was a Darwinophobe creationist who championed

polygenesis; Confucian bureaucracy is not an exciting, sustaining foundation of poetic virtue. Such fundamental discrepancies made naive inquiries about Pound exasperating, as is clear at the end of Basil Bunting's "On the Fly-Leaf of Pound's Cantos": "There are the Alps, / fools! Sit down and wait for them to crumble!" (Bunting, 37). However lofty Bunting's intended compliment, the increasingly bald fact is that without an ongoing present tense—students, teachers, critical interest—the Alps-like *Cantos* would be slowly crumbling in high-density storage. The Alps as epic metaphor are one thing; Hatlen's achievements are more fundamental to poetry.

10. Heroic modes and codes, which are at the root of much Poundian poetics, are not useful in registering the scale of what Hatlen achieved. He was not a colossus stretching from Terrell to Friedlander; a better frame in which to think about him would involve a non-naive negative capability, combined with a taste for efficacy, making sure something interesting happens, the best that can be done under the circumstances.

11. aware the future is extremely near

12. The language of Friedlander's poem is appropriated and the poem is signed by a registered Flarfist, but a reader expecting Flarf would only be happy with the title, "PLEASE HELP / US IN TEXAS," which might at first seem the kind of message line heralding a free $42,000,000.00 if only you will supply a few personal numbers. However, as one reads, Flarf's expected pleasures (incoherence and sabotaged sincerity) are thin on the ground, if not missing altogether: "Two years ago // My high school / Sophomore got on / An Ezra Pound // Listserv to get / Help on his / Research paper." Perhaps the uncontextualized informality of the pronoun in "My high school / Sophomore" can be read as wrong, naive, unconscious—*your* high school sophomore? Who are *you*? How do you have a *sophomore* in your possession? But the embattled pragmatism of the message continues to reveal itself as consistent—sincere, in Zukofsky's term: "We // Have tried following / The procedure exactly / At least 15 // Times to get / Off. We've been / Nice. We've been // Mean." We're reading a single voice, exasperated but still trying to make things work—and doing it quite skillfully. A parent whose child wrote a paper on Pound remains entangled in the listserv. But doesn't the end of the poem suggest a happy outcome? "Poets / Are great, but // Quite frankly, we / HATE Ezra Pound. / Can you help?"

We read this in a book by a poet who is also an editor of *Paideuma* and *Sagetrieb*: isn't the implication that the poet-editor has not merely appropriated and lineated the language, but has also understood it and then—the highest stage of reading according to both Dante and Pound—acted on it? I haven't discussed this with Friedlander, so it's speculation on my part, but it's hard to imagine getting such a clear email and not fixing the listserv problem.

Poetry making things happen: isn't that to realize Pound's dream?

13. Etude 54 is not especially Poundian, as a poem—a poem that Friedlander wrote, that is. The Williams of *Paterson*, Book Two, turning things over to Marcia Nardi so extensively, is a much closer ancestor—and the counterpoint of speech rhythm set against the transhuman threes (tercets of three-word lines) is also Williams-ish. My claim is this: Etude 54 shows us that Pound 2.0 is not based on formal features. What *is* Poundian is the conjunction of ethical forces brought together so sharply at the end: (1) poetry is a primary pleasure ("Poets // Are great"); (2) poetry articulates specific, historical grievances ("Quite frankly, we / HATE Ezra Pound"); and (3) poetry activates its readers ("Can you help?").

14. Burton Hatlen helped poetry, and helped us.

13

Bathos and Mind Reading

As a poetic term, *bathos* had a quiet life for over a millennium and a half as a minor synonym for *hypsos* (the sublime) in Longinus's treatise "On the Sublime": "We must begin now by raising the question of whether there is an art of sublimity or profundity" [. . . ei estin hypsos tis e bathous techne] (2.1). Logically, *hypsos* and *bathos* could have been opposites—high vs. low—but in terms of scale they were similar. The sublime: very high; the profound: very deep; thus either could signify the scope Longinus found compelling.

In the eighteenth century bathos underwent a fundamental antithetical shift when Pope, in *Peri Bathous* (1727) and *The Dunciad* (1728; 1742), plucked it out of obscurity and made it a crucial topic for literary battle, as he attacked specific contemporaries and mock-categorized their poetic habits with elaborate scorn. Longinus had also discussed unsuccessful attempts at sublimity (bombast and insipidness were his principal targets), but failure was not where his interest lay. His critical efforts were in the service of enthusiasm: the sublime, a sudden sense of euphoric expansion, emanating from the great soul of the writer and sweeping over the reader. It was an irresistible contagion, not unlike the epidemic spread of irrational emotion that troubled Plato about poetry, except the phenomenon Longinus was extolling took place, not in public space, but in the personal scale of library literacy. To the contrary of either ancient, Pope's bathos did not display any adhesive power; it marked the sundering of bathetic writer and discerning reader. Bathetic readers may have communed with bathetic poets, but that was merely a symptom of the ills of the literary marketplace. The discrimination of the critical reader was the poetic value Pope was fighting for. Bathos could be called an anti-collaboration, produced by the reader's acuity upon the writer's obliviousness. It could not be produced individually. To paraphrase Shelley: a poet cannot say, I will compose bathos.[1] Bathos was postscriptive; it was not born until the critical label was affixed. It was the rejectamenta of a poetic system in which perfectability (of the heroic couplet, for instance) was a reasonable aspiration.

Bathos was a polemical instrument. Pope was intervening to correct contemporary poetic taste, sarcastically employing large-scale epic machinery in *The Dunciad* to discredit Theobald, Cibber, et al. But the efficacy of this weapon ensured its obsolescence: with the fading of his targets into obscurity, the stridency of his polemic ceased to resonate. Over the next century, if we take Shelley's sense as emblematic of the changed conditions—"the mind in creation is as a fading coal . . . when composition begins, inspiration is on the wane" (Shelley, 527)—any notion of poetic perfectability became irrelevant. It's not surprising that under such circumstances bathos-spotting would subside into a minor spectator sport. By the twentieth century, anthologies such as *The Stuffed Owl* or *Pegasus Descending* were designed to amuse readers, not obliterate enemy poets. No longer an index of poetic damnation, bathos might be the result of a serious poet's carelessness or miscalculation—here, straight from the heart of Wikipedia, is Dryden's description of the setting for *Albion and Albanius*: "The cave of Proteus rises out of the sea, it consists of several arches of rock work, adorned with mother of pearl, coral, and abundance of shells of various kinds. Through the arches is seen the sea, and parts of Dover pier." Or it might be the product of a century of linguistic change, as when Emily Dickinson, describing the eyes of a dying tiger, writes, "His Mighty Balls – in death were thick –" (*Pegasus*, 229). Smirking at such an after-the-fact pun seems a low but not deeply sinful amusement, and the article on bathos in the 1993 *New Princeton Encyclopedia of Poetry and Poetics* is a short one, as befits a phenomenon of modest salience. Bathos, we are told, produces "the (unintentional) effect of sudden transport from the sublime to the ridiculous" (127).

With the benefit of hindsight we can detect in this small article, written mostly by Harold Bloom, the beginning of a second antithetical shift in the meaning of bathos. As any proper encyclopedia entry must do, the article gives an account of prior changes while acting as a shield against any further change. We are told of bathos's reversal of meaning from Longinus to Pope, but are then told that any further changes in meaning will not be correct: "Also common, though less so, is the use of the word for a deliberately contrived effect of pathos manqué or any kind of deliberate anticlimax, whether ironic, gay, or serious. This usage is now perhaps best avoided in evaluative crit., where its evident subjectivity makes it vulnerable to attack" (127–28).[2] Anachronistically, we can read a lot into that second adjective, "gay."

The literary-bureaucratic tone of this should not mask its tricky tangle of assumptions around subjectivity.[3] What is being misnamed as bathos is, we are told, "a deliberately contrived effect of pathos manqué or any kind of deliberate anticlimax." In other words, if it's deliberate, don't call it bathos: bathos should be reserved for an effect of which the writer is unaware.

It's no surprise, however, that poetic encyclopedias are ultimately of little use in holding back the tides of poetic change. During the second half of the twentieth century, and especially in our contemporary moment, something like bathos has emerged as a widely employed and applauded tonality that is clearly being used deliberately by poets. I say "something like bathos" because it's a fuzzy, elusive category.

If one credits the etymological residue of words, it might seem that the notion of low would be central to whatever constellation of meanings we want to assign to this new bathos, but I don't think this is so. The low, in various instantiations (writing that is vernacular, democratic, secular, embodied, carnivalesque, quotidian, popular, etc.) has, for centuries, been a locus of poetic renovation. Think of Dante's turn away from Latin to the vernacular, Shakespeare's mastery of class registers, Wordsworth's "real language of men," Williams's "speech from the mouths of Polish mothers"—familiar tales, certainly. What to many contemporaries of Wordsworth seemed a thoroughly unpleasant aesthetic moment—"on the wet and slimy foot-stone lay / The useless fragment of a wooden bowl"—turned out to anchor a long-lasting ethical seriousness, as subsequent generations accepted and amplified Wordsworth's emotional judgment in the next line: "It moved my very heart" (Wordsworth, *Oxford Authors*, 33). As with *King Lear*—"Thou'lt come no more, / Never, never, never, never, never. / Pray you undo this button" (V, iii, 308–10)—high seriousness is not ill served by being directly juxtaposed to the low. Over the long, variously handled, reproductive series of readings and rereadings, it is undiluted loftiness that turns out to be the more endangered species: work that cranes too steeply toward a heroic ideal reveals itself as historically brittle—for example, Robinson Jeffers, Clyfford Still.

The following passage from *Paterson* offers a clear example of the revivifying immediacy of the low. There are, of course, hundreds of examples in Williams, but here the contrast with the immediate context is especially interesting. The final phrase, quoted from a young girl speaking to her friend as she carries a flowering branch, rescues this overblown passage where Williams is juggling his epic themes (the Falls, water, language) with ponderous insistence. His own poeticizing flirts pretty heavily, it seems to me, with the old sense of bathos as he spreads his theme of eddying water across the air and even onto the poor girls' hair. But this lyrical huffing and puffing is transmogrified brilliantly at the end:

> Two halfgrown girls hailing hallowed Easter,
> (an inversion of all out-of-doors) weaving
> about themselves, from under
> the heavy air, whorls of thick translucencies
> poured down, cleaving them away,
> shut from the light: bare-
> headed, their clear hair dangling –

Two–
        disparate among the pouring
waters of their hair in which nothing is
molten–

two, bound by an instinct to be the same:
ribbons, cut from a piece,
cerise pink, binding their hair: one–
a willow twig pulled from a low
leafless bush in full bud in her hand,
(or eels or a moon!)
holds it, the gathered spray,
upright in the air, the pouring air,
strokes the soft fur—

                    Ain't they beautiful! (17–18)

The relation of the elements from Dryden's example of bathos is reversed. There, the would-be sublimity of Proteus's gem-studded heroism was suddenly brought down to the ridiculous by the intrusion of Dover pier. Here "Ain't they beautiful!" is the equivalent of Dover pier, but the effect is not at all ridiculous: it is the uncontradictable real. There is a shock of distance between the poet's language and the quoted speech of the girls, but it is their simple enthusiasm that uses language well, not the overelaborated gesticulating of the poet. It's as if Williams has staged, at his own expense, a lesson in his poetics: beauty is direct.

Despite the rhyme in altitude, the low is not congruent with the new bathos in any simple way. The low provides the effect of immediacy, while the new bathos, whatever its surface character (which may change rapidly and radically), requires complex construal on the part of the reader. The varieties of substitution, masquerade, and frame-breaking that the new bathos proposes are not easily dealt with via objective (i.e., conventional) literary categories.

When Keston Sutherland, in a 2001 article, writes, "Every feature of language identified by Pope as bathetic, is now a defining and admired feature of our poetry," it is not hard to think of supporting evidence for his claim (Sutherland). Even though I find soon enough that I think differently of the quality Sutherland is pointing to, the new bathos, to give it a placeholding name, makes an effective reconstellating device.

Quite a range of John Ashbery's work seems central to what I'm getting at, and I will be focusing on it here; but related tonalities can be found throughout the New York School (pick your generation); the new bathos is one mainstay of

Charles Bernstein's work, though it's less frequent in the work of other Language writers; and it's the very soul of Flarf. Whether this new bathos, however qualified, will in the end be a useful term is a vexed question, since for Pope bathos was an unconscious defect (again, unconscious on the writer's part), while, in the past half century, bathos has been deployed by poets quite consciously. But we should remember that bathos has once before changed into something like its own antonym, so a second reversal may not be foreign to its antithetical nature. And at any rate, as an initiating move, the new bathos usefully avoids the usual binary of progress/reaction.

Ashbery's ascension to the status of major poet is of course familiar: the publication of *Self-Portrait in a Convex Mirror* (1975) with its bouquet of major awards; and, among examples of praise, his canonization by Harold Bloom in *Agon* (1982). A prescient sense of the new bathos can be found in a much lesser-known moment. This occurred in 1977 in the early years of the Bay Area Language writing scene, when a former undergraduate student of Bloom's, William Graves (Yale classmate of Language writers Kit Robinson, Steve Benson, Alan Bernheimer, and Michael Waltuch), gave a talk in the Bay Area Talks series titled "The Bathetic." Graves's talk dealt mostly with Pope but ended with a quick glance at New York School writing as bathetic. In the relentlessly innovative atmosphere of the Talks, this was a striking gesture. Graves juxtaposed a quote from Scriblerus, "The Lords above are angry and *Talk big*," with this of Frank O'Hara: "I am assuming that everything is *all right* and very difficult" (Graves's emphases). He concluded by mentioning Ashbery's then-recent *Three Poems*, with its "almost continual revitalization of clichés. . . . The Sublime and the Bathetic there are everywhere, but evened out, naturalized, accepted" (Graves, 119).

The common account of Ashbery's reception makes his early use of avant-garde techniques (fragmentation, syntactical dislocation, etc.) in *The Tennis Court Oath* (1962) the major flash point in his oeuvre, with Language writers celebrating it and Bloom (among many others) actively disliking it. However, the notion of a neo-bathetic Ashbery would divide things up more unpredictably. There is certainly more going on in Ashbery's poetry than the sublimity of "Self-Portrait in a Convex Mirror."

Bloom's Ashbery is singularly without bathos, as will be evident in Geoff Ward's account. Bathos is not directly mentioned, but, almost as good, the anti-bathetic word *pathos* is prominent (as it was in Bloom's definition, above, where he mentioned "pathos manqué"). Ward quotes Bloom's reaction to hearing Ashbery read "Wet Casements": "Only the pathos of the traditional phrase 'immortal wound' seems to me adequate to my response. For me, it had joined the canon directly I heard it" (Ward 131). Ward brings his incredulity at Bloom's reaction to a pointed close by quoting the sudden eruption of bathetic vocabulary in

"Wet Casements," an otherwise bathos-free poem: "it appears somewhat naive of Bloom to reduce these lines to the record of 'the loss of a beloved name, or perhaps just the name of someone once loved' (Wearing *falbalas*?)" (133). Ward does not use the word *bathos*, but *falbalas*—italicized and exhibited without further comment as self-evidently preposterous—is pretty close. "What Bloom sees as the poem's heroic project is exactly the false idealism it most mocks: Bloom fails to see this because he fails to see the wit of 'Wet Casements.' Indeed, he fails entirely to see the wit in any of Ashbery's work" (134).

To say the least, there is wit in Ashbery's work. But *wit* is a word that is all too easily recuperative in this context, suggesting a low-cost way of transforming new bathos into conventional excellence. We could say that old-style bathos presented the reader with language, thinking, cadence that was strikingly incompetent, not so much uneducated—since naïveté could be considered natural and uncorrupted—as undereducated; and that the new bathos knowingly appropriates such features, but with all immediate appeal to judgment suspended, allowing effects that are emotionally, intellectually, and stylistically improbable to build up. This would amount to stylistic revivification, a virtue applauded by Russian formalists, New Critics, modernists, Language writers, et al. But aren't there cases where Ashbery powers his bathyscaphe to regions far below those we can recuperate by taking them as wit?

For instance, in the calypso section of "Variations, Calypso and Fugue on a Theme by Ella Wheeler Wilcox," when Ashbery writes, "The Great Wall of China is really a thrill / It cleaves through the air like a silver pill" (*The Double Dream of Spring*, 26), why is the uninitiated reader wrong to find this silly? Close reading will not furnish much of a defense. One could conjure up complexity, pointing to the mismatch of the lines, how the first line's promise of pure doggerel is slyly balked by the next line's failure to keep to the anapestic trot in the final foot. How about the unusual "silver pill" with its *l* sounds vying for the ear's attention amid the clang of the thrill/pill rhyme? Or the clash between the huge, ancient, stationary wall and the tiny, speeding, space-age pill? But such details finally offer scant camouflage for the couplet's obtrusive silliness.

And why is silliness a problem? Ashbery himself, discussing Frank O'Hara's early poems, cites a similar couplet of O'Hara's—"At night, Chinamen jump / On Asia with a thump"—and comments, "A poet who in the academic atmosphere of the late 1940s could begin a poem [that way] was amusing himself, another highly suspect activity" (O'Hara, viii).

True enough: O'Hara's emphatic refusal of seriousness is impossible to miss. But Ashbery's remarks go on to suggest qualities beyond humor: "One frequently feels that [O'Hara] is trying on various pairs of brass knuckles until he finds the one which fits comfortably. It's not just that it is often aggressive in tone—it simply doesn't care" (vii–viii). What if we take the couplet not merely as something amusing, but as a pair of brass knuckles? Are they comfortable? And for whom? Is the reader as comfortable as O'Hara presumably was?

For contemporary readers, "Chinamen" is a stereotype that is hardly mitigated by being set in such a childish jingle. I assume, though, that for a reader in the late forties, the word would have been more directly uncomfortable, pointing as it did to geopolitical inflammations, recent (World War II, Hiroshima) or looming (the imminent Korean War). When the poem as a whole is read, however, things change considerably. One can see how, from O'Hara's point of view, the combination of silliness, aggression, and the hard-to-define exoticism furnished by the blatant chinoiserie would have made for a particular kind of comfort. Brass knuckles—for protection—might be one image; or one could say O'Hara is creating noisy distractions in order to allow for the emergence of something tender, sentimental, and forbidden—a gay love poem:

At night, Chinamen jump
On Asia with a thump

while in our willful way
we, in secret, play

affectionate games and bruise
our knees like China's shoes (O'Hara, 13).

Read in this light, a different quality emerges from the opening couplet. It still pivots upon a stereotype, but one out of the mythological physics of midcentury folk culture, a Midwestern playground factoid that I remember from my own childhood in the 1950s (not many years after O'Hara wrote the poem): if everyone in China jumped up and down simultaneously, the earth would be knocked out of its orbit. This frame creates an absurd, Cole Porter–like wit, whose message is something like: "we're together and it knocks the earth out of orbit." Love and bathos are not separated out; the persistent trope of "China" allows for taboo physical detail to be mentioned and simultaneously disavowed by the absurdist rhyme:

The birds push apples through
grass the moon turns blue,

these apples roll beneath
our buttocks like a heath

full of Chinese thrushes
flushed from China's bushes. (13–14)

Even the final couplet, which at first may be taken as conventionally lyrical—

we couple in the grace
of that mysterious race

—ends with an insistence on the Chinese stereotype as a kind of tutelary spirit.

But I see that I have in some sense "rescued" this early O'Hara poem, keeping it neo-bathetic but making the bathos strategic, (guardedly) communicative, and almost heroic in its historical context. For more recalcitrant bathos, simultaneously obtrusive and evanescent, I want to return now to Ashbery's "Variations." But first, two points: (1) the poem, like many other Ashbery poems, is hardly typical of his work; and (2) the poem, whose parts are so thickly threaded with bathetic moments, is increasingly hard to perceive as bathetic when read as a whole. Karl Kraus wrote that the more a word is stared at, the more remote it becomes. Here, and with Ashbery's use of bathos in general, the bathetic moments are very obvious, but the more closely they are attended to, the less bathetic they seem.

The "theme" that the poem posits for itself is a quatrain whose banality is hard to miss:

For the pleasures of the many
May be ofttimes traced to one
As the hand that plants an acorn
Shelters armies from the sun. (Ashbery, *Double Dream*, 24)

John Shoptaw, in his excellent discussion of "Variations," mentions I. A. Richards's influential 1925 essay "Badness in Poetry," where a Wilcox poem is cited as a quintessence of bad poetry. And here, even before we read this quatrain, its dignity, such as it is, is fatally compromised by Ashbery's title (itself a mini-screwball comedy). The rather arty proposition of "Variations" is immediately sideswiped by the next two musical movements, "Calypso and Fugue," with this unlikely three-movement musical concoction further encumbered by being predicated on "a Theme by Ella Wheeler Wilcox"—one of those tripartite literary names from early in the last century that furnishs a sonorous punch line to some unstated joke about literary vanity. Compare, in "Daffy Duck in Hollywood," a similar moment: "the fertile escritoire of Helen Topping Miller" (Ashbery, *Houseboat Days*, 31).

However, just reading the next three lines is enough to change this target for sarcasm into something more open-ended. If we take the musical form offered by the title as an initial premise, we can hear Wilcox's quatrain not as a specimen of bathos, but as a common everyday tune. Such "hearing" goes against the grain—we have to suspend our evaluative sense—but if we can do so then Wilcox's quatrain rehearses two thoughts, one extremely familiar and both of them happy: (1) mighty oaks from little acorns grow (i.e., all personal, childish deficits may be made whole); and (2) one person can do something that will please large numbers of people (an especially pleasurable thought for a poet). Under this regime of bathetic reading the following lines, instead of registering as weird, rather excessive parody, become inventive tonal variations, one to a line, with the only rule being radical change:

> And in places where the annual rainfall is .0071 inches
> What a pleasure to lie under the tree, to sit, stand, and get up under the tree!
> *Im wunderschönen Monat Mai* (*Double Dream*, 24)

Structurally, to use an analogy from a different sphere, it is not unlike taking the trivial theme written by the music publisher Diabelli and making it the basis for utterly transformative variations, as Beethoven does in the Diabelli Variations. (To avoid misunderstanding: there is nothing in the poem that could possibly be construed as referring to Beethoven! But transferring aesthetic structures from lofty sites into bathetic contexts is a signature Ashbery move: compare the use of the God/Satan paradigm from *Paradise Lost* as an underlying grid in "Daffy Duck.")[4]

The opening three lines take the tree that Wilcox's heroic "one" had planted as a poetic fact, though, given the arid conditions, the flourishing of the tree is utterly improbable. Nevertheless, the "pleasures" and "shelter" that the tree provides are maintained assiduously across the tonal shifts. Such continual inventiveness makes me suspicious of any unified description of Ashbery's writing. Even so perspicacious a reader as Shoptaw describes the variations as emanating from an "enthusiastic paraphraser, a simplified personality," mentioning "'The Skaters' and 'The Instruction Manual'" as similar examples (108). But neither the quasi-autistic voice of "And in places where the annual rainfall is .0071 inches" nor the punctilious elaborator of "What a pleasure to lie under the tree, to sit, stand, and get up under the tree!" fits with the Heine line quoted in the third line.

The next passage puts a temporary halt to such tonal shifts on the local scale. In terms of a rhythm of attention, this brief irruption of continuity is as unpredictable as the tonal discontinuity of the prior three lines:

> The feeling is of never wanting to leave the tree,
> Or predominantly peace and relaxation.

Do you step out from under the shade a moment,
It is only to return with renewed expectation, of expectation fulfilled

The lines suggest a kind of nineteenth-century-German-inflected translationese. The subtle wrongnesses of "predominantly" being out of position, and of "Do you" used in place of "If you," display the most careful attention to each syllable. As the passage goes on, a doppelgänger of sincerity becomes ever more apparent—perhaps to the point of sincerity. Note how the arboreal wish fulfillment returns in the "chestnut" hair:

. . . Insecurity be damned! There is something to all this, that will not
  elude us:
Growing up under the shade of friendly trees, with our brothers all
  around.
And truly, young adulthood was never like this:
Such delight, such consideration, such affirmation in the way the day
  goes 'round together.
Yes, the world goes 'round a good deal faster
When there are highlights on the lips, unspoken and true words in the
  heart,
And the hand keeps brushing away a strand of chestnut hair, only to
  have it fall
back into place again. (24)

Shoptaw, echoing I. A. Richards's term of critique, calls these "stock responses," which must soon be set aside: "Even the nostalgic respondent [in Shoptaw's reading, this would be the speaker of the entire opening section], however, realizes that the maturation process necessitates relinquishing one's stock responses" (108). While it is true that the end of the "variations" presents us with totally altered conditions—

For later in the vast gloom of cities, only there you learn
How the ideas were good only because they had to die,
Leaving you alone and skinless, a drawing by Vesalius.
That is what was meant, and toward which everything directs:
That the tree should shrivel in 120-degree heat, the acorns
Lie around on the worn earth like eyeballs, and the lead soldiers shrug
  and slink off.

—rather than a narrative of aesthetic maturation (inferior stock responses being abandoned for sadder, more realistic truths), I would propose a different model. Of course "highlights on the lips," "unspoken and true words in the heart," and the ever-brushed-back "strand of chestnut hair" are stock, bathetic phrases. But in Ashbery bathos has a self-canceling quality. Gravity is suspended; up and down, the sublime and the bathetic, cliché and novelty, become relative. The language cannot be taken seriously and yet we do take it seriously—or, better: we follow it with careful attention and real pleasure.

Two caveats: The abolition of the high/low axis does not equate to any post-modern abolition of affect, nor is it necessary to rescue the poem's significance by invoking the poet's psyche. Such periodizing assertions as Fredric Jameson's—which found a "movement from the older *Nouveau roman* to that of Sollers or of properly 'schizophrenic' writing, or from the primacy of Stevens to that of John Ashbery," where reification has "penetrat[ed] the interior of the sign itself and liberat[ed] the signifier from the signified, or from meaning proper"—seem quaint now (Jameson, 200).[5]

Earlier, I mentioned that reading the new bathos requires complex construal on the part of the reader. So, here in my discussion of "Variations," I note that I have been suggesting that Ashbery, just as he said of O'Hara, was amusing himself in the Great Wall of China / silver pill couplet (and of course not just there), and that by following the structural prompts of the poem, we can reread what at first looks like Wilcox's banal quatrain as providing sturdy possibilities for pleasure (wish fulfillment perhaps) and poetic invention. In a moment, I will be quoting Ashbery giving some autobiographical background to the writing. None of this, though, should be construed as a brief for the primacy of Ashbery's sensibility, or as positing a critical goal of reconstruing the poet's feelings.

It *does* help one's reading to be familiar with Ashbery's work; there is obvious value to placing his work in historical context, knowing that he is, among other things, a gay poet whose career is both pre- and post-Stonewall; personal anecdotes are not fatal to reading. But all this is only to say that when we read poems we use what psychologists call a "theory of mind"—mind reading. This does not translate into unproblematic communication. Quite the opposite in fact: at any moment one must be ready for a plethora of art strategies and frame-breaking gestures. (Minds are complicated to read.) Poems are simultaneously acts issuing from a personally, historically, culturally, and poetically located mind carrying out certain procedures (John Cage's intention as an art-maker might be to short-circuit his immediate subjective intentions); and they are transpersonal linguistic artifacts that do not only refer to their origin. With Ashbery's poetry the effects are very rapid and unpredictable: the continual semantic surprises and tonal non sequiturs call for heightened attention.

However one tries to pin it down in a description, Ashbery's bathos has been highly influential. Compare Ron Padgett's "The Austrian Maiden" (which could plausibly be read as a gloss on the Ashbery lines I have just been looking at):

I wish I had blonde hair
and was a maiden, on a farm, in Austria,

in the nineteenth century, on a sunny day,
with rosy cheeks and blue eyes, just

like those Nazi images of healthy farmgirls.
But are my great-grandchildren going

to be monsters? Then I will have none.
I will milk the cow and tell Hans

and the others to keep their mitts off me.
I will fill my evening hours with the sad music

of Schubert and the sad poetry of Heine.
It will be so beautiful. (Padgett, 22)

A few quick points: The power of "Ain't they beautiful!" in the *Paterson* passage came from Williams's shocking lack of irony. Here, "It will be so beautiful" is twenty-first-century bathos. It is thoroughly hedged as to whether or not it's serious. It does not sound as if we're being told: "Schubert and Heine are part of the soil that fostered Hitler; there is no document of culture that is not simultaneously a document of barbarism." (Or, perhaps, if that *is* being suggested, the suggestion has to be swaddled in bathos because a stern lecture would merely seem trite after having been heard so often.) True beauty—Heine and Schubert—has to be unreproductive (as in "keep your mitts off me") to avoid proving Walter Benjamin right and bringing Hitler into the art sanctuary. The calendar-illustration rhetoric Padgett carefully uses here gives us only a simplified beauty (a "stock response," in Richards's terms), which is "sad."

Turning back to "Variations," of the many bathetic effects, I will mention two more. One occurs at the juncture of the calypso and fugue sections. The calypso is bathos at its broadest:

So my youth was spent, underneath the trees
I always moved around with perfect ease

I voyaged to Paris at the age of ten
And met many prominent literary men

Gazing at the Alps was quite a sight
I felt the tears flow forth with all their might . . . (Ashbery, *Double Dream*, 25)

This goes on at length but ends on a note that is harder to read as simply parodic, even though the defective language is blaringly audible:

And trust in the dream that will never come true
'Cause that is the scheme that is best for you
And the gleam that is the most suitable too. (27)

"The dream that will never come true"—can't that be taken as a synonym for poetry (cf. the willing suspension of disbelief)? The fugue section then begins: "'MAKE MY DREAM COME TRUE.' This message, set in 84-point Hobo type, startled in the morning editions of the paper: the old, half-won security troubles the new pause" (27).

The rapid shifts from phrase to phrase are playful, but at the same time they can be taken seriously; and when they are the effect can be as startling as an 84-point headline. Note, too, how this prose disregards the parodic tone of the prior stanza and plucks out the "dream" to begin with. It is structurally similar to the way the tree in the Wilcox quatrain was taken as poetic fact.

The second moment I will discuss comes at the end:

> "My dear friend," he said gently, "you said you were Professor Hertz. You must pardon me if I say that the information startles and mystifies me. When you are stronger I have some questions to ask you, if you will be kind enough to answer them."
>
> No one was prepared for the man's answer to that apparently harmless statement.
>
> Weak as he was, Gustavus Hertz raised himself on his elbow. He stared wildly about him, peering fearfully into the shadowy corners of the room.
>
> "I will tell you nothing! Nothing, do you hear?" he shrieked. "Go away! Go away!" (29)

Ashbery wittily arranges it so that the Professor's ill-tempered explosion ushers us out of the poem. What can the reader do after reading "Go away! Go away!" but, in fact, go away? Such wit points us back to funny and sophisticated species of authorial intent that suffuse Ashbery's work. But for bathos's sake, let's also posit that, just as the interlocutor already knows Professor Hertz's identity, we too know that Professor Hertz occupies an oracular position at the end of the poem. (Cf. the Grecian urn speaking at the conclusion of Keats's "Ode.") In an email, I asked Ashbery about this passage. He replied: "The Gustavus Hertz passage is from 'The City beyond the Clouds, or Captured by the Red Dwarfs,' by Roy Rockwood, 1925.[6] I just learned the author's name myself from a footnote in the forthcoming Library of America collection of my poetry. I had hitherto known only the title, having found a page from the book on a sidewalk in New York while writing the poem. Pretty bathetic, huh?"[7]

To find a loose page on the sidewalk is not totally unlike finding one of Sibyl's scattered leaves. Whereas Williams's found speech is the truth (and the beauty) of his situation, Ashbery's oracle is at once nostalgically ridiculous (1920s adventure prose) and unknowably sublime. Pretty bathetic, huh?

My admiration for and pleasure in Ashbery's work seems to have driven me away from the problem of a bathos that cannot be recuperated by attuned reading. To at least gesture toward this issue, let me end with a glance at "Theme Park Days" in *Chinese Whispers* (2002), a prose poem which begins with a transgressive, possibly unsalvageable gesture: "Dickhead, they called him, for his name was Dong, Tram Van Dong." The clash in tonalities, especially the insertion of the puffily heroic "they called him, for his name was" amid the grade school crudity of laughing at the Vietnamese surname—is that funny? I find it so, but shouldn't I be nervous about that? The poem, however, goes on from there without any overt gestures of poetic recuperation. The speaker, Tram Van Dong, reveals his fake heart, which is merely "a heart-shaped disk" that he takes out from "the small judas in his chest"; the disk is newspaper "crudely stapled together" with "'spirit writing'" (in scare quotes) on one side, "ancient stock-market quotations" on the other. But when this patently false figure speaks, as he does for the rest of the poem, the results are both witty (note the grim refrain from Beckett's *Endgame* that is applied sardonically to "the critics," for instance) and beautiful: "Delphic squibs caparison the bleak afternoon and the critics love it, eat it up, can't get enough of it. 'More pap! More pap!' Have a care, though, lest what I tell you here trespass beyond the booth of our conniving. Yet it will spread, as surely as an epidemic becomes the element we have chosen to live in: our old infectious experiment" (9).

I will call a provisional halt here, with the proviso that the dialectical image of poetry as both private container—"the booth of our conniving"—and unpredictably spreading contagion does not resolve the poetic and social issues that the new bathos brings up. Many contemporary poets, most notably the Flarfists and the Conceptualists, are challenging any settled agreements on what readers might find acceptable.

14
The Poetry Hoax and Poetic News

There have been many varieties of hoax; I am concerned here with the kind that aims to teach a lesson. This type of hoax is made by an expert, targets those claiming expertise, and is revealed by an expert; but it is not just a matter for experts. A wider audience is addressed. It is a malicious pedagogy, constructed to display a facade of credibility before exploding in the faces of its targets, who are then revealed as incompetents. While this hoax may display great novelty, it is a conservative enterprise, teaching the non-expert audience what it knew already. It is a pedagogy founded on enforcement of existing boundaries.

Compare these two hoax revelations: "For some years I've been troubled by an apparent decline in the standards of intellectual rigor in certain precincts of the American academic humanities. So, to test the prevailing intellectual standards, I decided to try a modest . . . experiment" (Sokal, "A Physicist Experiments with Cultural Studies," 62); and "We decided to carry out a serious literary experiment. . . . For some years now we have observed with distaste the gradual decay of meaning and craftsmanship in poetry" (Heyward, 137).

These statements were made fifty years and ten thousand miles apart, but the gist is the same: standards have fallen, expertise has been compromised, hence the need for a hoax. The first was written by NYU physicist Alan Sokal in 1996 explaining why he wrote "Transgressing the Boundaries: Toward a Transformative Hermeneutics of Quantum Gravity," a mélange of fake physics and theory-speak that he got published in *Social Text*. The second was written in 1943 by James McAuley and Harold Stewart, Australian poets who created the anti-modernist Ern Malley hoax. But despite the similarities ("decay of meaning and craftsmanship"; "decline in the standards of intellectual rigor") a poetry hoax does not work like a science hoax.

Whatever the merits of Sokal's critique of postmodern theory,[1] his credentials as a physicist ensured that the science in "Transgressing" was, and will remain, genuine nonsense. The Sokal hoax teaches at least that much, which is a claim the Ern Malley hoax cannot match. When Malley's book, *The Darkening Ecliptic*, was first revealed to have been authored in eight hours by two poets, James McAuley and Harold Stewart, didactically aiming to write nonsense, it was a successful hoax: the poems and their supporters looked ridiculous. However, a half century later, the work is printed complete in a major anthology of Australian poetry, which gives more pages to the hoax poet Ern Malley than to the real poet McAuley; Stewart does not appear. The Sokal hoax remains a hoax; *The Darkening Ecliptic* has become poetry. Yet compared to other examples of what might be called poetry hoaxes, it is the most hoaxlike: the most didactic, the most polemical as to what is and what isn't legitimate poetry. So if it isn't a hoax then the notion of poetry hoax is in trouble. But first some specifics.

The Sokal Hoax: Reaffirming the Boundaries

The central joke of Sokal's piece was that, as "Strawberry Fields" has it, "nothing is real." Sokal dressed this up in postmodern regalia: "physical 'reality,' no less than social 'reality,' is at bottom a social and linguistic construct. . . . [S]cientific knowledge, far from being objective, reflects and encodes the dominant ideologies and power relations of the culture that produced it . . . truth claims of science are inherently theory-laden and self-referential." The full inscrutability of science was wielded to show that time and space were no longer binding categories: "In mathematical terms, Derrida's observation relates to the invariance of the Einstein field equation $G_{\mu\nu} = 8\pi G T_{\mu\nu}$ . . . . The key point is that this invariance group 'acts transitively': this means that any space-time point, if it exists at all, can be transformed into any other. In this way the infinite-dimensional invariance group erodes the distinction between observer and observed; the π of Euclid and the G of Newton, formerly thought to be constant and universal, are now perceived in their ineluctable historicity" ("Transgressing the Boundaries," 217–18, 222).

Presenting nonsense coated with expertise is the first half of the two-step polemical pedagogy. Two groups are addressed: the targets of the hoax (the *Social Text* intellectuals) and a wider readership. After step one, the intellectuals are the advanced group: they may not be able to make much of $G_{\mu\nu} = 8\pi G T_{\mu\nu}$, but they do know that it can be interesting when long-accepted constants are destabilized by being shown in their ineluctable historicity. After step two—the revelation that the science was bogus—the general readers move to the head of the class and the intellectuals are given dunce caps. Common sense has been confirmed: to the non-expert reader, ineluctable historicity and $G_{\mu\nu} = 8\pi G T_{\mu\nu}$ are equally opaque. But such incomprehension is actually knowledge. The general reader has already passed the test (always already, as the saying goes); incomprehension was and is the correct answer. For the intellectuals the lesson is that transgressing the boundaries of the disciplines, deploying language from outside the area of one's intellectual training, is foolish.

That is the sum of the hoax's lesson. It does not teach topology or quantum mechanics, only that these subjects cannot be reached by mere vocabulary. A sphere of specialized practice is defended from encroachment by illegitimate experts, with commonsense judgment the ultimate court of appeal. Sokal scored points from both sides: as a physicist he could produce scientific howlers with polemical bite rather than scientistic babble; but that his theory-speak got published also counted. Physics was a hard science requiring an expert to draw the line between significance and nonsense; anyone could master the pretend skill of writing theory.[2]

Ern Malley

The Ern Malley hoax intended a similar lesson: any idiot could instantly produce the gibberish that was modernism. The hoaxers, James McAuley and Harold Stewart, were two of the best-read and most ambitious young poets in Australia; their target was Max Harris, editor of *Angry Penguins* and an enthusiast of Surrealism, Jung, Dylan Thomas, Eliot, Auden—all things European and modernist.[3] To hoax Harris, McAuley and Stewart concocted *The Darkening Ecliptic* and its author, the working-class modernist Ern Malley who died of Graves' disease at twenty-five, a poetic meteor like Chatterton, Keats, Rimbaud. The manuscript was accompanied by a well-pitched cover letter from the querulous philistine sister, Ethel. Harris fell for it and published the poems in *Angry Penguins*, trumpeting Australia's first modernist genius.

Word got out quickly. There was some debate over the quality of the poems despite the hoaxers' hostility, but basically the hoaxers won. *The Darkening Ecliptic* was published as a book; the magazine *Angry Penguins* was sued for obscenity by the government, which won; Harris was fined; *Angry Penguins* could not be sold in South Australia. Harris was broken as a writer and what *Angry Penguins* represented was knocked back for decades in Australia.

On the other hand, a copy of the infamous issue found its way to the Grolier Poetry Book Shop in Cambridge, Massachusetts, where John Ashbery read it in 1945. He later said, "I liked the poems very much. They reminded me of my own tortured early experiments in surrealism, but they were much better" (Heyward, 232). In 1961, he, Harry Mathews, Kenneth Koch, and James Schuyler published Malley in an issue of *Locus Solus* devoted to poetic collaboration. The hoaxers McAuley and Stewart may have tried to write gibberish, but from a post-Ashbery perspective, the odd specificity of the language and the speed of frame and tone shifting are what jump out; it is the gibberish aspect that is harder to perceive, like aging graffiti only intermittently legible.

But in the short and local term, McAuley and Stewart were authoritative in defining the work as a hoax:

> We produced the whole of Ern Malley's tragic life-work in one afternoon. . . . We opened books at random, choosing a word or phrase haphazardly . . . [weaving] them into nonsensical sentences. We misquoted and made false allusions. We deliberately perpetrated bad verse. . . . The alleged quotation from Lenin. . . , "*The emotions are not skilled workers*", is quite phoney. The first three lines of "Culture as Exhibit" were lifted . . . from an American report on the drainage of breeding-grounds of mosquitoes." (Heyward, 138–39)

The *New York Times* made this last revelation the substance of their headline: "Drainage Report Gems Culled In Report Called Tremendous" (Heyward, 154). But the whole poem in which the drainage report appears complicates any simple irony:

"Swamps, marshes, borrow-pits and other
Areas of stagnant water serve
As breeding grounds . . ." Now
Have I found you, my Anopheles!
(There is a meaning for the circumspect)
Come, we will dance sedate quadrilles,
A pallid polka or a yelping shimmy
Over these sunken sodden breeding-grounds!
We will be wraiths and wreaths of tissue-paper
To clog the Town Council in its plans.
Culture, forsooth! Albert, get my gun.

I have been noted in the reading-rooms
As a borer of calf-bound volumes
Full of scandals at the Court. (Milord
Had his hand upon that snowy globe
Milady Lucy's sinister breast . . .) Attendants
Have peered me over while I chewed
Back-numbers of Florentine gazettes
(Knowst not, Lucia, that he
Who has caparisoned a nun dies
With his twankydillo at the ready? . . .)
But in all of this I got no culture till
I read a little pamphlet on my thighs
Entitled: "Friction as a Social Process."

What?
Look, my Anopheles,
See how the floor of Heav'n is thick
Inlaid with patines of etcetera . . .
Sting them, sting them, my Anopheles! (Heyward, 255)

I have to squint a bit to read "deliberately perpetrated bad verse" here, but I can list some intended provocations: the mosquito prose splayed into lines; the address to the seemingly tragic "Anopheles" (rhyming with "Mephistopheles" but naming a malarial mosquito) followed by a hint that "the circumspect" could figure this out; the tissue paper clogging the municipal facilities (think: kids toilet-papering a house); the wild swings in diction in the final parenthesis with its absurd adage; the teenage naughtiness of the thigh-centric "Friction as a Social Process."

A post-Ashbery reader will not boggle at "he / Who has caparisoned a nun dies / With his twankydillo at the ready": the semantics may be frat-boy transgressive, but the vocabulary is volatile. Similarly with the "phoney" quotation, "The emotions are not skilled workers": surely there are many occasions when this is an apt observation. It's too bad Lenin didn't say it.

Ashbery had more sources than Ern Malley to learn from. But dropping a monkey wrench into the bizarrely sentimental seems quite Malleyesque; for example, when Ashbery takes the lines "the wonder of the day / when the child discovers her first hand" and makes them into "the wonder of the day / when the child discovers her first dead hand" (Ashbery, *The Tennis Court Oath*, 41).[4] But reading Malley simply as a prophet of the New York School neutralizes his sting. McAuley and Stewart may have been energized by constructing his lifework, but Malley is not a figure of fun when he semi-quotes Hermann Göring ("Albert, get my gun") or when he identifies with the malarial mosquito that was, in 1943, decimating Australian troops in New Guinea. As I say, the hoax is a malicious pedagogy.[5]

Malley identifies with another insect as well: the bookworm, "a borer of calf-bound volumes." In this, he resembles one of his creators, Harold Stewart, who "would sit in the public library transcribing [a poet's] entire *oeuvre*. . . . Hart Crane and Mallarmé were . . . absorbed this way" (Heyward, 51). Malley is a transcriber, too, but as he miscopies Lorenzo's sweet talk to Jessica from *The Merchant of Venice*, he has a spasm of disidentification. Lorenzo is saying, "Look how the floor of heaven / Is thick inlaid with patens of bright gold" (V, i, 58–59); but Malley, from his own "sodden breeding-grounds," cannot aspire to such poetic gold. He breaks off, transmuting gold into "etcetera" and wishing malaria upon the happy couple.

Malley's scorn derives from his isolation, a trait he inherited from McAuley and Stewart. They were neither fascist nor communist, and voice that neither/

nor position through Malley: "I have heard them shout in the streets / The chiliasms of the Socialist Reich / And in the magazines I have read / The Popular Front-to-Back" (Heyward, 261–62). Their many-stranded misappropriation of the new and the foreign shows the hoaxers to have been well informed about what was happening on the other side of the world, exemplifying Pound's dictum that "artists are the antennae of the race" (*ABC*, 81). But unlike the Poundian ideal, McAuley and Stewart kept tabs on the news in order to deform it and to shoo it away. They were defensive antennae, an early warning system to detect incoming threats. Their hoax position was both appetitious (modernism is global and takes on the present, so they can use anything) and conservative (modernism is poisonous). They meant to write bad poetry, but they tried so hard that, for that eight hours, their writing practice, luckily, transgressed the boundaries of their poetics.

A World without Hoax Poetry

McAuley and Stewart wrote in their historical context and their actions continue to refract through subsequent contexts, from Ashbery's reading in 1945 to my interest here. All writing and reading positions are time-bound. Ern Malley has already sympathized:

> Remember, in any event,
> I was a haphazard amorist
> Caught on the unlikely angles
> Of an awkward arrangement. Weren't you? (Heyward, 251)

Aren't we readers of poetry, of whatever stripe or vintage, "haphazard amorists"? Don't we all construct our tastes, our poetic judgments and pleasures, out of what history, fate, geography, chance have thrown our way? Don't poetic relations often manifest "unlikely angles" (William James–Gertrude Stein)? Aren't the "arrangements" often "awkward" (Zukofsky–Pound)?

Reading Ern Malley no longer elicits the hoax cry, "This is too preposterous!" The position of outraged consensus is an evanescent site of judgment: Malley's poems now seem sharply legible. But this is not a simple victory for the assimilative powers of poetry. If Malley, the leading hoax poetry candidate, cannot now be said to have produced hoax poetry, then there is no hoax poetry, there are only hoax poets, which in turn cues the question: isn't this because all poetry is something of a hoax? Sidney's defense of poetry, the poet "he nothing affirmeth, and therefore never lieth" (Sidney, 198), can be subject to inflammatory reversal: poems never lie because they contain no news.

But "news" means many things. Poems can be cultural news; and poetic hoaxes, in the looser sense, have been newsworthy. A short list of the non-Malley hoaxes would include Araki Yasusada (1997), *hibakusha* (atomic-bomb survivor) and innovative poet; the "Spectra" poets Ruth Knish and Emanuel Morgan (1916), constructed to ride in the slipstream of Imagism's brief vogue; Sappho's imagined pupil Bilitis, whose salacious, novelistic lyrics surfaced, perfectly preserved, in 1894 as *Les Chansons de Bilitis*, complete with learned footnotes quoting cruxes in the "original" Greek; Thomas Rowley, an invented medieval monk whose poems were inscribed on old parchment by the teenaged Thomas Chatterton in the late 1760s; and Ossian, the "Scottish Homer," whose supposedly third-century epics began to appear in 1760 via the putative translator James Macpherson.[6] What unites these figures is their non-existence, and the public outcry, of large to modest proportions, that it caused.[7] False paratextual information was disseminated; readers were fooled and, with the exception of the Spectra case, commentators were alarmed by the duplicities. But once hoaxes were cleared up, what the hoax poets supposedly wrote remains poetry, in some cases—Yasusada, Spectra—not wonderful poetry, but in others quite influential: Chatterton was a crucial instigation for Coleridge and Wordsworth; Ossian's impact was enormous. He may not have existed, but his poems and epics such as *Fingal* were certainly poetic news.[8] In the 1760s Thomas Gray was "*ecstasie* with their infinite beauty" (Groom, "Romanticism and Forgery," 1627); in 1818, when it had been clear for decades that Ossian was a production of James Macpherson's, William Hazlitt listed Ossian as one of the major poetic works in the world (along with Homer, the Bible, and Dante); Oscar Wilde's mother was an enthusiast, which is why Oscar's middle name is Fingal (Macpherson, iv–v). And I predict that twenty-first-century readers who appreciate estrangement via translation and other procedural practices will be interested in "Walter Scott's speculation . . . that Macpherson thought every word of his Ossian at first in Gaelic, before writing it down in English. There is indeed reason for believing that a fair portion of 'Fingal' was concocted in synthetic Gaelic . . . and that—in so far as it originated with him—Macpherson was . . . translating himself" (Gaskill, 11).

But if the poetry of the hoax poet Ossian is still poetic news, that doesn't mean that all poetry stays news. McAuley and Stewart's attempts at preposterousness may have been fragile, but some of the celebrations of prior poetic dispensations leave longer-lasting traces: I think that I shall never see / A poem lovely as a tree; In the land of Gitchee-Gomee, / By the shining Big-Sea water; A poem should not mean / But be; Mumbo Jumbo will hoodoo you. These inertial commons of poetry—or should it be wastelands?—will be filled out differently by different readers, but reading them forces the sobering recognition that, yes, this in fact was poetry.

Impatience with such facts has, from the Romantic era to the post-avant-garde present, fueled the innovative tradition. There have been high-minded exhortations toward nature (precise information, awakened bodily intelligence), but the anti-poetic is often part of the process, as poets make use of the low, rural language, the wrong, camp, Flarf: whatever is illegible to the reigning modes of reading. Such provocations want readers to recognize them and are thus something like the opposite of hoax poetry. Their news is that the non-poetic can be poetry: Jack Spicer's "The goop / is like mulberry soup" (Spicer, 123) or Ashbery's "The Great Wall of China is really a thrill / It cleaves through the air like a silver pill" (*Double Dream*, 26). The silliness is obtrusive, but for those who know Spicer's work, "goop" sounds its despairing, jokey chord (there is no poetic brotherhood, no group—only goop); Ashbery's readers know that the clunkiness of these lines is another example of his wide formal repertoire.[9]

These are matters of poetic knowledge: in one sense quite obvious, but in another sense specialized. A cynic might suggest a comparison with the Sokal hoax, and ask us to imagine its physics eventually being recognized as acceptable. But this cannot happen: falsifiability is foundational to science. Phlogiston used to be scientific fact; now it is a curious error. Poetry, if imagination cannot be falsified, only accumulates. There may be finite room in anthologies, libraries, and readers' minds, and over the long and wide haul poets fall out of fashion; but the local skirmishes of fashionability are merely makeshift fulcrums masquerading as development.

The cynic is voicing the old critique, straight from Plato: there is no poetic knowledge; poets are merely vectors of affect; the rhapsode Ion can recite Homer but, like all advocates of the poetic, he is in thrall to poetic deceits. Plato's charge has been answered by Aristotle, by Sidney, by the Romantics, by modernists, and by contemporaries. Such a continuity of answer suggests an equally forceful impingement of the question.

Pedagogic Poetry

It would only be a reader who knew nothing of the conventions of the dramatic monologue who would find it problematic that, in "My Last Duchess," it is Robert Browning, not the Duke of Ferrara, who is the source of the words of the poem. However, even in such an obvious example, it is not simply a matter of readers knowing that the poem is an imaginative act and therefore beyond issues of factuality. Readers do give themselves over to Coleridge's "willing suspension of disbelief" (Coleridge, 169), but only when the detail seems right. Lecercle's discussion of "encyclopedia" is apropos: "the broad sense of a set of beliefs and elements of knowledge which reader and author bring to bear on the text" (Lecercle, 4). When the reader's encyclopedia is augmented by the poet's, the poem is pedagogic.

With Pound's "Homage to Sextus Propertius," provocation and pedagogy go together:

> My orchards do not lie level and wide
> as the forests of Phaeacia,
> the luxurious and Ionian,
> Nor are my caverns stuffed stiff with a Marcian vintage,
> My cellar does not date from Numa Pompilius,
> Nor bristle with wine jars,
> Nor is it equipped with a frigidaire patent;[10]
> (209)

Pound is writing to be noticed: there is only one moment in the suite of twelve poems as baldly ahistorical as "frigidaire patent," and he makes sure that it appears in the opening poem. In isolation, this post-classical refrigerator has something of the cultural aggression of an Italian Futurist dismissing the past; but Pound is not a full-throated futurist: he is also emphasizing the antiquity of the classics to discomfit the general audience. The frigidaire is preceded by lines which bristle with unfamiliar specifics: "Phaeacia" is an exotic place name—the vowel string "aea" does not occur in standard English; "Ionian," "Marcian," and "Numa Pompilius" do not belong to any knowledge-territory familiar to the early twentieth-century reader. While Pound castigated Milton as in thrall to Latinity (*ABC*, 29), here he emphasizes the Miltonic post-positional adjective, "the luxurious and Ionian," setting it off on its own half line. He is insisting on both antiquity and contemporaneity.

This wide vista makes poetry pedagogical, echoing Aristotle's answer to Plato that poetry, expressing the universal, is more philosophical than history, which only expresses the particular. But where Aristotle opposes the particular to the universal, Pound, good modernist that he is, unites them. In being accurate to the specifics of its time and place (Phaeacia, Numa Pompilius), good literature transcends time and place (the frigidaire patent); it "STAYS news" (*ABC*, 29).

With "frigidaire patent" Pound leaves the door slightly open to hoaxiness, but beyond this line "Homage to Sextus Propertius" is far from a hoax. Pound is passionately didactic, showing readers that just as Propertius wouldn't play the part of imperial poet at the beginning of the Roman Empire, so the contemporary poet with a grasp on history, ethics, and poetics should scorn the European imperial powers in World War I:

> Annalists will continue to record Roman reputations,
> Celebrities from the Trans-Caucasus will belaud Roman celebrities

And expound the distentions of Empire,
But for something to read in normal circumstances?
(207).

Authentic Trauma

For Pound, writing "Propertius" in wartime London, normal circumstances were already nostalgic; but such nostalgia allowed him to voice a civic rhetoric that could disparage war as uninteresting news from the imperial peripheries. In the intervening century-plus, the wide persistence of trauma has made such a stance untenable, and just how well poetry can record this trauma has become a continuously pressing question.

To pick a stark example, and one that intersects with the hoax question: How have poems registered the atomic bomb? I will cite four examples: William Carlos Williams's "Asphodel, That Greeny Flower" (1952); Frank O'Hara's "Why I Am Not a Painter" (1956); Yasusada's "Mad Daughter and Big-Bang" (1997); and an excerpt from Hara Tamiki's *Summer Flowers* (1946).

In its opening statement "Asphodel" presents the most plausible model for poetic news that I know:

My heart rouses
    thinking to bring you news
        of something
that concerns you
    and concerns many men. Look at
        what passes for the new.
You will not find it there but in
    despised poems.
        It is difficult
to get the news from poems
    yet men die miserably every day
        for lack
of what is found there.
    Hear me out
        for I too am concerned
and every man
    who wants to die at peace in his bed
        besides.
(*WCW II*, 318)

When Williams wrote these lines, poetry had recently been pushed to the unfamiliar precincts of the American front pages by Pound's public agon: his fascist radio speeches during the war, the aborted treason trial at the war's end, and the journalistic firestorm over his being awarded the Bollingen Prize in 1949. Williams's forced withdrawal from consideration for the position of poetry consultant to the Library of Congress in 1952 had been something of a public event too, though in this he was, as usual, overshadowed by Pound.

In "Asphodel," after decades of absorbing, chafing against, and seconding Pound's lessons, Williams offers a more socially nuanced and ethically capacious correction to Pound's sense of poetic news. Where Pound brooks no obstacle to legibility—poetry IS, and it STAYS, news—Williams makes its reception specific and contingent: an embodied reader either gets the news and can die at peace, or doesn't and dies miserably. Williams's claim recognizes failure as one of the structuring possibilities of poetry.

The vocabulary couldn't be plainer, but what the lines are saying is slippery. It's not hard to place it in poetic history: this is the American idiom that Williams supported in the face of Pound's and Eliot's Euro-historical erudition. But even though *news* and *get* are the most basic American words, they are not simple. Why is it difficult to get the news from poems? Lack of expertise? "People don't get how to read poetry; they read for plot or imagery and don't get what makes a poem news." Circulation problems? "It's hard to get the crucial poetry books in local libraries and bookstores." Or are pedantic imaginations, inflexible libidos, and tin ears impervious to poetic inspiration? "They just don't get it." This sense makes news transcendent, like the good news of the Gospel.

I am continually struck by the claim these lines make; familiarity does not flatten it. At times I can find it inspiring, to use that suspect word. It is not simply saying that poetry can enrich any life—easy to agree with; the claim here intends a wider reach, beyond an established audience to society at large, and thus it is harder to believe. The news from poems can answer the sharpest personal and the largest social demands? What kind of answer would that be? Would wars stop, to allow for harmonious deathbed scenes on a universal scale? Or, like the audience listening to Homer in the *Ion*, is my feeling of inspiration simply a link of contagious excitement, attached to nothing more than Williams's feeling of excitement?

Coming into dialogue with Socrates, Ion is certain of poetry's emotional power and epistemological plenitude. Its power is undeniable: the evidence is there in his body and the bodies of others. When the poem is pitiful, he weeps, the audience weeps; when it is horrific, his hair stands on end, their hair stands on end. He also believes that his prize-winning recitations of Homer give him access to the skills represented in the poems, until Socrates shows him that what he considered his knowledge is neither his nor knowledge, that his words are shaped "not by art or science . . . but by . . . divine possession" (536c). In the *Republic*, Plato spells out the implications: poetry's power is dangerous; its audience helplessly follows emotional scripts sprawling promiscuously across ethical boundaries.

In "Asphodel" poetry arrives via inspiration: "the words / made solely of air / or less, / that came to me / out of the air / and insisted / on being written down" (*WCW II*, 325). While there is no Socrates in "Asphodel," nor any magnetized audience, there is the poetic enthusiasm: "My heart rouses / thinking to bring you news." But what news? It remains unspecified: it fills Williams with enthusiasm, but ultimately he cannot translate it out of his enthusiasm. Possibly the news *is* nothing but his enthusiasm. Lack of content can be a virtue, since breadth of address seems the point. The news concerns "you"—Williams's wife Flossie—and "many men," who suffer "every day" from the want of this news. But such universalism suffers a blow when, just a few lines after announcing that he has crucial news for her, the poet has to beg Flossie to keep listening: "Hear me out," a refrain which is varied throughout the poem. Perhaps she tunes out because the news seems only addressed to a male public ("all men"), with the additional, singular, aggrieved wife addressed privately for reasons of domestic tranquility.

"Asphodel" is neither a critically fashionable poem nor a poetically fashionable one. While it is celebrated for its opening lines, and praised (and panned) for its depth of sentiment, it is not particularly modernist. It is a poem written in weakness (age, depression, electroshock). Age, memory, and approaching death are predominant themes: in Greek myth, asphodel grows next to the Elysian fields. It's prolix, words are repeated carelessly, the rhetoric is clumsy. The moments when Williams addresses Flossie are mostly strained: "You have forgiven me," he asserts at one particularly mawkish moment.

But as with everything Williams wrote, "Asphodel" attempts to incorporate fact, notably the atomic bomb. However, it does this by reducing it to a rumor of cataclysm, which is then made "poetic" with clumsy, poeticized sleight of hand as Williams splits the actual devastation caused by the bomb into "heat" and "light":

in an eternity
          the heat will not overtake the light.
                    That's sure.
That gelds the bomb,
          permitting
                    that the mind contain it.
This is that interval,
          that sweetest interval,
                    when love will blossom,

come early, come late
        and give itself to the lover.
Only the imagination is real!
(*WCW II*, 334)

Decades earlier, the author of *Spring and All* had warned against such stale metaphors: "Crude symbolism is to associate emotions with natural phenomena such as anger with lightning, flowers with love" (*WCW II*, 188). One of the myriad descriptions of imagination in *Spring* is apropos: "Imagination is not to avoid reality, nor is it description nor an evocation of objects or situations, it is to say that poetry does not tamper with the world but moves it—It affirms reality most powerfully and therefore, since reality needs no personal support but exists free from human action, as proven by science in the indestructibility of matter and of force, it creates a new object, play, a dance which is not a mirror up to nature, but—" (234–35). In "Asphodel" the unscriptable force of the bomb flattens this to a brittle assertion: "Only the imagination is real!"

I realize that in criticizing "Asphodel" for its handling of the bomb, I am sliding from poetic to historical news, and thus I could be said to frame the issue in Zhdanovian terms, where the superstructural poem must be judged by how well it matches the already-defined real world. Such show trials are not useful. But an opposite conclusion, where the poem is detached from referential demands, employs a similar Zhdanovian binary, separating the spheres instead of forcing them together. Nor will splitting the difference produce some semi-referential middle ground where the structures of news and poetry can be durably reconciled: they are incommensurate. The "sweetest interval" in "Asphodel" names poetic autonomy, which history will always undo. The poem's invocation of poetic news may inspire poets (it does me), but the rest of the poem cannot bring news of the atomic bomb.

My second example is Frank O'Hara's familiar "Why I Am Not a Painter" (1956). It is far from a hoax, but formally and tonally it can give the impression of not fulfilling any of the contracts poets are supposed to honor. Incommensurabilities are its fuel. O'Hara starts off asserting that he is a poet, not a painter, but the turn in the latter third of the poem occurs as he claims genuine poetic powers: "I am a real poet." This genuineness comes, not from O'Hara writing the poem we are reading, but his having written another poem, "Oranges," which is actually twelve poems and is actually in prose, as in the French prose poem. But *this* poem, "Why I Am Not a Painter," is prosy in another sense; it is insistently faux-naive. There are the line breaks: "he / says"; "I look / up"; "It is even in / prose"; "I call / it"; and there is the diction that is deliberately inadequate: "There should be / so much more, not of orange, of / words, of how terrible orange is / and life" (O'Hara, 261–62). And then there's the vocabulary, which is beyond aggressively simple: in the last phrase, O'Hara tramples decorum with the glee of a proto-Flarfist, saying big things clumsily.

But of course the mistakes I'm spelling out here are all part of the wit of the poem. O'Hara breaks the primary commandment of his poetic era—charged, unique language, significant form at all points—because he is so confident of the significance of his and Mike Goldberg's—the painter's—art. Some of the lines in "Why I Am Not a Painter," if they occurred in a poem by a high school junior, might activate the pedagogic sensibility. "He / says"—you should consider the integrity of the line; and while you're at it, watch out for accidental repetition: in the second stanza you've used "drop in" three times and "go" five. But such teaching would be obtuse: this is a real poem, by a real poet, its ontology all the more secure because—just like "Oranges" doesn't mention orange and Goldberg's painting "SARDINES" doesn't have sardines in it—"Why I Am Not a Painter" is never "poetic" in any but the falsest way.

Another way to grasp the real poetry of "Why I Am Not a Painter" is to think of the distance between the ordinariness of life, expressed in unproblematic language ("I drink; we drink . . . / . . . I go and the days / go by") and the terribleness of life, expressed in melodramatic language ("how terrible orange is / and life"). The terribleness of life cannot be written. Trauma is kept off the page, out of the poem, off the canvas. It is mysterious—in the closet, so to speak. Is it the atomic bomb, Auschwitz, McCarthyism, sexual preference? The poem won't tell.

Araki Yasusada's poems purported to both bring and to *be* the news. There was to be no interval between the messenger and the message. The affair was superficially like the Malley hoax, but ultimately no experts were dethroned nor were any lines sharply drawn by the ambiguous rhetorical address of the work. To give a quick synopsis: notebooks of a hitherto unknown and now deceased poet, Araki Yasusada, surfaced in 1996, translated into idiomatic English but containing many indications of Japanese provenance. The work was accompanied by an unusual narrative: Yasusada was a *hibakusha*, a survivor of the bombing of Hiroshima, but his disjunct poems were unlike those of any other survivor. Late in life he had enthusiastically discovered Roland Barthes and Spicer, displaying an appetite for poetic experiment and theory that placed him on the innovative side of the divide between language and self (or text and experience, or defamiliarization and communication). But as a *hibakusha* Yasusada had full rights on either side of the divide. His poetry was innovative, but it was also the quintessential "poetry of witness," to use Carolyn Forché's term for work produced by "significant poets who endured conditions of historical and social extremity during the twentieth century" (29). Poems of witness themselves bear "the trace of extremity within them, and . . . are, as such, evidence of what occurred" (Forché, 30).

Doubled Flowering opens with this poem:

MAD DAUGHTER AND BIG-BANG
DECEMBER 25, 1945*

Walking in the vegetable patch
late at night, I was startled to find
the severed head of my
mad daughter lying on the ground.

Her eyes were upturned, gazing at me, ecstatic-like . . .

(From a distance it had appeared
to be a stone, haloed with light,
as if cast there by the Big-Bang.)

What on earth are you doing, I said,
you look ridiculous.

Some boys buried me here,
she said sullenly.

Her dark hair, comet-like, trailed behind . . .

Squatting, I pulled the
turnip up by the root.

*[In the aftermath of the bombing, many survivors moved into the foothills of the Chugoku mountains surrounding Hiroshima. This was the case with Yasusada and his daughter.]
(Yasusada, 11)

The translators' bureaucratic prose is a crucial frame, undergirding the extremity of Hiroshima. Forché's introduction to *Against Forgetting*, her anthology of poetry of witness, begins with a similar gesture, quoting "the coroner's report for corpse #12: 'Cause of death: shot in the nape. In the back pocket of the trousers a small notebook was found soaked in the fluids of the body and blackened by wet earth. This was cleaned and dried in the sun'" (Forché, 29). The notebook contained the last poems of the Hungarian poet Miklós Radnóti. He was real, Yasusada was not, but the same rhetorical structure governs both accounts. The poetry of witness needs two voices: an authenticator and the poet-witness. Read without its note, the Yasusada poem could be a dream, or a Williamsy meditation (the final line break, "the / turnip," is pure Williams) inflected toward Surrealism. The note reframes it as heroic witness.

Yasusada's amalgamation of poetic antagonisms was interesting to many, and his poems were accepted by a wider range of magazines than was usually open to one poet. What followed was more interesting: rumors that there was no Yasusada. A consensus soon emerged that the author was Kent Johnson, a contemporary American translator and poet. Wesleyan University Press dropped publication plans, but the results of Yasusada's nonexistence were publishable and within a year Roof Books issued *Doubled Flowering*, gathering the now-pseudographic writing. There were some initial reactions—editor Arthur Vogelsang called it "essentially a criminal act" (Yasusada, 130); for John Solt, translator of Japanese poetry, it was "Japanesed crap" (131)—and an overview by Marjorie Perloff, who showed how careful reading might have revealed some of the historical impossibilities: there were no scuba divers before World War II; in 1925 there was no Hiroshima University for Yasusada to have attended, etc. ("In Search of the Authentic Other," 148–68).

Ron Silliman's pre-hoax comments on Yasusada are expert: "There's an elevation in tone . . . that reminds me more of Michael Palmer than Spicer, perhaps because the translators are all Hiroshima poets (one of whom seems to spend half of each year in Sebastopol). . . . These works kept me up last night and probably will again" (149). The contrast with the Sokal hoax is marked: far from having his authority diminished by having placed his detailed poetic knowledge in enthusiastic service of the supposedly Japanese poems, Silliman furnishes a post-hoax blurb for *Doubled Flowering* in which he agrees with Perloff: "The 'scandal' of these poems lies not in the problematics of authorship, identity, persona, race or history. . . . This book makes the argument for anti-essentialism. That it has done it so well infuriates folks with a proprietary interest in categories. Thank you, Araki Yasusada!"

By authenticating Yasusada, Perloff and Silliman are granting him a place in the anti-mainstream arena. From such a vantage, "Yasusada" is an instantiation of the tradition, going back at least to Whistler, of American artists not letting half knowledge derail their enthusiastic engagement with Asia. Pound's *Cathay* and Noh translations are notable results. This makes the issues of expertise and knowledge, so definite in the Sokal hoax, fuzzy. If knowledge of Japanese poetry, not to mention the experiences of a *hibakusha*, is not crucial, then judgments like Solt's "Japanesed crap" lose their bite and *Doubled Flowering* becomes textbook anti-essentialism, while it can also claim to provide imaginative experience of the atomic blast.[11]

But it seems a pallid claim if we compare it to a poem of Hara Tamiki, a *hibakusha* who survived Hiroshima:

Here is my typographic evocation of the poem:

flAshIng *rUbblE*
whItE *EmbErs* fIrE
trEmEndOUs **ArEA**

chArrEd InflAmsEd
rEd *dEAd* cOrpsEs'
jErky *rhythms*
ExIstEd OncE? *EvErythIng cOUld* hAvE ExIstEd?
OnE flAsh *tOrE* **It** *Off*, wOrld **Is**
thAt hOrsE *stOmAch* swOllEn **lIkE** sO
bEsIdE knOckEd **OvEr** *strEEtcAr*
bUrnIng *wIrEs* st**Ink**

I do not read Japanese and so am simply gesturing toward what I read in John Whittier Treat's *Writing Degree Zero*, where I learn that Hara's *Summer Flowers*, a prose account of being bombed in Hiroshima, suddenly switches to poetry written in katakana, a "Japanese syllabary used for transliterating foreign words and native slang." Treat comments, "The orthography is strange, and the poetic language stranger" (149).

Estrangement, *ostranenie*, and the like have become comfort food in innovative circles. Hara's displacements seem to have been more local: *Summer Flowers* was the euphemistic title for what was originally named after the Japanese word for the atomic bomb. But under the rule of American censors it was illegal to write about the atomic events; *Summer Flowers* only got through because it was published in an obscure magazine.[12]

15

A Williams Sound-Script

Listening to "The Sea-Elephant"

Williams has remained a foundational poet for me. The exuberance, variety, and transparency of his formal experimentation; the surprising eloquence amid his sometimes bumptious democratic stylistic affirmations; the breadth of his knowledgeable enthusiasms; the unflagging straightforwardness, both in and out of experimental modes—there are many ways that the writing remains of the greatest interest. However, during the decades that I have been reading his work, there have been the lesser moments in poems I value highly; the not particularly notable pieces; and the downright clunkers like "Tract": "I will teach you my townspeople / how to conduct a funeral—" (*WCW I*, 72).[1] My judgment is not unshakable, but it is instantaneous.

"The Sea-Elephant" has moved from somewhere in clunker/not-interesting territory to become a poem I find quite fascinating. This is not due to any perspicacious reading on my part; it's because I listened to Williams reading it.

This experience has split "The Sea-Elephant" into different objects. As a poem on the page, its quatrains enact the typical Williams tussle between syntax, prosody, and lineation. The four-line boxes display a visual metric that has little relation to the sound, at least as Williams himself voiced it in the recordings we have:

> Trundled from
> the strangeness of the sea—
> a kind of
> heaven—
>
> Ladies and Gentlemen!
> the greatest
> sea-monster ever exhibited
> alive (*WCW I*, 341)

Here, as throughout much of Williams's verse, we can read (i.e., see) his polemic as he uses democratic American materials to attack that double-headed ogre of his poetics, England, an opponent that was both passé (sonnets, iambic pentameter) and more fashionably advanced than Williams's own work (think: *The Waste Land*). Against this, Williams wields American speech and unpredictably lineated quatrains—Cubist-lite? precisionist?—art-identified, at any rate. In the twenty-first century, after decades of Williams's wide influence across American poetry, such quatrains look formally innocent, but for many readers a century ago the variation of line length (from "the strangeness of the sea" to "heaven") and the unusual line breaks such as "of / heaven" and "exhibited / alive" were startlingly modernist (Bochner, 162–81). And as for content, a poem about a sea elephant at the circus was echt American.

A similar polemic can be detected in the oral performance, but in that medium the poem takes up the battle quite differently, dramatizing Williams's American materials and anti-Eliotic poetic desires in a suite of socially distinct voices, with what I call a "poetic" voice recurring amid irruptions from a circus carny, the sea elephant, a fussy woman, and ending with the poet breaking out in a sarcastic parody, halfway to a falsetto.

It is the sound of "The Sea-Elephant" I will read here—specifically, a 1952 recording of Williams reading the poem to an audience at Princeton. In an earlier online version of this essay (Perelman, "A Williams Sound Script"), to make clear what that vocal suite ("poet," carny, sea elephant, woman, semi-falsetto) sounded like, what those printed words were also sounding, I quoted the performance via a link to the 1952 recording of Williams reading the poem, and all subsequent quoting in the piece was conducted via sound clips. On the screen, there were only MP3 links, making clear that sound, not text, was the topic. Here, the subject remains "The Sea-Elephant" as sounded in that 1952 reading, but the format dictates that all quotation happen in print. The following is what I hear as the sound of "The Sea-Elephant," with an invitation to access the MP3:[2]

Poet: Trundled from the strangeness of the sea—a kind of heaven—

Carny: (*nasally*) Ladies and Gentlemen! the greatest sea-monster ever exhibited alive the gigantic sea-elephant!

Poet: (*non-nasal*): O wallow of flesh where are there fish enough for that appetite stupidity cannot lessen? Sick of April's smallness the little leaves—Flesh has lief of you enormous sea—Speak!

Sea-Elephant: (*bellowing*) BLOUAUGH!

Poet: (feed me) my flesh is riven—fish after fish into his maw unswallowing to let them glide down gulching back half spittle half brine the troubled eyes—torn from the sea.

Woman: (In a practical voice) They ought to put it back where it came from.

Poet: Gape. Strange head—told by old sailors—rising bearded to the surface—and the only sense out of them is that woman's

Woman: Yes it's wonderful but they ought to put it back into the sea where it came from.

Sea-Elephant: (*loudly bellowing; audience responding with shrieks and gasps*) BLOUAUGH!

Poet: Swing—ride walk on wires—toss balls stoop and contort yourselves—But I am love. I am from the sea—

Sea-Elephant: (*smaller bellow*) BLOUAUGH!

Poet: There is no crime save the too-heavy body the sea held playfully—comes to the surface the water boiling about the head the cows scattering fish dripping from the bounty of . . . [*falsetto*] and Spring they say Spring is icummen in—

Somewhat like the relationship between a musical score and a performance, this is less informative than the recording; the whole channel of immediate hearing, both musical and profoundly social, is missing. But the distance from my transcription to the printed quatrains of the poem does at least suggest something of the difference between sound and text.

Sensory Basics

It takes only the briefest introspection to be reminded of the foundational difference between listening to and reading a poem. To bracket the complexities memory would bring in, let's make it a poem read or heard for the first time. I will also bypass the complexities of neurological processing and speculations about the tangled relations of sight and sound. I am concerned here with the middle ground of conscious human perception.

The principal difference is that reading is voluntary, whereas, with listening, there is a basic secondariness. While I can listen carelessly or even with hostility and thus have some secondary control over the sense being made, nevertheless, the speaker's words, affect, timbre, timing, volume, pitch contour, and intonation are primary physical facts that I must have already processed to even be hearing them. With reading, on the other hand, nothing happens unless my eyes activate the poem, and any instant that desire flags, reading ceases. On a bad day, with a poem I'm not interested in, my reading motor may stop every few seconds. It's not exemplary behavior, I grant. But stuttering or not, reading provides a more capacious temporal vantage than listening. While construing the clumps of letters at the focal center (i.e., reading words), my eyes simultaneously register a dim sense of the words and spaces on the rest of the page or screen. This sense of the rest of the page is unfocused, to be sure; nevertheless, it means that, in a bare way, to read is to see a short way into the near future (and, symmetrically, into the near past). When listening, I'm more confined to the present, though there is some local sense (lasting maybe five seconds) that holds the sound together while syntax and semantics are being construed.[3]

Beyond such facts of sensory processing, in my own experience there is a primary difference: my emotional stance toward what I read is critical, hard to please, while much of what I hear I tend to like. I'm a much more generous listener than reader. Am I home to two distinct sensory beings? Or does reading push in the direction of privacy (autonomy, solipsism) while listening is irreducibly social?

It's tempting to dramatize the reading/hearing difference. William James writes that the separation of one mind from another is absolute: "Neither contemporaneity, not proximity in space, nor similarity of quality and content are able to fuse thoughts together which are sundered by this barrier of belonging to different personal minds. The breaches between such thoughts are the most absolute breaches in nature" (James, 226). Can James's eschatological language apply to a more counterintuitive breach: the intimate breach within a single mind between the eye and ear, reading and listening?

Possibly so; but then again, maybe not. It's a breach that is constantly traversed. As we listen to the poet read the written poem, we can attend to slips and surprising emphases, but these are simply matters of performing a score. Any distance between reading and hearing is continually normalized by the fact that we are forced by the language we use to say "The Sea-Elephant" is the same sequence of words whether it's read or heard—that is, the same poem.

Granted: a poem (printed) is a poem (heard) is a poem. But that does not mean the differences between poem printed and poem heard cannot be quite surprising. In what follows I will explore the different territories of listening and reading without mapping them onto one another.

Listening has fundamentally changed my judgment of "The Sea-Elephant," not only adding qualities I had missed in reading it but eliminating an irritating fuzziness that only existed on the page. Reading (at the "high end" at least) is in the service of exact reproduction. Take two quite different examples from arts that can be perceived by reading: music and poetry.[4] The first is Olson's familiar claim in "Projective Verse" that the projective poet is to use the typewriter to make the page a score, thus unifying the written and spoken poem (Olson,

Collected Prose, 245–46). The second is an antique anecdote I picked up from record jackets: Brahms is asked if he's going to the concert; No, he says, adding that he's just read the score and heard a perfect performance in his head—it would only get botched in the concert hall. Distinct as Brahms and Olson are, reading is an exact activity for both. The guarantors of this exactitude are the poem on the page and the musical score, both of which present the occasion for a perfect, reproducible performance.[5]

My initial reading experience of "The Sea-Elephant" on the page, as I try to reconstruct it, was far from perfect. But its imperfection supports my sense that reading aims at exactitude. As far as I can remember, I never would actually finish reading the poem. My reading eye would always bump off it, noticing only the quatrains, mostly two- or three-word lines with single-word lines appearing unsystematically, reinforcing my sense that Williams's line breaks were always a seat-of-the-pants operation. But the only specific that stands out as I try to remember those non-readings is one irritant: "Blouaugh!"

I had never liked reading Williams's nonlexical moments: poem XX of *Spring and All*: "The sea that encloses her young body / ula lu la lu" (*WCW I*, 222–23); the 10/30 entry from *The Descent of Winter*: "To freight cars in the air . . . pah, pah, / pah pah, pah, pah, pah, pah" (*WCW I*, 301); "The Trees" (*WCW I*, 337–38); and "For a Low Voice" (*WCW II*, 153–54), among others. And of course not to forget the locus classicus from *Paterson*: "And, derivatively, for the Great Falls, PISS-AGH, the giant lets fly! good Muncie, too" (*P*, 10).

These moments were all downers, but the "Blouaugh!" in "The Sea-Elephant" was especially annoying. Some non- or half-linguistic sounds are easier to read than others. "Ula lu" and "pah" at least look precise—one knows what they are supposed to sound like. But what is "Blouaugh!" supposed to sound like? Is it one syllable or two? Is it "Blow" + "augh!" or more like a stretched-out "Blog!"? Not being able to tell instantly (and "Blouaugh!" appears three times in the poem), my eye would always push away toward a different page.

But listening has changed that. "Blouaugh!" is no longer an ungainly phonetic blur to vex the exacting private reader: in the recording, its three different noises are key moments in the tragicomedy of phallic poetics that is being performed in front of, and ultimately performed with, the audience.

Here, I will be a phonological docent for this performance—a performance that, as I say, completely changed my sense of the poem, making it into a specific event, more capacious and less self-similar than the printed poem. To my ear, this version resolves some of the awkwardness of the poem, redeeming its touching openness from the bumpy satire it keeps falling into. This essay is an homage to this performance moment.

But we need to remember that the temporality of the situation is multilayered. The poem was written in 1929; an older Williams is reading and commenting in 1952; and I was able to retrieve that voice via twenty-first-century technology.[6] It is as if the technologies of sound reproduction have reversed the moment of Pisistratus—the tyrant of Athens who, the lore has it, instigated whatever process it was that got Homer written down, transforming the *Iliad* and *Odyssey* from variable oral poems into fixed texts.[7] Here, with Williams's poem, the fixed letters of the text are reopening to performed variation.

Typical of oral performance, Williams makes a mistake in the reading, dropping the "too" from "too-heavy," but that is of little note. More significant are the social, sonic, and rhetorical dimensions clearly dramatized by the sound-script. A second performance of the poem is also available on PennSound, from a reading in 1955 at UCLA where Williams sounds much more stroke-damaged, still a trouper, but forcing the same sequence of social tones and dramatic turns through a voice that cannot pronounce or modulate all that well. Nor does it sound like he's seeing the page very clearly.[8]

But this less felicitous version makes clear that, despite the differences between performances, Williams is performing the same sound-script (i.e., the same sequence of voices and the same schema of accentuation in the phrasing). The second version takes longer (2:15 as opposed to the 1:52 of the 1952 version), and is tough sledding—especially if you go on to listen to the long (7:40) comment where Williams slowly discusses the variable foot and his invention of the stairstep line (which "The Sea-Elephant" does not use), then rambles on about the need for American poets to overcome iambic pentameter, which he tries to define but gets wrong. It is interesting evidence (if any more were needed) of how central an obsession metrics were for him from before the Imagists of World War I to the end of his life, although listening to the earlier reading must remind us of the crucial fact that his practice would often, as it does here, far outstrip his theory.

In the Homeric situation, in presenting the poem, there must have been different levels of performance, from a bare-bones narrative with basic ornamentation (epithets to fill out the meter) to a full-dress elaboration—did they charge by the simile? Somewhat in that spirit of such mutability, I am proposing, tongue not totally in cheek, that we consider the 1952 performance here (the poem plus Williams's comment) as a fuller-dress version of "The Sea-Elephant."

To underline my interest in the comment, I will print it at the end of this piece, lineated to mime the printed poem. The transcribed comment contains almost exactly the same number of words, so my lineation works nicely until the last quatrain. As with my presentation of the sound-script as dramatic speech, by making Williams's comment into a "Williams" poem I want to dramatize both the distance between text and voice and, at the same time, a transmutability that cannot be perceived by eye or ear separately. Listening to and reading a poem are two different sensory activities, but, at the same time, they are evidence of the same thing: the poem.

In giving my sense of the 1952 performance, I will be counting in the bits of audience participation that are audible. My sense of how the second sounding of "Blouaugh!" is unique comes from the audience reaction, as the listeners dissolve into screams and laughter when they rehear it bellowed louder and longer than the first time: Williams really roars it out, which immediately causes the audience to involuntarily echo it back, shrieking and laughing. In this almost instantaneous call-and-response, both the poet-as-sea-elephant and the audience are expressing wants and fears via the lower half of the phonological apparatus, without much syllabic fuss at all from tongue, teeth, and lips. An ad hoc oral negotiation is audible: a kind of playground contract has been established on the fly. It's as if the poet has said, "I've scared you again (shouting like a sea-monster), but you'll recognize that there's nothing scary, I'm not a sea elephant, you're not a fish, you're not a victim of the raging appetite whose crudity I've forced you to hear again." The audience laughs and screams like children on Halloween, shocked into a skittish glee by the unpredictable irruption of the now-recognizable (and thus semi-tamed) monster.

Audio Tour

To one whose knowledge is produced and ratified by reading, the sonic medium is elementary and vague: the poem feels "trundled from the strangeness of the sea." We no longer read Williams for line breaks and all the poetic-scholastic drama those decisions entail; quarrels over metrics are replaced by social agons. We no longer hear Williams railing against iambic pentameter, which he once called the medieval masterbeat (*RI*, 219). Through the history of Anglo-American modernism, to iamb or not to iamb was a charged matter—"To break the pentameter, that was the first heave" (Pound, *C*, 532)—but in the sonic universe of "The Sea-Elephant" such battles cease. "[T]rundled from the strangeness of the sea" is a well-balanced floating stretch of regular beats, which could be a snatch of iambs, or of trochees, indifferently. In the sonic universe poems are not machines made of words, as Williams's oft-repeated claim has it; rather than the word, the phrase becomes the unit, with contestatory foregrounding of various social voices.

In the naive, echoey world of sound, what does it matter if we hear TRUN dled / FROM the / STRANGE ness / OF the / SEA—catalectic trochees (final syllable missing)—or TRUN / dled FROM / the STRANGE / ness OF / the SEA—acephalous iambs (first syllable missing)? Either way, "trundled from the strangeness of the sea" is a symmetrical stretch of stressed/unstressed syllables enclosed by stresses, which is then followed by its inverse, "a kind of heaven," a symmetrical stretch of stressed/unstressed syllables enclosed by non-stresses. What could sound more sealike, womblike (trundle bed, bundle of joy), than the sum of these two phrases with their syntax withholding the subject of the sentence and thus reinforcing the sense of unending suspension?

Poet: Trundled from the strangeness of the sea—a kind of heaven—

The subject of the sentence then bursts upon us, fulfilling, in some technical sense, the syntactic contract. The sentence-construing listener is owed one subject (something is trundled from the sea, but what?), which is then provided:

Carny: (*nasally*) Ladies and Gentlemen! the greatest sea-monster ever exhibited alive the gigantic sea-elephant!

What the ear hears, though, is not syntactic completion but the brash interruption of a different intonation, the carny's strongly nasalized voice. At least, that's what's in the sound-script: during the 1952 performance Williams himself does not initially realize he is inhabiting a different speaker until he is halfway through the phrase.

No more saline, womblike non-difference: we are now addressed as gendered beings: either ladies or gentlemen. And the fractures don't stop there: we're customers, we're classed (we're at the circus), and we're regional (as the Bronx/Jersey nasality informs us). Via accent and denotation, the carny's voice has made it clear that the greatest sea monster ever exhibited alive is, precisely, not Moby Dick. We're outside of literature, it might seem.

But the poet cedes no ground. He grabs the mic back and, using a slightly lower pitch and non-nasal seriousness, pronounces the fact that, although the poem has just quoted commercial speech, it nevertheless has serious designs on articulating the poetic sublime:

Poet: (*nonnasal*) O wallow of flesh where are there fish enough for that appetite stupidity cannot lessen? Sick of April's smallness the little leaves—Flesh has lief of you enormous sea—Speak!

Carny and poet both speak of the sea elephant, pointing to a monster. The carny uses the American commercial vocative, addressing the customer, offering mastery for a quarter. In reaction, the poet addresses the sea elephant using the vocative: "O wallow of flesh." For the poet the sea elephant is a sublime wallow of carnality, Pig Cupid's big brother,[9] an ally in the fight against *The Waste Land*; it is usefully unambiguous against some genteel April which often seemed to Williams to have Eliot's copyright on it. "April is the cruellest month" is itself ironic, but Williams often disregarded this to attack the month itself, here and in poems such as "April Is the Saddest Month" (*WCW II*, 117), which depicts, with lighthearted but clinical precision, the aftermath of dogs mating.

But beneath his cynicism Williams also shows himself jejune, smitten with spring, Keats-ish. (This happens throughout his career; it is not cancelled out by his increased sophistication.) Via a sonic pirouette (leaves = lief), what were the trite symbols of spring, "the little leaves," become a site of his own desire as he insists that "Flesh has lief of you." "Lief" is a word, though not one the ear hears much at all: an odd, rusty adjective, adverb, even an obsolete noun ("dear," "sweetheart"), but mostly used in the Shakespearean "I had as lief. . . ." Here and elsewhere Williams uses it as his own idiosyncratic noun to indicate leafy utopian permission. In "Asphodel" he writes: "A thousand tropics / in an apple blossom. / The generous earth itself // gave us lief. / The whole world / became my garden!" (*WCW II*, 313).

But if the fight aims to rescue modern poetry from docility (descriptive seasonality), "Flesh has lief of you, enormous sea, Speak!" makes an odd battle cry. If the goal is to bring poetry and the present closer, then might not the carny be more contemporary than the poet? Maybe the poet, tangled up in lofty desire by long *e*'s (leaves, lief, enormous sea, Speak!) had better give the mic back to the sea elephant:

Sea-Elephant: (*bellowing*) BLOUAUGH!

Does one hear this as rebuke, release, self-satire, or affirmation? We can imagine a scale of earnestness stretching from the religious awfulness of the Thunder's "DA" near the end of *The Waste Land* to a bad boy pretending to puke on the marble floors of culture. The primary aggression could be directed at the carny ("O blasphemous venality of the commercial world, BLOUAUGH!"); at Eliot ("O pedantic smallness of poetic ambition, BLOUAUGH!"); or at himself ("O overblown poet commanding the enormous sea to speak, BLOUAUGH!"). All sound plausible.

The poetic voice's subsequent elaboration will not resolve any ambiguities. It begins in the first person as if the poet were ventriloquizing the sea elephant,[10] but quickly switches perspective to the poet observing the sea elephant:

Poet: (feed me) my flesh is riven—fish after fish into his maw unswallowing to let them glide down gulching back half spittle half brine the troubled eyes—torn from the sea.

Just as it is not easy to tell if BLOUAUGH! was a cry of ejection or incorporation, desire and disgust are not disentangled here. Is this eating or spitting up? Authoritative, kingly appetite or childish puking? This equivocation extends even to the idiosyncratic verb "gulching back": the sea elephant's gullet is an insatiable gulf that vomits fish back out.

As if to comment on such gorging messiness, another voice is heard:

Woman: (In a practical voice) They ought to put it back where it came from.

On the page, the enclosing parenthesis, "(In a practical voice)," is meant as a stage direction for voicing. Awkward as it seems on the page, it demonstrates that Williams was thinking of the poem as a sound-script. For the listener, however, the phrase is simply redundant. Here, the sarcasm of Williams's tone is dominant, and it's hard not to assimilate this woman to a stereotype of the antibody matron. This sense is quickly reinforced by repetition, as we soon hear the woman again, a little bit more emphatic as she dismisses the poet's mention of the mysteries of the sea elephant as an old gender-bending mermaid:

Poet: Gape. Strange head—told by old sailors—rising bearded to the surface—and the only sense out of them is that woman's

Woman: Yes it's wonderful but they ought to put it back into the sea where it came from.

Having set up this woman as a satirical target, Williams then uses the full volume of the sea elephant against her. There is no ambiguity here: this is the sea elephant as emblem for Williams's rejection of domesticity:

Sea-Elephant: (*loudly bellowing; audience responding with shrieks and gasps*) BLOUAUGH!

As if the sea elephant had just spoken for him, the poet uses the beast's undifferentiated massiveness to dismiss all craft and cleverness. The immediate referent for the following would seem to be trained seals (Williams wrote "The Sea-Elephant" after a visit to the circus in 1929), but it also seems emblematic of Williams's lifelong struggle with line breaks.

Poet: Swing—ride walk on wires—toss balls stoop and contort yourselves—
But I am love. I am from the sea—

Rather than engage in such prosodic cleverness, why not just bellow one's own presence? You other trained, contorted poets may worry over the damn line breaks, but for me it's all desire, all the time. At least, that's what poet-as-sea-elephant is saying. In fact, the actual line breaks on the page are an excellent species of Williams's own prosodic contortions:

Swing—ride
walk
on wires—toss balls
stoop and

contort yourselves—

The third time the sea elephant speaks,

Sea-Elephant: (*smaller bellow*) BLOUAUGH!

it becomes an approved cry of triumph, of appetite asserting its priority. But positivity is harder to pronounce. Sea elephants can interrupt poems, but they don't do as well at writing them. Williams tries to make the sea elephant emblematic of his own poetic enterprise, indulging in a small fantasia of hetero carnal bliss:

Poet: there is no crime save the too-heavy body the sea held playfully—comes to the surface the water boiling about the head the cows scattering fish dripping from the bounty of . . .

But the bounty of such triumphant identification proves ephemeral and the poem suddenly switches without warning back to literary polemic. The target is some vague bolus of Pound (whose catchy but ultimately nondescript satire is quoted: Winter is icummen in [*P/T*, 120]), Eliot, and ye olde Britishness. The poem ends with finicky, aggressive sarcasm:

Poet: (falsetto) and Spring they say Spring is icummen in—

This makes the audience laugh (of course, the Blouaugh!s, the carny, and the woman had softened them up).

Throughout the reading, Williams seems to have had a strong hold on the listeners. (This will become even clearer in the comment.) Williams's repertoire of vocal manners in the poem is not utterly divorced from the carny's behavior: both are examples of aggressive outreach. The product the carny is urging on the public is a sight of the sea elephant; with Williams, the product that is recommended is his poetry. And if we remember the context of Williams's career at the time of the writing, this final sarcasm can sound rather sour, a grumpy realization of his secondary position. Rather than a kingly sea elephant disporting in the sea, the poet is a married man in New Jersey, probably taking the kids to the circus. Aggrieved masculinity chafes within petty rituals. It's 1929, and poets still have to write about spring.

The intense deformation of the poet's voice at the end makes an odd conclusion. The emotional level—what old-fashioned terms the sonic universe brings to mind!—seems not far from grade-school sarcasm. Perhaps some of Williams's polemic is directed toward his own practice as a poet—he could be conflicted about his own partially repressed Keatsianism—but is the inarticulate aggression of the sea elephant any way forward? The fall in volume of the third "Blouaugh!" suggests the trope is getting a little tired already.

My following lineation of the spoken 1952 comment is presented as if it were a Williams poem, something on the model of Louis Zukofsky's "'Mantis,' An Interpretation":

> My wife
> tells me I read the
> rougher pieces. Every
> man
>
> hates to expose
> himself in
> the . . . public (I
> was
>
> going to
> say . . .) [*laughter*]. You don't
> like to reveal
> the
>
> more sensitive . . . feelings you
> may
> have perhaps.
> It's always
>
> easier
> to be a
> little . . . a
> little
>
> rough. At least it's a
> way of
> being
> timid, I

suppose, showing
your timidity anyhow.
Because modern, the modern poet, such
a

one as I am, at
least, does
not seek the
temple.

There
are those—and
I don't mean
to

belittle them—such as
Ezra
Pound, who are always—or
T. S. Eliot,

or
some of
the French, the distinguished
poets

of
the past, W. B.
Yeats, they
carry about with them

an aura that
is
poetry it seems. Forgetting
[*louder*] that you

are the
poetry for god's sake! Let
'em come down
to

you and
lift
you up! Anyhow, it's
very attractive

to have
these wonderful
people stand above you
and make you

feel
like a worm. [*loud, long laughter*] Uh? There're
other things. Poetry
in

the past
has been gusty [gutsy?],
it's been rough,
it's been

Villon,
it's been parts of Shakespeare.
It
isn't only that

temple thing.

The way the audience picks up the vulgar suggestion in Williams's nearly whispered rumination, "to expose himself in the . . . public," shows how closely they're listening. This was not an isolated trope for Williams. Discussing another reading (NYU, 1949) where "he had read one or two confessional pieces that he had not intended to read, he told the friend who had arranged the reading that he felt like he had been 'talking into a felt mattress.' Confessing in public felt as if you have pulled 'back your foreskin (if you have one) in public'" (Middleton, 84).

However, the moral here, to my ear at least, is not that Williams is an unreconstructed phallic monster. "The Sea-Elephant" can certainly be read as a phallic attack on femininity/feminization, but in the comment Williams finds his wife's remark informative, and it leads him to a complex perspective on his own aggression. To be rough is to display one's timidity: "It's always easier to be a little . . . a little rough. At least it's a way of being timid, I suppose, showing your timidity anyhow." Semantically, what follows is a non sequitur. Logically, this explanatory "Because" is puzzling. The intertwining of masculine display/fear is caused by arguments over poetic decorum? But on the emotional level, such sudden leaps into the arena of modernist authority have been occurring throughout the poem.

In what follows, Williams begins with an earnest attempt at decorous discussion, "the distinguished poets of the past" who are not to be belittled. But while Williams is not (ostensibly) belittling them, they, as we hear next, have already belittled him. Warming to the rage he's about to vocalize, he shouts out his most paradoxical poetic credo: "Forgetting [*louder*] that you are the poetry for god's sake! Let 'em come down to you and lift you up!" I find this very moving, if permanently complex. One can take it as another version of the real language of people, but that doesn't account for much of the substance of the poem, or the framing. The audience is the poetry, but needs the poet (apparently in a superior position) to lift them up. I will not attempt to untangle the complications of this. Again, my intuition (the same faculty that saw Williams's strengths and flaws as a baggy unity at the beginning of the essay) suggests that this may be an unresolvable knot. It might be useful, in fact, to keep it tight.

The poet may be in a superior position, lifting the audience up, but, typical of Williams's sudden reversals, his next position is low indeed: "Anyhow, it's very attractive to have these wonderful people stand above you and make you feel like a worm." The audience's loud laughter is ultimately as impossible to parse singly as any of the "Blouaugh!" moments. But it is plausible that what animates the listeners' explosion of pleasure is a sudden sense of the kinship of the sea elephant and the worm. Both fit easily into the tragicomedy of phallic authority we've been hearing. The audience's pleasure is palpable, fleshing out Williams's insistence that the audience is the poetry.

16

Alice Notley and Poetic Inheritance

The notion of a poetic generation is a convenient shorthand in places—Romantic poets are divided into first and second generation to remind students that Blake, Wordsworth, and Coleridge were decades older than Byron, Shelley, and Keats. But to move beyond a suggestion of family resemblance and claim the first generation engendered the second, in any sense that can be materially specified, would seem an unproductive literalization of what was merely a colorless trope of mental convenience.

Alice Notley's 1980 talk, *Doctor Williams' Heiresses*, insists on such literalization:

> Poe was the first one, he mated with a goddess. His children were Emily Dickinson & Walt Whitman—out of wedlock with a goddess. Then Dickinson & Whitman mated—since they were half divine they could do anything they wanted to—& they had 2 sons, William Carlos Williams & Ezra Pound, & a third son T. S. Eliot who went to a faraway country & never came back. From out of the West came Gertrude Stein, the daughter of the guy who wrote the 800-page novel & the girl who thought maybe rightly that she was Shakespeare.[1]

This faux-naive fable goes on to narrate a one-page history of American poetry, starting with Poe-Whitman-Dickinson and leading—via Stein, Williams, Frank O'Hara, and Philip Whalen—to Bernadette Mayer and Notley herself. *Heiresses* as a whole is an aggressively intimate polemic about the value of Williams, celebrating a poetry kept vivid by staying enmeshed in wide social experience (which included women and babies). The talk has not circulated widely, so I will be quoting it at some length here.

The tone of this opening fable may at first sound naive but it is a splay of different registers. Short phrases, vocabulary at easy-reader level ("Poe was the first one"), fairy-tale diction ("a faraway country")—this is for children, even young children. But then again this is obviously addressing an adult audience—us. We know, or are addressed as if we know, that Eliot became a British citizen and that Stein grew up in Oakland. In "the girl who thought maybe rightly that she was Shakespeare," we are assumed to hear the allusion to Virginia Woolf's creation, Shakespeare's sister. Woolf's polemic was built around an absence: "Let me imagine, since the facts are so hard to come by, what would have happened had Shakespeare had a wonderfully gifted sister" (Woolf, 46). Notley, even as she evokes this, pulls us a step beyond into a situation where the sister is not only real, but is in fact Shakespeare: "the girl who thought maybe rightly she was Shakespeare," where the impersonal authority of "maybe rightly" suggests that what we are hearing is a fact, that Shakespeare *was* his own sister, or that Shakespeare *was* her own sister, however you want to comb out the semantic suggestion. Such ambitious gender leapfrog is playful, but the histories and counter-histories that make such thinking palpable are adult matters.

I hear a third register as well, neither fairy tale nor adult, more like a strategic deployment of an adolescent tone: "—out of wedlock with a goddess" (excited gossiping); "they could do anything they wanted to" (rebelliousness); and "the guy who wrote the 800-page novel" (ostentatious forgetfulness). In addition, what triggers my sense of this in-between space is the implied world of poetic mating/marriage. It is a rude, preposterous construction suggesting the lilt of playground proto-adolescence: "Walt and Emily in a tree, K-I-S-S-I-N-G." Notley goes on:

> Gertrude Stein and William Carlos Williams got married: their 2 legitimate children, Frank O'Hara & Philip Whalen, often dressed & acted like their uncle Ezra Pound. . . . Now O'Hara & Whalen were males that were male-female, as were many of the children of Williams by various goddesses & of Gertrude Stein & some gods. Olson was too big to be male-female as he would have liked. (Notley, *DWH*)

As the account moves closer to her own time of writing, Notley strategically stops naming poets: they are simply "all males" and "very many." Names only reappear at the end:

> Anyway it was striking how there were no females in this generation; & the first children of the male-females & of Olson & their other brothers were all males, and there were very many of them because of their fathers' incredible promiscuity. But the male-females also produced a second wave of children of which there were many females. These females could not understand how they came to be born—they saw no one among their parents & brothers who resembled them physically, for the goddesses their father mated with were evaporative non-parental types. As a matter of fact

> these females couldn't even believe that their fathers *were* their fathers. They came to indulge in a little ancestor worship—that is they each fell in love with a not too distant ancestor. One of them, Bernadette Mayer, fell in love with Gertrude Stein. And the one named Alice Notley fell in love with her grandfather, Williams Carlos Williams. (*DWH*)

Marriage/mating between famous names producing famous offspring, with evaporative goddesses serving as background continuity—on the surface this is a heteronormative fairy-tale genealogy; but, again, the address is to those who know that Dickinson and Whitman never married and that Stein was childless. We are meant to see the heteronormative costuming as flimsy; we are meant to note the contortions needed to keep the fundamental polarity of man/woman intact, so that it is necessary to use "male-female" to indicate that O'Hara was gay. The fable ends with polemic seriousness as Notley names herself and Bernadette Mayer, placing both in the arena with the named ancestors.

Heiresses collages disparate materials: the fable is followed by casual, sophisticated conversation between unnamed persons who it is hard not to take as Notley and her husband Ted Berrigan. This is followed by excerpts from Williams's *I Wanted to Write a Poem*, excerpts from a Notley interview, and a long letter from Bernadette Mayer reacting to the opening fable but dwelling more on real-time pregnancy and pediatrics than poetry. The talk ends with Notley addressing Williams directly. Poems and lines of Williams's are interspersed throughout. Though the talk explicitly praises Williams's poetry for its vivid speech, such juxtaposition of differing textures is another Williams technique. The overall effect of *Heiresses* approaches the resolute untotalizability of, say, Book Four of *Paterson*.

Heiresses was part of Notley's 1980 residency at 80 Langton Street in San Francisco, and it was published by Lyn Hejinian in her Tuumba pamphlet series: thus both talk and text appeared in contexts associated with the coalescing Language scene. Early in her career, Notley was already a major figure in the St. Mark's scene. Though the talk is rarely explicit about these groups, *Heiresses* now reads as an articulation of a fundamental opposition between a poetics foregrounding the poet writing in real time versus writing that foregrounds textuality. The boundary between the second-generation New York School and the Language scene was far from ironclad and many crossover figures could be cited. Nevertheless, in those days it was an easily felt difference.

In reading *Heiresses* as articulating such a distinction, I am ignoring Notley's disclaimer. Soon after the opening fable, she denied it had any specific intention: "I can't remember anything about what I was thinking about Williams & women writers 2 years ago. It was just a crackbrained theory so I could write some works then" (*DWH*). But even this shrugging-off sentence seems consonant with New York School poetics: pragmatic devotion to art; everyday diction; pointed disinterest in articulating an explicit poetics. As O'Hara famously put it: "Nobody should experience anything they don't need to, if they don't need poetry bully for them. I like the movies too. And after all, only Whitman and Crane and Williams, of the American poets, are better than the movies. As for measure and other technical apparatus, that's just common sense: if you're going to buy a pair of pants you want them tight enough so everyone will want to go to bed with you" (O'Hara, 498).

Poetic Transmission

One of the things I hear in O'Hara's "common sense" advice is an eroticized translation of Williams's poetic struggles with measure and the variable foot. Certainly, O'Hara never separated art and erotics. Take the early "Memorial Day 1950":

> Fathers of Dada! You carried shining erector sets
> in your rough bony pockets, . . .
>   And those of us who thought poetry
> was crap were throttled by Auden or Rimbaud
> when, sent by some compulsive Juno, we tried
> to play with collages or sprechstimme in their bed.
> (O'Hara, 17)

While O'Hara always seemed to have imaginative access to the beds of his heroes, Allen Ginsberg at times insisted on a lineage that only works by physical contact: "Neal Cassady slept with [Gavin Arthur] occasionally . . . and Gavin Arthur had slept with Edward Carpenter, and Edward Carpenter has slept with Walt Whitman. So this is in a sense in the line of transmission. . . . Kerouac's heterosexual hero [i.e., Cassady] who also slept with somebody who slept with somebody who slept with Whitman, and received the Whispered Transmission, capital W, capital T, of that love" (Ginsberg, *Spontaneous Mind*, 317). (And Ginsberg slept with Cassady, it should be added.) The Whispered Transmission, which Ginsberg capitalizes for the ear of the interviewer (and the eye of subsequent readers), does not travel via the page. Poetic knowledge is reproduced by physical contact.

Ginsberg's sense of Williams's work was equally physical. More than the poem on the page, Ginsberg values Williams's own enunciation. The last line of "The Clouds" trails off into ellipsis: "Plunging upon a moth, a butterfly, a pismire, a. . . ." (*WCW II*, 498). In an interview, Ginsberg quotes the line by imitating Williams's pronunciation rather than the "a" that is printed on the page:

> "Plunging upon a moth, a butterfly, a pismire, hupp." And then he waved his hands in the air—he just gave up. So I suddenly realized it was just like somebody talking in a bar, not finishing the sentence but just giving up with a gesture of impatience, and that it was a syntactical fact of speech that had never been written down before in poetry—and so I realized that his poetry was absolutely identical with speech. (Ginsberg, *Spontaneous Mind*, 268)

Listeners often receive a more sharply focused impression when hearing a poet read, but here Ginsberg is suggesting that the poet's body is where the poem exists.

In *Songs for the Unborn Second Baby*, a long poem of Notley's that she refers to in *Heiresses*, Notley toys with such notions of contact. The gist of the following section of the poem is an unambiguous diatribe against Williams the swaggering male:

> male principle of the poetry, you earnestly sexed
> character of your poetry fucking
> me across the decades like we
> poets like or centuries why aren't you
> my obstetrician, are you?
> for they forgot us a midwife
>
> but you're right, Bill Williams, I won't
> take it
>   your flattery, I hate
> Venus, you
>   can't flatten me, further
> you betray me with your fragrant
> infidelities to Floss and I toss off our
> whiskies to your impalement (*Songs*, n.p.)

But there's local ambivalence in the passage: "why aren't you / my obstetrician, are you?"; "infidelities" that are not flagrant but "fragrant"; and especially this: "fucking / me across the decades like we / poets like." Take out "like we / poets like" and we would have Williams as the classic male victimizer, the "earnestly sexed / character of [his own] poetry" fucking things up for Notley decades later. However, "like we / poets like" tugs against such easy resolution. "We poets" unites Notley with Williams: both are poets who like "fucking . . . across the decades." It's hard to pin down subject positions in lines as fluid as these, but Notley is writing from at least two situations at once: as objectified female she is getting fucked over, while as poet she is involved in some mutually pleasurable poetic intercourse transcending time and place.

In the final section of *Heiresses* Notley mentions *Songs* and its anger against Williams. She speaks directly to Williams with a similar mixture of anger and intimacy as *Songs* displayed:

> I typed up all of your poem "Asphodel, That Greeny Flower," & Honey that took a long time. In that bad time there was always you. To love as a poet & to love & hate as a man. Immobile pregnant & isolate & unhappy, I didn't need to read about your attractions to women other than your wife. Your reasoning seemed specious & was enraging. . . . But I wrote my poem & I used for its form your *Paterson* & an O'Hara ode & those Cantos . . . & it is held together by flowers, as "Asphodel" is—we had a bewilderingly luxuriant garden there—& by the presence of the opposite sex "you" & by the will to write poetry. I want to say this only for me I think, I think whoever hears this knows it & knows all about you—(Notley, *DWH*)

Though address here is intimate—Notley's I talking to Williams's you—Notley claims it is still public. But a characteristic effect of second-generation New York School poetry occurs when the private context overrides public knowledge. Another example of what I'm getting at here comes from earlier in the talk:

> —I can't remember anything about what I was thinking about Williams & women writers 2 years ago. It was just a crackbrained theory so I could write some works then.
>
> —Why are you working up to writing some incredibly baroque lecture? You should be worrying about whether or not your panties are gonna fall down while you're giving it. (Notley, *DWH*)

I feel that I know the speakers here are Notley and Berrigan, and I predict that many others would agree. Where does my knowledge come from? It's a mix of publically available information (from reading their work), personal acquaintance, and the intermediate sphere of contact with many others who were involved in various degrees with their work and their lives.

This gradient between public and private knowledge is displayed in the two emblems in Berrigan's remark: there's the baroque lecture (public knowledge) and the fallen panties (private, but in public view). The panties are of course the interesting alternative:

> —Which pair should I wear in case they do?
>
> —Your Philip Whalen black & white calligraphy panties with lower case letters stitched along the seams . . . [ellipsis in original] Why don't you do something easy like play some records of Williams reading
>
> —Ah, they've all heard those records.
>
> —Are you kidding? Young poets haven't heard shit—they all turn up their noses at the Caedmon records because they got famous on the Dylan Thomas records. Which is why we liked them. (Notley, *DWH*)

In a comic but learned register, the first half of Berrigan's answer provides the same display of private poetic inheritance. Philip Whalen stitches calligraphy only on Alice's panties. Even if they fall down, they would titillate but not "instruct" the gaping students.

The reported conversation ends on a thoroughly pedagogic note:

> . . . he consolidated a lot of what you knew already, but he allowed you to be fast, perky, sassy, talky, all these different ways that had to do with talking, in one poem. He helped you to be as fast as you are. And to consolidate these voices you were hearing in your head & in the house & on the street & put them in the same poem. Getting it off Williams was like getting it authentic & not a little thirties-movie-modern like in Frank O'Hara . . . [ellipses in original]
>
> —My theory had something to do with being for awhile the female to his male. You could use him without sounding like another imitation Williams poem. And how could you not use him since he was the greatest one? But you could use him to sound entirely new if you were a woman. It was all about this woman business. I thought we didn't need to read women—I mean find the hidden in the woodwork ones—so much as find the poems among whatever sex that made you feel free to say anything, including your own anything. (Notley, *DWH*)

An absolute connection with Williams is the source of this poetic autonomy. An emblem of this is the early Williams poem Notley quotes in between the conversation I have just cited and the opening fable. The fable ended with the statement that "Alice Notley fell in love with her grandfather, William Carlos Williams"; the poem that immediately follows shows Williams in love with his [grand]daughter:

Youth and Beauty

I bought a dishmop—
having no daughter—
for they had twisted
fine ribbons of shining copper
about white twine
and made a tousled head
of it, fastened it
upon a turned ash stick
slender at the neck
straight, tall—
when tied upright
on the brass wallbracket
to be a light for me
and naked
as a girl should seem
to her father.
(*WCW II*, 166)

This reads many ways. (1) The poem personifies and sexualizes the mop, but also gives a detailed physical description of it. (2) Williams is satirizing his own libido: a *mop* makes him think of a naked woman? (3) He is exploring a forbidden fantasy, but situating it in a safe context. (4) The poem demonstrates "the imaginative qualities of the actual things" (*IM*, 67) as it displays shifting modes of declaration: description of mop, evocation of incestuous desire, metaphorical transformation of the mop into a light and back into a naked daughter—all the while using a lofty rhetoric of the sublime ("for they had twisted"; "to be a light for me"; and the quasi-Homeric "fine ribbons of shining copper"). (5) Williams is working on his line breaks. (6) For all its shiftiness and transgression, this is a poem in which gender assignments remain fixed: there is no suggestion that the poet is going to mop the floor; nor does the final maxim, that a girl should seem naked to her father, carry much impact beyond its naughtiness. It seems a bluff by a poet who does not have a daughter. Williams in this 1916 poem is displaying, precociously, the mid-century pattern Rachel Blau DuPlessis aptly finds in Olson, Creeley, and Ginsberg: "the desire to alter male possibility but not question female social positions" (DuPlessis, *Purple Passages*, 91).

What I am most emphasizing here, though, is the intimacy Notley is claiming by placing the poem where she did in the talk, framed to dramatize the impossible but compelling union of her and Williams's poetic bodies. This fronting of private knowledge, contact, inheritance, and membership in a select order of poetic authenticity was an antithetical gesture to some of the practices of the Language scene. Williams was as crucial a figure for Language writers as for Notley, but the admiration was for a more textual poet.

In another moment in *Heiresses*, Notley writes:

> We still haven't caught up with what Williams meant by the variable foot . . . Variable foot is maybe about the dominance of tone of voice over other considerations—I do my poems from here 'cause I talk from here—haven't you ever talked to anyone? I'm not an oracle or a musical instrument or a tradition or a bellows or even a typewriter: I am a tone of voice, warming, shifting, pausing, changing, including, asserting, exulting, including, including, turning & including. I break my lines where I do, as I'm being as various as my voice should be in our intimacy. I'd like there to be something as firm as you to push my voice into in its best most natural place, that would really be measure. (*DWH*)

Notley distinguishes "tone of voice" from the classical model ("an oracle"), the Romantic ("a musical instrument"—Shelley and Coleridge's aeolian harp, say), the Eliotic ("tradition [and the individual talent]"), and the Olsonic ("bellows" = the breath; "typewriter" = the poet using the typewriter to score the precise timing of the poem's enunciation). The typewriter—a machine that produces textuality—points to Language writing as well.

Notley's description culminates: "a tone of voice, warming, shifting, pausing, changing, including, asserting, exulting, including, including, turning & including." A single vividly alert body is the source of this variousness, and the varieties of tone flesh out a unified stretch of experience. It was such unities that Language writers aimed to disrupt through many of the techniques they were using at the time (the new sentence, collage, syntactic fragmentation).

It strikes me now, in the twenty-first century, that neither tone of voice nor textuality does justice to why Williams stays interesting. The following passage from *Paterson* cannot be reduced to either "Williams the poet" or to "words on the page" without having the life drained out of it:

> Invent (if you can) discover or
> nothing is clear—will surmount
> the drumming in your head. There will be
> nothing clear, nothing clear.
>
> He fled pursued by the roar.
>
> Seventy-five of the world's leading scholars, poets, and philosophers gathered at Princeton last week . . .

Faitoute ground his heel
hard down on the stone:

Sunny today, with the highest temperatures near 80 degrees; moderate southerly winds. Partly cloudy and continued warm tomorrow, with moderate southerly winds.

Her belly . her belly is like
a cloud. a cloud
at evening .

His mind would reawaken:

He Me with my pants, coat and vest still on!

She And me still in my galoshes!
(*Paterson*, 85)

Bodies Writing Poems

In 1980, Notley's insistence on locating poetic history in her body seemed very different from the poetics of Language writing, where the transpersonal social composition of language was foregrounded. But choices that seemed stark twenty-five years ago have not proved to be mutually exclusive. As a coda here, I want to compare two contrasting emblematic poets to suggest how contingent any division is between text and body.

What has resonated most unescapably from Eliot's "Tradition and the Individual Talent" is his championing of impersonality. As we are told near the end, "To divert interest from the poet to the poetry is a laudable aim" (Eliot, *Selected Prose*, 42–43). But that essay has contributed greatly to the mystique surrounding the person of Eliot; throughout, Eliot hints at a private gothic narrative of personal danger. There is the coy aside that, "of course, only those who have personality and emotions know what it means to want to escape from these things" (43). "Escape" is a charged word, and it turns out that escape is not possible. He has already been captured, as the familiar quote indicates: "not only the best, but the most individual parts of his work are those in which the dead poets, his ancestors, assert their immortality most vigorously." Eliot adds a stern (but odd) emphasis: "And I do not mean the impressionable period of adolescence, but the period of full maturity" (38). The vigorous, assertive dead, more real than the live poet, reappear at the conclusion of the essay: the poet "is not likely to know what is to be done unless he lives in what is not merely the present, but the present moment of the past, unless he is conscious, not of what is dead, but of what is already living" (44). The normative message here is that great poetry is timeless. But a different scenario can be deduced: a vampire taking over a living body, which makes great poetry not so much timeless as undead. In a later essay Eliot gives us more information about the victim (himself). The initial assault is during the "impressionable period of adolescence": "Consider the adolescent reading of any person with some literary sensibility. Everyone, I believe, who is at all sensible of the seductions of poetry, can remember some moment in youth when he or she was carried away by the work of one poet. Very likely he was carried away by several poets, one after the other" (*Selected Prose*, 101–2). In the essay, we learn the identity of one seducer: "I was intoxicated by Shelley's poetry at the age of fifteen" (86).

Compare O'Hara's "Ave Maria." There the adolescent artistic awakening takes place at the movies, where "the soul / . . . grows in darkness, embossed by silvery images" and the young artist learns "where candy bars come from": knowledge which is "as gratuitous as leaving the movie before it's over / with a pleasant stranger whose apartment is in the Heaven on Earth Bldg / near the Williamsburg Bridge" (O'Hara, 372).

But isn't this apples and oranges? The young Eliot is carried off by the poets he reads; the young O'Hara is—in the poem's scenario, at least—willingly carried off by a person. And isn't that the difference between their work? For Eliot, poetry needs contact with the "mind of Europe" (*Selected Prose*, 39); in O'Hara's "Personism: A Manifesto," poetry needs "love's life-giving vulgarity" (O'Hara, 499). The seduced Eliot reads Shelley; the seduced O'Hara has great sex at the Heaven on Earth Bldg.

What about the Heaven on Earth Bldg—did earthly activities go on there or was the whole thing just imaginary? For readers who want to salvage the wit of "Ave Maria" from the thought that it is based on pedophilia, it is tempting to read the "pleasant stranger" as an outrageous thought experiment counterbalancing the equally exaggerated Norman Rockwell family that is teased throughout the poem ("Mothers of America," "oh mothers you will have made the little tykes / so happy," etc.). In such a reading the "pleasant stranger" is merely a complexly naughty ogre, while the poetic payoff is the non-ironic phrase "darker joys," with its unspecified virtues.

But for most of O'Hara's poetry the strategy that de-realizes the "pleasant stranger" is exactly wrong. It is hard to imagine celebrating his poetry with the enthusiasm it deserves while still considering "12:20 in New York," "a hamburger and a malted," and the "bottle of Strega" (325) as poetic symbols or as props for some reality effect.

The charisma of "Personism" comes from O'Hara's verve in taking complex matters of poetics and exemplifying them as concrete situations in daily life. Aesthetic questions are brought back to how the person feels, which, after all, is the original meaning of *aesthetic* in Greek—not that O'Hara showed all that much interest in the classics. For him, most poems tasted as bad as mother's overcooked roast beef and felt as bad as the exasperated lectures she delivered while ladling out the gravy: "Too many poems act like a middle-aged mother trying to get her kids to eat too much cooked meat, and potatoes with drippings (tears)" (O'Hara, 498). This seems to be much the same house that "the young tyke" escaped in "Ave Maria." How to judge poetry? By how much you like it. The canon of American poetry that O'Hara endorses is tiny: "only Whitman and Crane and Williams . . . are better than the movies." Would you rather see *Rebel without a Cause* or read *Lord Weary's Castle*? If you don't need poetry, bully for you. At this point it seems that, when it comes to poetry, the person is all-determining. The manifesto is entitled "Personism," after all, and was written immediately after O'Hara wrote "Personal Poem": "Personism . . . was founded by me after lunch with LeRoi Jones on August 27, 1959, a day in which I was in love with someone (not Roi, by the way, a blond). I went back to work and wrote a poem for this person. . . . [Personism] puts the poem squarely between the poet and the person, Lucky Pierre style, and the poem is correspondingly gratified" (499).

In the midst of such a celebration of the personal, where even the poem is granted personhood as the "gratified" middle partner, a "Lucky Pierre" in a sexual daisy chain, it is easy to miss the emphasis O'Hara puts on the *im*personal. Personism, he insists, "does not have to do with personality or intimacy, far from it!" (499). Even though the originary moment of Personism involved a real telephone call to the beloved, address in the Personist poem remains virtual. The phrasing is tricky: "I was realizing that if I wanted to I could use the telephone instead of writing the poem, and so Personism was born." I suppose this can be read as O'Hara realizing that he "*could* [my emphasis] use the telephone," followed by his (unmentioned) actual use of the phone, and thus that Personism involves mixing real-time conversation with written address. But in the less strained reading he doesn't pick up the phone, which suggests that "Personism was born" as a shock of compensation at the poet's absenting himself from the everyday circuits of felicity.

If we buy the claim that Personism has nothing to do with intimacy, that "it's all art," then O'Hara can be seen to be saying something rather close to Eliot's claim that "the emotion in [the poet's] poetry will be a very complex thing, but not with the complexity of the emotions of people who have very complex or unusual emotions in life" (10). I am not suggesting that Frank O'Hara is T. S. Eliot's long-lost twin; but comparing them suggests how interlaced the putatively opposed notions of "poet" and "poetry" are.

To return to Notley and the differences between her poetics and those of Language writing: as I said at the beginning of this section, to contrast Notley's embodied poetics with the social textuality of Language writing has become a blurred shorthand. There are many examples of foregrounded language or foregrounded embodiment on either side. In Ted Berrigan's *Sonnets*, an exemplary second-generation New York School work, textual manipulation—extensive recycling of lines and phrases—is central. Conversely, if Steve Benson's performance-generated pieces—for example, many of the pieces in *Blue Book*—do not emphasize the moment-by-moment existence of the poet, nothing does. Selections could be made in which Bernadette Mayer was a Language writer, Kit Robinson a second-generation New York School poet. And what about Clark Coolidge, who, at the time Notley was presenting *Heiresses* at 80 Langton Street, was a beacon of textual activism for many Language writers? His affinities through the sixties and into the seventies were with the second-generation New York scene. The larger point is this: Without the example of Williams there would have been neither Language writing nor the second-generation New York School.

17
Speech Effects
Talk and Transcription

Talk has its charm, evanescent but persistent.

Driving around Philadelphia on July 19, 1996, I heard a few minutes of funk singer George Clinton being interviewed on National Public Radio by Terry Gross. It was an "archive" Fresh Air program from 1992—or was it 94?—now being rebroadcast in conjunction with the release of Clinton's new CD, "The Awesome Power of a Fully Operational Mother Ship." Or was the original broadcast timed to promote "Mother Ship" ("Mothership?"), and the repeat presentation timed to promote some new release? Talk is evanescent, especially when it comes from a more or less unfamiliar quarter.

Clinton spoke of his early involvement with Parliament. Other Motown groups—the Temptations, Gladys Knight and the Pips—had tightly organized choreography and costumes. Body size was important: the Temptations were each exactly six feet tall. Parliament, on the other hand, were different heights; it wasn't easy to keep shirts ironed and ties clean; their dance routines weren't as tight as those of the Pips or the Temptations. After a certain point attempts at patching together some kind of uniformity were abandoned and "We threw down the suit and wore the bag."

Transcribed from memory now, those words look blander and odder than they did at the time, when they conveyed real charm—funking around on stage in a garment bag, rather than aspiring to the machined, upwardly mobile libido of the Temptations and their matched suits. Clinton's own vocal routines during the interview seemed quite rehearsed. He had clearly given these kinds of interviews often; he was comfortable as a public figure and knew audiences would appreciate hearing some casual inside information, even if it didn't come from all that far inside. He possessed a melodious ease in speaking across community boundaries: what he said sounded good. Commodified though they were, his speech-routines were a pleasure. Besides being "the root of all evil"—what word is less likely to be used as a term of praise in contemporary poetics?—

commodities can, after all, be a source of enjoyment. Clinton's mastery of his own social trajectory was audible in his speech: amused and amusing, entrepreneurial, laid-back, interesting.

I will discuss examples of speech intersecting various literary genres—a David Antin talk poem; Kerouac's transcription of taped speech; the Bay Area Talk Series—and as I do I want to keep the potential charm of talk in mind. Talk is the most mixed of media: social, embodied, formulaic, spontaneous, conflictual, identificatory. Speech can be the most efficient way to communicate—"*talk* to me." And it can be quite the opposite—"stop blathering and *say* something!" The tones and rhythms, the prosody of perspicacious speech are tokens of possible agency, however local, within the conflictual grids of the contemporary socialscape. These conflicts are as densely coded within the hierarchies of publishing and circulation as anywhere: the evanescent charm of talk is hard to recover in printed speech. Nevertheless, here, in print, I want to remind readers of its existence.

1)

My investigation of the talk as genre is grounded in reconsideration of the San Francisco Talk Series and the collections of talks I edited in the early eighties, *Talks (Hills 6/7)* and *Writing/Talks*.[1] The Talks (to retroactively capitalize them) exist as independent critical documents; they also can be read as a partial record of the history of the Language writing scene—multiform as that scene was.[2] Some of them, especially Ron Silliman's "The New Sentence" and Lyn Hejinian's "The Rejection of Closure," were sites where influential notions were first presented: though it is the modified, identically titled essay that has circulated. It makes sense that the talk, as a form for criticism, would seem sketchier than an essay. But the Talks contain possibilities that are not explored elsewhere by the ranges of Language writing practice: dramatic and rhetorical effects that depend on an unambiguous notion of person and that go against the grain of much of that practice.

Before turning to the Talks, I want to mention some antecedent figures from the New American poetry—David Antin, Allen Ginsberg, and Jack Kerouac—and some related forms. The talk is very much a middling genre. Made out of speech but often later constituted by writing, its amorphous territory is bounded by poetry readings, performance art, teaching and other academic procedures, interviews, and entertainment. It can focus around one speaker, a few, or a group; it can be an act of criticism or an art performance; it can connote professionalism or anti-professional spontaneity. As a recording of mixed group intention, it lacks the focus that solo acts of writing have, whether these arise from authorial decisions or pre-established procedures. But a different level of intention is created by the fact that a talk has been recorded, transcribed, and published. This elevation of the speaker's words pushes the talk closer to the interview, where we reproduce George Clinton's words because they belong to George Clinton.

In poetry over the last decades the spoken has become, if not primary, then certainly prominent. Since the 1960s, voice has been valorized across a wide range of aesthetics—from Charles Olson and Allen Ginsberg, who make breath a key element of composition, to the workshop notion of voice. But this quite mixed chorus praising sound ultimately reads from a printed score. Whether the voice is pronouncing spoken word art or a double sestina, the words have almost always been organized prior to the performance.

David Antin's talk poems reversed this priority, originating as improvised speech. "what am i doing here" (1973), the initial poem in his first book of talk pieces, is a twenty-page transcript of a spoken improvisation that covers a range of loosely interlocking subjects and stories: writing versus talking; an acquaintance who dated a man who had a tattooed penis; Antin letting a very paranoid friend borrow his car; a discussion of scientific terminology from an antifoundational viewpoint. The deliberate casualness of the segues lasts on through to the end, which, though earlier themes are remembered, is not a climactic summing up of previous themes; instead, a poetic credo is casually pronounced:

> as a poet i was getting extremely tired of   what i considered an unnatural
> language act   going into a closet   so to speak   sitting in front of a
> typewriter   because anything is possible sitting in front of a typewriter and
> nothing is necessary   a closet is no place to address anybody[3]

In the standard regimes of writing there is a time lag between production and reception of words. By making spoken improvisation the site of creation, Antin wanted the two times to coincide. The transcription imitates this immediacy by avoiding capitals, punctuation, apostrophes, and flush left and right margins, and by using spaces to mimic the pauses between phrases. The spaced clumps of lowercase letters aim to designate nothing more than sonic immediacy.

Antin's typography had a second target however: normative prose and the authority of conventionalized discourse. The issues were as can be seen from the blurb on the back cover:

> For the past few years the poet and art critic David Antin has been performing spontaneous "talk poems," . . . "I see my talking pieces," says Antin, "as philosophical inquiries to which I try to bring the resources of language, not only my own language, but natural language in its natural set-

> ting, or one of its natural settings—talk. I've been a poet, critic, linguist, and engineer, and though this knowledge informs the book, it is not the work of a professional.
>
> "*Talking at the Boundaries,*" he continues, "asks questions about life, about art, about the nature of experience . . . All of the pieces in it began—like most talk—as improvisations on particular occasions in particular places . . . as an improvisation is not in 'prose,' which is an image of the authority of 'right thinking' conveyed primarily through 'right printing'—justified margins, conventional punctuation, and regularized spelling—this book has been printed without recourse to such appeals . . . Shakespeare's father's name is recorded in eighty-three different spellings . . . he himself spelled it four different ways in his own will."

The title of the book is a bit like Shakespeare's (Shaxpear's) signature, since it changes depending on where one looks: on the front cover and the top of the back, it is *talking at the boundaries*; the Library of Congress publication data give it as *Talking at the boundaries*; but inside the blurb and inside the quotation marks that designate Antin's own words, the typography is the most normative: *Talking at the Boundaries*. These variations seem the product of contemporary print bureaucracies rather than any echo of free-wheeling Elizabethan attitudes toward the written word: a lowercase title acquiring an initial capital from the Library of Congress and a second capital from an editor at New Directions following the dictates of the style manuals.

The words appear in quotes and the phrase that introduces the quotation is "says Antin." But the words seem less spoken than written for a blurb. It is a rather blunt irony that these words claiming the necessity of typographic freedom for speech are writing set into justified blocks of prose, with their appearance in quotation marks merely designating that they are Antin's intellectual property, rather than his speech.

Antin calls talk natural: it is "natural language in its natural setting," whereas temporally separated writing is "an unnatural language act." But speech does not exist in a pure state of nature: issues of property and prestige frame and occupy the phrase pulse of the talk pieces. For each piece, Antin writes an introduction in the same format as the talk poems themselves, with the addition of italics. The preface "what am i doing here" begins:

> *this poem-talk was improvised at the san francisco poetry center on the occasion of a joint reading by jerome rothenberg and myself in april 1973   we had each been asked by kathy fraser to provide some sort of statement about our own work to provide something of a context for the audience and for kathys introduction   i had suggested that i had always had mixed feelings about*

> *being considered a poet "if robert lowell is a poet i dont want to be a poet if robert frost was a poet i dont want to be a poet if socrates was a poet ill consider it"* (1)

While Antin uses typography to connote language in its natural setting, the reference is never unprofessional, with each introduction mentioning a particular venue: "*the philadelphia art museum and moore college were cooperating on a series of talks set up loosely to coincide with the duchamp retrospective*"; "*i had to stop in new york to talk to people at the acquavella gallery who were putting on a matisse show*"; "*i was tired of riding on planes so i decided to take the bus to south bend where i was going to be talking at notre dame*" (25, 51, 87).

Antin's use of quotation marks around the Lowell-Frost-Socrates statement in the first introduction seems anomalous. In general, he uses lowercase letters even to the point of courting awkwardness: "*ill*" is more easily read as an adjective than as the contraction of "*i will*," so that "*if socrates was a poet ill consider it*" at first suggests "ill-considered." Does Antin allow the quotation marks to interrupt the lowercase regime because he needs to specify speech acts? But while the subsequent speech act of his talk "what am i doing here?" takes up the next twenty pages, the phrase "*if robert lowell is a poet i don't want to be a poet*" was not spoken in the course of the talk. It was, he writes, a "statement" provided to the audience. Though it's in quotation marks, it's doubtful it was spoken before the reading. Poets almost always begin with a remark or two before reading; but how would a talk-poet draw the line between introductory patter and the performance itself?

I'm poring over this phrase because it is one of the most memorable statements in the book. With all the straightforwardness of speech, Antin is kicking Frost, the late king, and Lowell, the current king (as of 1973), out of the realm of poetry. It is not pure speech that is doing this, however, but situated speech requiring the addition of quotation marks, which are not sonic at all, but markers of intellectual property. With his talk poems, Antin is proposing a reconfiguration of the literary field; the quoted sentence announcing this is thus nearly as important as the poems themselves. It is more than a real-time phrase uttered to a real-time audience, it is a social-literary act.

Margreta De Grazia has shown that quotation marks used to have precisely the opposite valence as today: in Elizabethan times they designated cultural commonplaces, which would be marked amid blocks of print so that the phrases by Aristotle, Augustine, et al. could be copied into commonplace books. Our current usage arose along with the entire panoply of individual rights. From the abolition of torture in state trials to the Fifth Amendment to the acceptance of intellectual property, the words of individuals were deemed inviolably specific; quotation marks were to defend them from being taken over by the state or by other individuals.[4]

In the blurb for *talking at the boundaries*, Antin said/wrote that the pieces arose "as improvisations on particular occasions in particular places." When he gave a talk in the Talk Series in 1978 at 80 Langton Street in San Francisco, the particular place completely changed the nature of his talk. Rather than an Antin monolog, it became a talk with a great deal of audience participation, to the distress of some who felt that Antin's artistic property was not being respected. Issues of power and literary genealogy were at stake. It was five years after Antin began to do talk pieces; *talking at the boundaries* had just been published by New Directions; the Talks had been going for two years; Antin was one of the first speakers from outside the Bay Area scene and had the most literary capital.

He arrived late due to a Bay Bridge traffic jam and, as organizer, I introduced him, as was usual, with a minimal comment—something like, "Here's David Antin." In hindsight, something a bit less naive, some mention of his monologic procedures and the polylogic ambience of the Talks would have been a good idea. But the clash that followed was lit up more luridly by my awkward minimalism. His talk, "Figures of Speech and Figures of Thought," began with his usual mixture of themes: in this case, classical Greek notions of metaphor, harmony, and negotiation; a long story about a coed who became anorexic; and a consideration of metaphor—anorexia as athleticism? anorexia as disease? But this cluster of themes was ultimately overshadowed by the interplay between Antin and the audience.[5] He never finished the anorexic's story, as he and the audience became embroiled in a discussion about the talk form and the usefulness or impropriety of audience participation; and in fact the talk was never transcribed and published.

To repeat, the blame for the blow-up is mine: a better introduction could have kept the monolog intact. But in a number of places Antin seemed to invite audience participation. He singled out audience members with extended mention: he opened the talk by mentioning Ron Silliman's tape recorder: "Now that Ron's recorder is working we're capable of doing it." He asked George Lakoff if Lakoff's new book was going to be about metaphor. He would react to laughter by extending an amusing riff. He spoke of an uncle also named David Antin, then contrasted name to definition by comparing the sentence "I wonder if Ron Silliman will be here tonight?" with "I wonder if there will be a Ron Silliman here tonight?" While initially he held the floor seamlessly, such nods to the audience gradually encouraged comments and suggestions to which he responded increasingly, so that after an hour Silliman, Lakoff, Tom Mandel, and I were asking long questions and illustrating points with extended comments. Near the end of the piece, Antin and Silliman had a long dialog about the form of the talk, with Silliman, in a comment that seemed to anticipate the clash to come, suggesting that Antin was not interested in innovation and was perhaps courting catastrophe to move forward. Antin replied that the formal catastrophe in the arts of discourse had occurred near the end of the eighteenth century when a fixed sense of the group being addressed disappeared.

The discussion had been amiably intellectual to this point; but the issue of group incoherence and a small version of rhetorical catastrophe began to materialize when one man said that he had felt very uncomfortable with the last hour's interruptions or conversation. He said that he could not see Antin's interlocutors, who were all sitting in the front row, and that Antin's work needed to be uninterrupted to succeed. As Antin was responding to this concern, he was interrupted by his wife, Eleanor Antin, who said that she had come to hear art and felt violated by the interruptions. "We're all prisoners of five guys. Is that what these things are? Everybody comes to hear these five guys?" Mandel challenged her characterization of the talks. Silliman said that both forms of talk—Antin's monolog and the Talk Series polylog—were valid and that the audience was witnessing a transition from one form to another. David Antin said that he had expected the interruptions and that he had been trying to find out how much negotiation was possible. The discussion grew crowded and loud; the tape recorder did not pick it all up. Here is my transcription of one moment:

Eleanor Antin: You're facing them [the interlocutors in the front row], David. Even for the young men here as well as for the women it's an extremely macho situation in which we are here, and you are looking at their faces; they're talking to you.

David Antin: [unintelligible—possibly suggesting Eleanor was free to leave]

Eleanor Antin: Oh come on! Where can I go? I came in the wagon; I can't go anywhere. [laughter] [much unintelligible, overlapping conversation] . . . I experienced it that way because they have more strength than we do. They talk louder; and I can't see their faces; and they're in the front, and I personally came for something else. I came to hear David Antin do an art work. And it was stopped before it even started, as it happens, he was in the middle of a rather horrific story about a young woman who died. And the story was just—pouf! Everyone interrupted it and it just ended.

This was followed by discussion about the physical space: the pillars blocking views, the difference between the front and the back rows. Eleanor Antin dismissed this more neutral material, switching pronouns in midstream, going from public to personal: "I felt violated, literally. Look, I came up here with him. He's willing to improvise his way, it's OK with him but *I know that you thought you were going to do an art work here. I know you did*."

There was more discussion; senses of endings and compromise were offered; David Antin said he was interested specifically in "the conditions that exist here. . . . I'm sorry, I don't feel violated" [laughter]. Eventually people stood up, continuing to talk, but the tape recorders were shut off.

This is only a fragmentary transcription-description of a two-hour event that would translate to something on the order of sixty to eighty pages of print. I'm pointing to one charged section near the end. But this was not just a collision between Antin's oral-based art and several poets involved with Language writing. Gender was obviously crucial. As was so often the case with the Talks, the alpha males were out in force.

There were also novelistic ironies: the status of the narrative—who knew the story and who did not; Eleanor Antin revealing its conclusion in the course of a complaint that her husband had been interrupted; husband and wife arguing over who was violated when he was interrupted. Her accusation that the regulars at the Talk Series had wrecked her husband's art was in a sense a reverse-reflection of complaints that Antin's talk-pieces had no art. Yet from the perspective of the regulars they were certainly art, and perhaps were, from that 1970s anti-narrative perspective, too artful.[6]

Where and when did the art occur? In the performance, or in the longer-term, diffuse space of the literary field? In this larger perspective Antin's redefinition of poetry would be confirmed by every new talk piece performed, published, referred to, imitated, challenged. The negotiation he hoped for at the Langton Street talk was just one item in a larger, scattered series of negotiations. This essay is, partially, another item in that series.

2)

Championing speech as the site of art, transcription was for Antin a necessary evil; in his insistence on lowercase minimal typography he privileged a more or less poetic look, somewhat cummings-esque, set against the normativities of prose. Jack Kerouac's transcription of conversations between himself and Neal Cassady (Cody) in *Visions of Cody* demonstrates how transcription can create art out of a speech event that was not originally conceived of as art in the slightest. Antin's talk pieces use print to present speech as the essence of poetry; Kerouac's transcriptions find writing in the midst of speech.

Here is a small moment. The subject is a letter from Cody's father. Jack wants to hear it; Cody insists on their reading it. They're talking about what they're reading; we're reading that talk, and behind it, getting glimpses of the somewhat bathetic letter of the father.

JACK. Let's hear his—because his —

CODY. Yeah but I want you to *read* it. Yeah that's what I'm tryin to say . . . it's real crazy. . . . See, here's the way he writes. You can always—he can't write on a straight line, see, and he's very slowly, carefully like a child, see . . .

JACK. (*reading*) Diana Pomeray

CODY. Lookit. . . . D.O. Arlington . . . *a-i-r—*

JACK. What does *D.O.* mean?
CODY. I don't know
JACK. Do?
CODY. Lookit, Airlington, see it's really north but he doesn't know, see
JACK. How to write an *n*?
CODY. I guess *n*—well, he does that but he might have, misunderstood, but here Airlington, *a-i-r-l-i-n-g*. . . . Airlington
JACK. Nappan who's that? That's the —
CODY. That's their name, yeah, care of Cody Pomeray, that's his address for the last fifteen years, it's Green on Market, see —
JACK. Market Street Denver (*because of Frisco*)
CODY. Yeah. . . . this letter. He usually only writes one page, he never puts any date or anything, see? "My dear"—see how he does it? (*laughing*) . . . "son and daurter" . . . . *d-a-u-r-t-e-r* —
JACK. Daurter
CODY. "Received—"
JACK. *R-e-c-d*!!
CODY. Yeah, he does that right. "Your most welcome" without an *e* (*laughs*) "and was . . . your most welcome . . .and was" (*laughs*) dig him, see?, that's formal, see, according to *him*. He's writing a nice, you know, literary— (*both laughing*)[7]

Kerouac transcribes four nights' conversation—ending with a radio blaring a midnight sermon to an empty room. The conversations are very dope-laden affairs, amusing at times but very "you had to have been there" at others. However, the transcription itself, as Allen Ginsberg points out in his introduction to the book, is artful and always interesting. Ginsberg claims significance for the transcripts for various reasons:

1. Vocal familiar friendly teahead life had never been transcribed . . .
2. Despite monotony, the gaps and changes . . . are dramatic.
3. It leads somewhere, like life.
4. It's interesting if you want the characters' reality.
5. It's real.
6. It's art because at that point in the progress of Jack's art he began transcribing *first* thoughts of true mind in American speech. (viii)

"First thought best thought" became Ginsberg's poetic credo; he almost always presented the truth-making spontaneity of the mind in tandem with the breath and the voice as the essential instruments a poet needs to cultivate and obey. And his assertion that transcribing the tapes was transformative for Kerouac's writing seems very plausible: the thoroughness of the transcript required even, relentless attention to, and affection for, every particular in the temporal stream—primary virtues of Kerouac's writing. His spiritual elan arose from that evenness. But it is a hazy assertion of Edenic virtue to say that what Jack and Cody *said* was a "first thought." To me, the transcript reveals the difficulties of speech ("yeah that's what I'm tryin to say"), the varying rhythms of the speakers' attention, and the bemused receptivity of careful transcription and punctuation. Attention is rapidly various: at times each speaker is responding to what the other said, or to what the other said two speeches back, or to the father's letter. The most elemental questions erupt out of nowhere—"How to write an *n*?"—and are answered by the wisdom of banal repetition—"I guess *n*." Misspellings and abbreviations turn into words: air, do. The provinces of speech and writing are interlaced as Jack and Cody critique the insufficient writing of Cody's father in their own insufficient speech—and yet the transcribing mind of Kerouac feels exemplary. "*R-e-c-d*!!" is fascinating as speech and as transcription. It shows the abbreviation Jack marveled at, "R-e-c-d"; while at the same time Kerouac the transcriber uses quotes, hyphens, italics, and a double exclamation mark to capture the pitying enthusiasm of Jack the speaker who spells out, letter by letter, the automatized, bathetic-noble attempt of Cody's father to be "literary." And then the book's hero, Cody, manifests his father's naïveté about writing by simply agreeing: "Yeah he got that right."

The transcription is what makes this interesting. It is not "first thought best thought"; it is novelistic (literary, lettristic), reanimating the past and adding a present perspective. Spelling out the speech accurately makes it public, but the transcription is also intimate. In the sentence "Market Street Denver (*because of Frisco*)" the phrase in italics is added to explain—to who? the world?—why Kerouac specified Denver when Cody would certainly have known it.

There are Market Streets in both cities, but Denver functions for Kerouac as locus of a Golden Age of Cody's adolescence, where cars were stolen and sex was ubiquitous, without consequences, and momentous. Even though Kerouac transcribed these tapes almost immediately—he and Cody discuss a transcribed moment from one night on the following night[8]—by being transcribed the conversations are put in the past. Kerouac uses the alphabet along with all normative resources of punctuation to preserve this past. This complex act, which governs the rest of his writing, is not "first thought best thought," it is rememoration: one-time life disappearing into writing.

3)

The Bay Area Talks were oriented toward the present and the future: the participants were attempting to construct a plural poetics in public. Talking out these writing values was at times clarifying, at times diffuse. The written talk that remains casts a dramatic, novelistic light on these thrashings-out. The variance between these dimensions and the poetics discussed keeps the Talks in an undefined space. Their specific forms differ: some were proto-academic essays; some were performance pieces; some were group discussions of poetics centered around an initial speaker with the audience chiming in, interrupting, suggesting detours, wrestling over control of terms and of the verbal arena—the Antin talk is an extreme version of this.[9] My methods of transcription differ as well. Of the talks I chose to print, most were edited "for clarity," which involved pruning at various levels. I tried to leave in a structure that was at some moments obvious but at others seemed detectable below the verbal surface or among the words: a dramatic negotiation of poetic value, acted out by author-speakers projecting various versions of a poetic space. To reveal this—and of course such a subterranean structure is my idealized projection—I removed words at all levels. "Ums" and "ahs" were deleted. Sentences were sharpened: "And—or it's, incredible affection . . . in a vacuum" became "Incredible affection . . . in a vacuum." Some sentences, digressions, interchanges were removed. And while every talk contained conversation, either throughout or at the end, some of the final conversations were not printed. In those cases, a reader's sense that the words were a speech act must become tenuous: "The New Sentence" (1979), for example, begins with the name of the speaker, Ron Silliman, printed in bold followed by a colon followed by the words of the talk; twenty-seven pages later the final word of the piece, even though it is followed by the date of the talk in italics, seems to conclude an essay, not a talk. And the reference to writing becomes even more pronounced in this case because Silliman wanted that final word, "PERIOD," printed in caps to suggest that the whole performance be thought of as one gigantic sentence.

If Silliman's talk is more written than spoken, Lyn Hejinian's "The Rejection of Closure" (1983) presents a case in which the talk format contains linguistic moments that can only occur as written speech. Where the essay ends with a conclusive assertion—"While failing in the attempt to match the world, we discover structure, distinction, the integrity and separateness of things" (Hejinian, 56)—the talk ends with a more comical example of openness:

> **Hejinian:** . . . And then, also, a whole other day could be spent talking about what the relationship of language is to desire, and how libidinous is speech, and all of that, which I've been thinking about a lot, especially after that panel discussion at Intersection, hearing people talk about how they felt about talking. And it really seemed like there was a connection, which I hadn't thought about before, but the more I think about it the more . . . [tape ends] (Perelman, *Writing/Talks*, 291)

At another point in the conversation, Benjamin Friedlander is quoted as saying, "Think of a Bach score. It's closure made as finite and compact as possible. There's no single reading, there's nothing you can take out of it, it's all there" [289]. In fact, Friedlander remembers saying "Think of a box score" (as in baseball), which is also closure with open possibilities of reading.

A third possibility: Steve Benson, in his "Views of Communist China" (1977), transcribed every identifiable noise during his performance piece. The performance, which needs to be remembered when reading the piece, involved layers of defamiliarization. Benson moved a few pieces of his furniture and some personal effects into my wife's and my loft and acted as if the audience was in his apartment. A second layer of defamiliarization: he framed this tour by some dramatic recitation of material taken from an article on Communist China. At the beginning and end of the piece he was "Master Ch'en" discussing his very oppressed early years, his pride at making his own radio, his fealty to the Party. In the middle he was Steve Benson conducting a tour of "his apartment" and at times of his libido and his writing practice. The familiar household stuff of a writer's apartment—books, mirrors, posters—and how all those objects might provoke real writing sparked intimate discussion. Here is a sample moment:

Benson: [. . .] the Pollock I wound up finally putting on its *side*, and —
Perelman: Why? Just . .
Benson: I've got, well, for a long time I —
Perelman: To knock a chip off its shoulder or something?
[laughter in group]
Benson: I had seen it regular for so long, and it was always just like an object, it was never like an all-over painting or it was never really an experience, it was too small, and it was too much, sort of, *over* there against the wall, kind of . . so . .
Dorothy Phillips:—a piece of paper?
Benson: Yeah.
Phillips: How do you put a piece of paper on its side. I just, can't —
Benson: Oh, I meant, like, well . . it's a horizontal composition, right? [laughter in group] So I put it up as a vertical composition.
Perelman:—sticking up from the wall . . like a shelf, you mean.
Francie Shaw: That's a great idea.
Benson: The Delacroix . . that, I mean, that was always just like a problem. It was like, here's this really frenzied white horse, and I sort of respected it or admired it but more just as an idea.
Barrett Watten: Do you have an overall strategy that's more uh, solid and compelling than any strategy having to do with any particular object?
David Highsmith: That's like asking him what he does for a living.

[laughter in group]
Two voices: What *do* you do for a living? (Perelman, *Hills*, 95–96)

Shklovsky's account of his discovery of defamiliarization—one day after years of ignoring a tobacconist's sign, he sees it set sideways and is shocked into vivid perception by the change—is possibly all-too-familiar to many. Here it is re-invented, by happenstance. And then, by being misunderstood, it becomes truly unfamiliar.

The talks were not always sites of misunderstandings; at times there were straightforward conflicts. In Charles Bernstein's talk, "Characterization" (1983), a rather far-reaching argument developed between him and Barrett Watten. The conflict was over definitions of the Language movement: Watten arguing for a constructivist model deriving from the Russian Formalists and Bernstein for uncontainable textuality.[10]

The piece began with Bernstein presenting a full-page *New York Times* spread with lots of white space: an elegy to an ad executive, "The real giants have always been poets / men who jumped from facts / into the realm of imagination and ideas. / / He elevated advertising to high art / and our jobs to a profession. / / He made a difference."

Bernstein: . . . I've always objected, actually, to the characterization of myself as a poet, much because of the way they have "He was a *poet* . . ." This idea of the poet being singled out. In fact, I've noticed recently that poster for "Jim Morrison, an American poet." . . . It's as if you want to say that Zukofsky is a great American poet, you would say that he is a "great American musician." . . .

Michael Palmer: It's interesting, too, that when Zukofsky is characterized as such, to distinguish that kind of "great American poet" from "the great American poets," let's say like Robert Frost, who people actually know about, it's then followed parenthetically by "a poet's poet." . . . it's at once "poet squared" but also "poet diminished."

Bernstein: You see this in respect to some American playwrights wanting to say that what they're doing is opera. Robert Wilson, in *Letter to Queen Victoria*, which he called an opera,—it was, to me, one of the best pieces of theater I've ever seen. But it had to be called an opera because it was so good.

Ron Silliman: There was a review in last Sunday's paper: "A 3-D movie good enough to be 2-D." [laughter]

Barrett Watten: You better look out or you might start doing a performance piece, Charles. [laughter] (*Writing/Talks*, 8–10)

Recall that Antin, too, disclaimed the profession of poet;[11] and that, in "Communist China," Watten asking Benson about an "overall strategy" was instantly perceived as asking about his profession, drawing a burst of nervous laughter. Although here in Bernstein's talk the initial jokes were genial, a similar uneasiness around the job description of "poet" is evident. No one wanted ad executives to claim high art status while also boasting of their professionalism; but no one could quite imagine what it would be like to claim the title of poet without the irony needed to beat the executives back from poetry's imagined social spaces.

Later in the talk, arguments over definitions of the poet's activity become more heated. I had asked Bernstein to do a close reading of a few lines of his poem "Standing Target." In the course of his response he cited some lines from another poem, "Part Quake" (*Islets/Irritations*): "They ridicule revolutionary theory / and sneer that having a correct / position is sectarian." If one has read much of Bernstein's work, it is difficult to read these lines as expressing his own position in any unironized way. He immediately qualified the unambiguous denotation, mentioning the dangers of Stalinism on the one hand, and the problem of having no position vis-à-vis material-historical situations on the other. Criticizing Deleuze and Guittari's romanticization of deterritorialized flows, he went on:

Bernstein: And that's why I disagree with the way language is characterized within French structuralist thought from Saussure to Derrida, in which language is thought to be divided in a polarity between the signifier and the signified, as two different things, and that the relation between the sound and the mental image is arbitrary. . . .

Watten: But that's two different meanings at two different times. When Saussure wanted to talk about the arbitrariness of the sign what he meant was that it was not mystic. He was trying to get rid of undue concern with etymology in 19th-century linguistics, and that's exactly what that means, and it doesn't mean *anything else*. I wish somebody would put it on a billboard someplace. . . .

Bernstein: Criticism insofar as it's provisional sets up terms. And those things do have value within their context, but when they get reified . . . then you have this monster. . . . Saussure has to attack etymology by proposing his things, just as I could be forced into attacking those things because of the monster that gets created from that.

It seems to me that criticism, rather than trying to establish fixed things . . . in its best exists at a provisional level, and that provisional quality doesn't need to be masked. But the wrinkle in it is that that masking has social power. . . .

Watten: Okay, Charles, I really think you should purge your vocabulary of phrases like "structural linguistics from Saussure to Derrida."

Bernstein: I should purge my . . . ?

Watten: You shouldn't allow yourself to say that. And that would be the answer to the whole thing. I mean, if you know better . . .

Kit Robinson: Why can't he say that? [17–19]

Robinson's question can be extended, and must be extended, in any poetics that will stand the test of time: no configuration of language can be ruled out. Watten's point, I take it, is that criticism is meaningless if not grounded by specific facts (i.e., Saussure's formulation was addressing a specific context, and this should be a given if we discuss Saussure). Yet, as Bernstein answers, criticism's own facts must remain provisional. Critical terms need play, in the physical, emotional, and semantic senses of the word, to remain useful across contexts. Watten's verb, "purge," seems to take Bernstein's lines, "They ridicule revolutionary theory / and sneer that having a correct / position is sectarian," unironically; I hear Watten claiming that editing, which could be called "vocabulary purging," was always necessary. But of course "purge" has been used in harsher contexts and can be taken as a marker of violence. And then again, it can be taken as a witty rejoinder: since you've brought up the Russian context, I'll express my desire for correct speech by urging you to "purge" your vocabulary of inexact generalizations.

"We threw down the suit and wore the bag." Signified and signifier; vehicle and tenor; shell and kernal. But the moral I am aiming at here is not binary; talk and writing are conjoined. The moment where Watten, Bernstein, and Robinson conversed is now being brought to our attention via the activity of my transcription and this meditation. Perhaps the original—low-quality tape-recordings now digitized at Penn Sound—will be accessed and reheard. But whatever written mediations and remediations occur, they will never uncover any original speech-sound, which was already mediated at the moment of utterance by the various listeners in attendance and their various sets of ears.

The talks lie between two long-lasting critical soundbites: Rorty's praise of liberal "conversation" (or, if you prefer, Graff's "teach the conflicts") on the one hand; and, on the other, the slogan of radical textuality and dethroned subject, Foucault's "What matter who's speaking?" In their opposite ways, both moments even out the field of utterance, either into a transpersonal grid, or an extended town meeting. The talks can be read as offering a useful supplement or roadblock to both of these too-regular solutions. They acted out in public space a dialogic dimension of poetry that usually remains private, in letters, comments after readings, lifted eyebrows, pointed silences. In supplementing the too-often monologic voice of poetry, the talks opened a precarious space between dominant voices and democracy, auratic performance and group participation.

But while such a space remains useful, this particular one was far from utopic: men talked much more easily than women, and different degrees of educational capital made for a painfully uneven floor. A number of people who attended the talks spoke (afterward, off the record) of being "terrified" to speak.

18
Zukofsky at 100

1. The session title, "Zukofsky at 100," suggests a crucially ambiguous vantage.[1]

2. Louis Zukofsky, person, would have been 100 this year.

3. But Zukofsky, the body of work—as in, "Have you read Zukofsky?"—is of indeterminate age.

4. Is a body of work born when the first attested or accepted work appears? If so, then we should start counting with the earliest work, "I Sent Thee Late," the 1922 poem that appears in "*A*"-18, and we should be celebrating "Zukofsky at 82."

5. Or does a body of work become a body only when the work stops appearing? In that case, though it feels harshly ironic, we should make the birth year of "Zukofsky the body of work" coincide with the year that "Zukofsky the person" died.

6. So if we count from the date of the last work, *80 Flowers*, and the publication of the completed "*A*," then it should be "Zukofsky at 26."

7. While 26 is poetically significant in the Anglo-American alphabet, 100 is the most august, barely reachable of the human-sized numbers.

8. For modernists seeking mastery, 100 beckoned.

9. In "An Instant Answer or A Hundred Prominent Men," Stein repeats "and one" 100 times (*GS I*, 484).

9a. Stein can always be being sarcastic: it isn't "A Hundred Prominent Women," after all.

10. For much of the time Pound was writing them, 100 was the magic number for *The Cantos*, given that it was the number of cantos in Dante's *Comedia*.

11. In our day, there's Bruce Andrews's *I Don't Have Any Paper So Shut Up (or, Social Romanticism)* and *Lip Service*, each with 100 sections.

12. Zukofsky was drawn to 100 as well: both "*A*"-22 and 23 contain 1,000 lines.

13. (1,000 is the epic version of 100.)

14. There's also the progression of his last planned projects: at the beginning of his eighth decade he begins *80 Flowers*, with *Gamut: 90 Trees* planned for the decade after that. Isn't 100 the teleological goal there?

15. (At this point, it's hard to resist Ron Silliman's prediction for the next project: *101 Dalmatians*.)

16. Why am I so drawn to that joke?

17. Is it because Zukofsky now stands for avant-garde mastery and completion, yet that oxymoron is particularly distorting when applied to him?

18. In resisting the equation Zukofsky = 100, I am also resisting the equation Zukofsky = 1.

19. And the equation Zukofsky = music.

20. This in the face of the fact that it is hard to miss the ubiquitous instructions to construe his work as a unified, musical totality.

21. I.e., "Each writer writes one long work whose beat he cannot be entirely aware of" (*A*, 214).[2]

22. I.e., the last words of "*A*"-24, the tiny coda written by Louis to Celia Zukofsky's *LZ Masque*: "the gift / she hears / the work / in its recurrence" (*A*, 806).

23. I.e., this from the Preface to "*A*"-19: "The form of the poem is organic—that is, involved in history and a life that has found by contrast to history something like perfection in the music of J. S. Bach" (*A*, 1–12, "Preface").

24. Celia's basic gesture in "*A*"-24—composing Louis's poetry, drama, fiction, and criticism into cadenced musical voices—insists on this analogy and grants Louis's words, originally written in various genres and various historical circumstances, the retrospective perfection of music.

25. That's "music" in the Paterian, Poundian sense: poetic "music."

26. My scare quotes around *music* make it plain that I am an apostate from this grand synaesthesic synthesis.

27. I am acting as the tritone, the augmented fourth, C/F#, *diabolus in mu-*

sica as the medievals had it, and will try to make audible my perception of the value of the dissonance I hear in Zukofsky.

27a. To paraphrase what he writes in "*A*"-6, perhaps "it has something to do with" his being Jewish (*A, 26*).

28. While this dissonance does not accord at all with the emphatic simplicity of his pronouncements on poetics, nevertheless it continues—in my ear, at least—to resound in the deadpan slippages, extravagant layerings, and uncoded leaps of much of his writing practice.

29. Zukofsky's critical practice is a set of protocols intended to suppress such extravagance.

29a. If you took *A Test of Poetry* as a bible of poetics, poetry like Zukofsky's would be the last thing you'd write.

30. In *A Test*, the Milton of *Samson Agonistes* gets a low mark for his "inability to leave words alone"; he is "infatuated with sound, thunder, and fury, and is 'building' a verse paragraph" (72); LZ puts scare quotes around "building," implying that yielding to verbal infatuation results in mere imaginary work on an imaginary building. (Think air guitar as opposed to the *St. Matthew Passion.*)

31. But as any reader of Zukofsky knows, he himself is infatuated with sound and with building verbal contraptions that had never been imagined before:

32. O dear cool you couldn't a virile—you couldn't a parent he—
salvé! take weight bone ah Jupiter act it open,
Janus, door! when Balbo thickened—serviced his benignant
ol' him—home say days hipped seized say next tenure heat—
how come fare runt hearsways 'n how the door serve very malignantly
posthumously poor wrecked torn father's young married son—eh.
(*Complete Short Poetry*, 299)

33. Of course, such un*Test*able extravagance does not resound everywhere in Zukofsky's body of work; a considerable portion is as verbally neat as *A Test* suggests is proper:

34. The miracle of his first job
On the lower East Side:
Six years night watchman
In a men's shop
Where by day he pressed pants
Every crease a blade
The irons weighed

At least twenty pounds
But moved both of them
Six days a week

From six in the morning
To nine, sometimes eleven at night
Or midnight;
Except Fridays
When he left, enough time before sunset
Margolis begrudged.
His own business
My father told Margolis
Is to keep the Sabbath.
(*A*, 152)

35. These passages from "*A*"-12 and *Catullus* were chosen at random.

36. Nevertheless it strikes me as an instructive coincidence that both involve fathers and that their respective styles match the degree of seriousness with which paternity is addressed.

37. The second passage is pious, taut with restraint.

38. The passage from *Catullus* is rife with vaguely anti-paternal, comic-phallic noises: "O dear cool you couldn't a virile," "couldn't a parent," "weight bone ah Jupiter," "ol' him," "posthumously poor wrecked torn father's young married son—eh."

39. But to simply split Zukofsky along a paternal axis of obedience and rebellion isn't sufficient.

40. Zukofsky's impiety is sly, a Talmudic impishness more profound than disobedience, an ecstasy of syntactic teleporting to no world that anyone lives in yet.

41. However, Zukofsky did in fact live in the historical world, inextricably, as one might say.

42. In trying to establish a place for his writing in that world he continually did two things:

43. in his critical work he would insist vigorously on an extreme decorum of style;

44. while in his poetry he would display his powers, of construction and of construal,

45. displays that were neither decorous nor indecorous: those categories don't apply.

46. *A Test* is a line on the CV Zukofsky submitted for some imagined position of permanent authority. For an unrecognized poet aspiring to be a major modernist there was a defined set of tasks, a sequence of labors that would authenticate the laborer as a true Hercules.

47. What did proto-Hercules have to do to become Poet Hercules?

48. In Milton's time the schedule of tasks for a major-poet-in-training was Virgilian:

49. first, eclogues,

50. then georgics,

51. and finally an epic.

52. In the 1930s when Zukofsky was marshaling his own forces Pound was his model and the requirements had changed. Now it was:

53. notable editorial intervention,

54. a collection of short poems,

55. an epic,

56. and a codified statement of poetics.

57. Pound remained the model of the poet for Zukofsky.

58. *Prepositions* was on Zukofsky's desk when he died, open at his essay on Pound.

59. When *Catullus* was published, Zukofsky wrote Pound, asking what he thought: "I understand Mary de R[achewiltz] has been receiving my Catullus translations in *Origin*—sometimes wonder what '/you/' might think of 'em if you <can> read 'em> <Don't matter what anyone else thinks—even the praise. Still obstinate you see" (*Pound/Zukofsky*, 218).

60. Thus Zukofsky's 1, his life, adds up to more than 1.

61. Zukofsky carries Pound on his back, like Aeneas carrying Anchises out of burning Troy.

62. Except there's no Roman Empire as a fated destination.

63. Zukofsky also carries Bach: "something like perfection in the music of J. S. Bach."

64. And not to forget Williams.

65. "Song of Degrees," section 5, begins, "William / Carlos / Williams / alive!" and ends with Billy the Kid

66. . . . torn,
shot
so quickly
it sounds
water
purls
a
high
voice
as with
a lien
on
the sky
that becomes
low now
frankly
water—
called also—
softly—
a kill

67. The lines just before this are

68. the
same word
that
may have,
to touch
two faces—
the heart
sees into—
of one
sound:
(*Collected Short Prose*, 148–51)

69. It's not just that Zukofsky's 1 always sounds with 2 faces, though it does—a not un-Yiddish sound, perhaps.

70. It's that Zukofsky's celebration of the poetically perfected life—"William / Carlos / Williams / alive!"—also contains the countervailing gesture: "a kill."

71. A little symbolic mathematics: if the authorized perfected lifeworks—Catullus, Bach, Pound, Williams—are 100 and the individual aspiring life—Louis Zukofsky—is 1, then the result should be that the poetry produced by that one life (Louis Zukofsky) will also be perfected, since 100 divided by or multiplied by 1 = 100.

72. But clearly that's not the case.

73. *Gai Valeri Veronensis Catulli* when divided or multiplied into English by Louis (and Celia) Zukofsky does not equal the purportedly perfect original.

74. Purportedly perfected forms, when divided or multiplied by Zukofsky, produce irrational numbers.

75. As he writes in *A Test*: "*The Sonnet Form* is *not* a matter of 14 lines, set rhyme scheme, 10 syllables to a line, alternating ascending accents, as the rhetoric books have it. *Sonnet* . . . implies the form of the short tune, to which certain Italian poets—Dante, Cavalcanti, and others—wrote words; . . . Dissociated from music, the *sonnet* became merely the poor versification of amateurs, without emotion or sense of the relation of the parts of a composition to the whole" (*T*, 67).

76. This statement comes from a poet who had, a few years earlier, written this:

77. Clavicembalo—Nine less two, Seven
Were the diggers, seven sang, danced, the paces
Seven, Seven Saviours went to heaven—
Their tongues, hands, feet, eyes, ears and hearts, each face as

Of a Sea looking Outward (Rose the Glass
Broken), Each a reflection of the other.
Just for the fun of it. And 't came to pass
(*Open, O fierce flaming pit!*)
three said: Bother,

Brother, we want a meal, different techniques."
Two ways, my two voices. . . Offal and what
The imagination. . . And the seven came
To horses seven (of wood—who will?—kissed their stomachs)

Bent knees as these rose around them—trot—trot—
Spoke: words, words, we are words, horses, manes, words.
(*A*, 42)

78. This sonnet would not fit happily to any Dantescan or Cavalcantian "short tune."

79. A crucial component of its deviation from "musicality" is its use of the conventional sonnet form.

80. Its relation to that form is not parodic, but para-poetic. The sonnet armature is a perpetual instigation for poetic display.

81. This seventh sonnet that concludes "*A*"-7 insists on the traditional rhyme scheme for the first two quatrains—Seven, paces, heaven, face as; Glass, other, pass, Bother (with the truer rhyme *Brother* enjambed to begin the next line)—but then, at "different techniques," stops rhyming.

82. Zukofsky loads onto the sonnet armature a remarkably diverse concatenation of verbal matter, social tone, and allusion to things inside and outside of "*A*."

83. What are some of the techniques employed?

84. The sonnet starts with the last word of a sentence, "Clavicembalo."

84a. It is an extremely odd sentence, by the way. It's not easy to tell where it begins, but my opinion is that it starts four lines back: "A sign creaked—LAUNDRY TO-LET— (creaked—wind—) —SUN— / (Nights?) the sun's, bro', no months' rent in arrear— / Bum pump a-dum, no one's cut out, pump a- / Ricky, bro', Shimaunu-Sān, yours is the / Clavicembalo" (*A*, 41).

85. Zukofsky mixes tonal registers: the language of mathematics ("Nine less two") with the singsong of a fairy tale ("Seven were the diggers . . . the paces Seven, Seven Saviours went to heaven").

85a. False messiahs taking the next plane out? "Saviour" with a *u* can only = Christ; but here there are seven.

86. He uses typography (clearly not a "musical" device!): capitalization to mythify and personify in a comic manner: "a Sea looking Outward (Rose the Glass / Broken)." By the way, in those last two words, the glass doesn't break until the line breaks. That's not a line break that's easy to conceive within the universe of Poundian/Zukofskyan "music." There's the dramatic use of white space and italics, parentheses too, for the reference to "*A*"-1, "(*Open, O fierce flaming pit!*)."

87. "Pit" there encompasses the Christian Hell of the *St. Matthew Passion*, a Hell Zukofsky doesn't believe in, sung to music he does believe in; the pit where the orchestra is playing, and the pit that the miners are locked out of.

88. There's the use of extra-poetic speech: "Bother, / Brother, we want a meal, different techniques." The voices of the unemployed are clear here, but Zukofsky folds his own poetic and social concerns into the quoted speech. It's hardly likely that a person who said, "Brother, we want a meal," would begin with "Bother, brother." Nor is it likely that the person asking for a meal would also ask for "different techniques." But Zukofsky at this time believed, along with Pound and many others, that to supply different writing techniques was at least as valuable as supplying physical necessities.

89. There's the use of phrase fragments to suggest fleeting, half-formed thoughts of great intensity: "(of wood—who will—kissed their stomachs)."

90. That last phrase especially is striking. "Kissed" sounds out a completed action, but it doesn't sound out the agent or the object. Kissing a stomach can be very innocent fun (making babies chortle), but it's hardly likely that, at the end of "*A*"-7, the poet was bringing in childcare duties. Outside of child-care, kissing a stomach is a charged erotic act. So who kissed which stomachs here? Did Zukofsky kiss, at least in the written world of these three words, the stomachs of the poetically invoked horses, or of the barely employed diggers, or of the wooden sawhorses?

91. Whichever it is, and it might be all three, there is great power of suggestion in the phrase, which is emphatically *not* clear or exact in the way that *A Test* demands.

92. My polemic here is not against Zukofsky's use of musical structures as analogies to instigate his writing. It is against the ahistorical and really terribly vague use of music as a transcendent praise term in poetics—such an impoverished sense of music. The actual practice of music, after all, has as tumultuous a history as poetry. Schoenberg had been writing twelve-tone music for more than a decade before Pound wrote *ABC*; the riots over Stravinsky's harsh polyrhythms were old news; Antheil's airplane engines had already roared.

93. Think of how we feel when "poetry" is used in such tepid, generalizing ways: the poetry of Robert Ryman's white canvases, the poetry of Joe DiMaggio's swing, the poetry of spring.

94. But my fulminations feel a bit quixotic when common sense reminds me that music is widely used in poetics to point to a quality that is exciting and beautiful—"those wonderful sounds good poetry makes."

95. Perhaps my final negotiating stance should be this: not to proscribe music or the use of 1 or of 100 but rather to urge that the lower limit of Zukofsky's famous integral be kept in mind.

96. If a poetic integral is a process that actually integrates, then the poetics that Zukofsky affirms will indeed touch on music while also being speech. It will exist between 1, the life, and 100, the completed work. Throughout that range, simultaneously.

97. Why is it good to focus only on the upper or for that matter only on the lower limit?

98. Instead, I propose a toast to the uncompletable gamut.

99. Bottoms up!

To Zukofsky at 100.

19
On "The Jewish Question"

Given the intractableness of the question of a connection between radical poetics and secular Jewish culture, it is fitting that my three approaches are incommensurate.[1] The first, based on Susan Handelman's scholarship, neatly divides Jews and Christians; the second, my own musings, agonizes about the possibility of any dividing line; the third, a sendup of homeopathic notions, may represent my own beliefs most accurately.

1. Susan Handelman posits a far-reaching distinction in *The Slayers of Moses*, drawing a contrast between the Rabbinic and the ancient Greek perspectives on language. For the Rabbis, word and thing were indistinguishable, while for the Greeks they were separate. The Hebrew *davar*, Handelman writes, means both word and thing, and for the Rabbis God was as much the producer of writing as maker of the world, and the Torah was as real as, if not more real than, the world. (Sometimes, quasi-heretically, God was more the product of the Torah than its author.) For the Greeks, in contrast, language was descriptive, belonging to the predicate, its function being to distinguish one substantive from another. Handelman sees this contrast between Jewish and Greek conceptions continuing into the Christian era, with the Church Fathers devaluing language in favor of "the Word." For thinkers such as Augustine and Origen, language was ultimately a barrier to the presence of Christ, the one and only Word. The advent of Christ's embodiment provided access to the spirit, superseding the letter. The desire to "escape from textuality," Handelman writes, "permeates Christian thought" (Handelman, 115).

Handelman uses this large distinction to frame an account of what she calls "modern literary theory," discussing Freud, Lacan, Derrida, and Bloom. I want to borrow her model and apply it to poetry, where it will be merely an analogy to divide poets into "Jews" and "Christians." Nevertheless, it will turn out to make sense in some surprising ways.

Coleridge is obviously Christian. In his famous distinction between imagination and fancy, the validated half, imagination, would be Christian ("a representation in the finite mind of the eternal act of creation in the infinite I AM [of God]"), as opposed to the denigrated part of poetic composition, fancy, which only plays with "counters" that are "fixed and dead" (Coleridge, 304–5), mere language—or, as one might say, Talmudic wordplay. Whitman would be Christian ("Who touches this book touches a man" [Whitman, 611])[2]; Pound would be Christian (pagan-Christian) with his insistence on the ideogrammic method as essential in capturing "thing-ness" in writing (and avoiding Talmudic "slither"—entanglement in verbiage). Zukofsky, happily living in and via letters ("z-sited paths are but us" [*A*, 563]), would be Jewish; Stein would be Jewish.

Would Ginsberg, Whitmanian that he is, be Jewish? We'd have to say no, since the body and the embodied voice are so clearly the origin, locus, and telos of his work. Even what at first look like his "language-centered" moments are directed, ultimately, past language. True, the following excerpt from the end of the first part of "Howl" starts with a focus on juxtaposition, verbal collage, and disjunction, and it could, in isolation, seem a glimpse of the new sentence: "who dreamt and made incarnate gaps in Time & Space through images juxtaposed." But as the long-breath sentence continues, something quite different happens:

> who dreamt and made incarnate gaps in Time & Space through images juxtaposed, and trapped the archangel of the soul between 2 visual images and joined the elemental verbs and set the noun and dash of consciousness together jumping with sensation of Pater Omnipotens Aeterna Deus
> [. . .]
> who rose reincarnate in the ghostly clothes of jazz [. . .] and blew the suffering of America's naked mind for love into an eli eli lamma lamma sabachthani saxophone cry [. . .]
> with the absolute heart of the poem of life butchered out of their own bodies good to eat a thousand years.
> (Ginsberg, *Collected Poems*, 130–31)

This is suffused with Christian vocabulary: "incarnate," "archangel," "Pater Omnipotens Aeterna Deus," "who rose reincarnate," and it quotes Christ's last words on the cross ("eli eli lamma lamma sabachthani"). And while the last line seems most directly a reference to Aztec sacrifice, isn't a heart that's good to eat for a millennium awfully close to the Eucharist?

It's really not fair to allow this concentration of Christologic vocabulary to nudge "Howl" into alignment with something like *Jesus Christ Superstar*. Nevertheless, it is a bit weird how explicitly Christian this seems, since Alicia Ostriker's reading of Ginsberg as Jeremiah always seemed suggestive and since Ginsberg the person always seemed (and sounded) vaguely Rabbinic (Ostriker, 28–31).

"Wichita Vortex Sutra" follows a similar pattern of moving from word to body. At first it seems linguistically focused, but the more emphatic frame is the body. It begins with an emphatic repeated insistence on language ("The War is language"): the bad magic of congressional language and the good magic Ginsberg hopes to create; and the rhetorical and political climax of the poem is "I make mantra of American language . . . I here declare the end of War!" (*Collected Poems*, 407). However, that mantra is ultimately *not* primarily language. Ginsberg uses his voice as an embodied sound to act on the language and change it, which will then change the world, stop the Vietnam War, pacify and enlighten the bodies of those who listen. The action is meant to reach from the poet's body to the bodies of those receiving the poem (listeners more than readers); the poem is a conduit connecting them:

> Not the empty sky that hides
>   the feeling from our faces
>   nor our skirts and trousers that conceal
>   the bodylove emanating in a glow of beloved skin,
>   white smooth abdomen down to the hair
>   between our legs,
>   It's not a God that bore us that forbid
>   our Being, like a sunny rose
>   all red with naked joy
>
> (405)

2. "You don't have to be Jewish to love Levi's" was the slogan in a series of NYC subway ads for rye bread a few decades back. There was a series of posters, each displaying a deliberately varied demographic of non-Jewish consumer: the African-American cop, the Puerto Rican broadcaster, the Chinese student, the WASP, etc., each one grinning while he or she held a corned beef on rye with a neat bite missing. Always the same bite, it seemed. Did it suggest circumcision and the unalterable singularity of Judaism? Or, on the contrary, was the bite evidence that the African-American cop, the Puerto Rican broadcaster, the Chinese student, the WASP, etc., had happily incorporated the Jewish bite as part of a large, mutual inter-assimilation? (Stomach as melting pot.)

Is there a Jewish radical poetic practice? In one sense, of course there is: "Jewish" can simply designate the fact that writers such as Louis Zukofsky, Gertrude Stein, Laura Riding, and Charles Reznikoff were Jews. It's a bit like choosing a fantasy sports team, or an astrological poets team: I'm on the Sagittarius team with Horace, Milton, Dickinson, Tardos. But if anything is wanted beyond this then the question quickly gets more vexing. Is there something Jewish about Zukofsky's, Stein's, Riding's, and Reznikoff's writing? If so, can the same or a similar something be found in the work of writers who were not born Jews? If not, is it just a matter of keeping score, tallying up how many Jews there are in our pantheons? Do fractions count? By parentage, Mina Loy was half Jewish, even William Carlos Williams was one-eighth (or was it one-sixteenth?).

If one accepts transhistorical analogy then there are many ways in which Rabbinical writing anticipates modernism and contemporary innovative writing. The rabbis were concerned with textuality, wordplay, and letterplay, and there is a thick tradition of semantic pole-vaulting over obstacles created by the absolute specificity of the words of the Torah. (And whenever verbal flexibility wasn't enough to do the trick, there was always the parallel oral teaching to turn to.) Such verbal exploration across the boundaries of what was previously accepted makes it possible to read the rabbis, by analogy, as innovative poets *avant la lettre.*

Such analogizing is a kind of assimilation, but moving chronologically backwards. Rather than second-generation Jews turning away from Jewish ancestry to become modern Americans, it's contemporary innovative poets discovering that their Jewish ancestors were poetic innovators. Another, more contentious example of genealogical back-formation occurs in the epigraph to *A Big Jewish Book*, where Jerome Rothenberg's translation makes the Talmud explicitly Poundian, not only using his famous slogan but also his emphatic capitalization:

> Rabbi Elieser said
> "prayer 'fixed'?
> "his supplication bears no fruit
> . . . .
> the question then came up: what
> is FIXED?
> Rabba & Rabbi Yosef answered
> "whatever blocks the will
> to MAKE IT NEW
>   (Rothenberg xv)

This pledges allegiance to a tradition, declaring that Pound *is* one's ancestor while erasing, forgiving, reframing, putting into perspective, bracketing his vigilant and vigorous anti-Semitism. A more direct encounter between the postwar innovative tradition and Pound would be Allen Ginsberg's forgiving embrace of the old modernist during their meeting in Venice.

Where Rothenberg's translation might simply be read as homage to Pound's poetics rather than to the person, Ginsberg's embrace was directed to Pound himself. It seems a similar gesture to his "mantra" moment in "Wichita Vortex Sutra": by means of the enlightened clarity of embodied action, Ginsberg will effect change. "I here declare the end of the War" ≈ I here declare the end of anti-Semitism (of Pound's, at any rate). Whatever change may or may not have been effected in Pound himself, the embrace is something of an emblematic moment in poetic history. Along with a range of other (literary) actions by Kenner, Olson, Zukofsky, among others, it insisted on placing Pound firmly in the center of the innovative tradition. But what, if anything, did it do with respect to "the Jewish question"? Did it do much to change the fact that, in poetry at least, anti-Semitism was a major characteristic of modernism?

It was not the most *modern* part of modernism, since it simply reprised the conservative-hysteric tradition, notably articulated by Richard Wagner, that saw Jewish art as irredeemably ersatz: Jews can't write real music, they can only ape techniques, and the more dexterous the imitation the more insidious for the unwary listener or reader. Pound writes: "Until [T. S. Eliot] succeeds in detaching the Jewish from the European elements of his peculiar variety of Christianity he will never find the right formula. Not a jot or tittle of the hebraic alphabet can pass into the text without danger of contaminating it" (*SP*, 320). That's Pound near his worst, but the aesthetic vehemence is of a piece with his saner railings; the dynamics are the same, though the referents differ. On a less specifically anti-Semitic note, Pound often defined his art, and to a lesser extent Eliot and Wyndham Lewis defined theirs, against unbounded exfoliation of verbalism. Pound writes in *Guide to Kulchur*, "When a code ceases to be regarded as an approximate expression of principles . . . and is exalted to the rank of something holy in itself, perversion ineluctably sets in. . . . Code-worship appertains properly to tribes arrested at nomad level" (*GK*, 164). And while it may seem that such identification of Jewishness with the ersatz is old hat, unfortunately, it flares up in such moments as Harold Bloom's essay that refuses the possibility of a "major" Jewish poet.[3]

Anti-Semitism does not permeate the multiform facts of modernism, of course. But it is there and, insofar as it is, doesn't it insist that Jewish writing, if it is *Jewish*, cannot be innovative, and that MAKE IT NEW is restricted to new testaments?

For decades, Pound had been hypervigilant about noticing who or what felt Jewish. Was Ginsberg's embrace of him enough to render that vigilance beside the point? What is involved in rendering anti-Semitism beside the point? Perhaps it is just personal: Ginsberg talking Pound into coming off it and accepting Jews. Or did Ginsberg, symbolically at any rate, cease being Jewish after the embrace? He forgave Pound as a Buddhist: "Anti-Semitism was just your hang-up." Isn't that phrase spoken from a perspective that is itself no longer hung up on Jewish identity? Does Ginsberg become trans-Jewish at this point?

Along with Zukofsky, Charles Olson, Robert Duncan, and Robert Creeley, Ginsberg is one of the *filii Poundiani*. And of course Ginsberg remains Jewish. Witness "Kaddish."

The insistent singularity of Jewishness is hard to avoid. After all, Judaism is not ecumenical.

Biographically, Stein *is* Jewish and Loy (née Lowy) *is* half Jewish. But in terms of poetics, what can be meant by the notion that Stein's and Loy's writing *is* Jewish? (Or, in Loy's case, half Jewish?)

If we read in terms of subject matter, things get clearer: Reznikoff's subject matter is often insistently Jewish; Loy's "Anglo-Mongrels and the Rose" explores the rift between Anglo and Jewish identities; "Poem beginning 'The'" brilliantly mocks Western philosophic and poetic traditions, with Zukofsky, who had just attended Columbia University via a narrow quota system, showing how a Jew could ace the modernism exam set by *The Waste Land*.

But that's Jewish subject matter or subject position more than Jewish writing. How is Stein's writing Jewish? Yes, there's the pun on Yiddish, "Yet Dish," and, I think, a few similar instances, but they are rare (and aren't there, equally rare, instances of anti-Semitism?). But what in Stein's poetics, style, mechanics, rhythm, could be identified as Jewish? If we simply leave it that Stein's writing is Jewish because of its ever-present textual play, then doesn't Joyce, starting from the "scrupulous meanness" of *Dubliners*, transform himself into one of the most Jewish writers of the twentieth century?

3. Another way of coming at Jewishness in innovative writing, what I'll call homeopathic Jewishness, will restore the commonsense fact that Ginsberg is a Jew, though in a non-commonsense way.

To present it requires a bit of autobiography. Back in hippie days, alongside such matters as macrobiotics, astrology, and the collective unconscious, I had a brush with homeopathy. There, besides the well-known notion of curing like with like (e.g., pills against poison ivy would contain minute bits of poison ivy), I learned or at least now remember learning that the more you diluted a homeopathic medicine the stronger it got. (It had something to do with the "molecular memory" of the water.) So, for low strength, dissolve a drop of homeopathic medicine in a pint of water. To make the medicine stronger, dissolve the same drop in a quart. Full strength would be one drop per gallon.

It was at a conference on Jewish-American writing at the University of Pennsylvania three decades later—after hearing much talk of hybridity and borders crossed, Yiddish as a porous anti-essentialist tongue incorporating other languages easily, vocabularies adopted and instantly changed, new boundaries embroidered with old and new shapes—my long-forgotten homeopathic lore suddenly resurfaced as an oddly amusing response to the question of being a Jewish-American writer. It was a punch line to some poetic, philosophic, or religious joke I haven't finished hearing yet.

Crudely, the homeopathic model says that the more diluted the Jewishness, the more Jewish the writer.

It can be objected that the homeopathic method is intensely circular, since the original homeopathic "drop" that it starts with is the biographical fact of a given writer's Jewishness.

Still, when the question is asked—"how Jewish is the writing?" —homeopathic poetics is equipped to provide an answer. It doesn't look for characteristically Jewish language or Jewish content—quite the reverse. It measures the amount of non-Jewish "water." The less overt Jewishness there is in the writing—the more diluted it is—the more Jewish the writing.

Take Reznikoff, where the central framework is often clearly Jewish and where there is a great deal of explicitly Jewish vocabulary and subject matter: *Jerusalem the Golden*, the shtetl narratives, not to mention the plain old religious stuff. For me, this is the lesser part of Reznikoff's oeuvre:

> I am Joseph, your brother, whom you sold into Egypt.
> And now be not grieved, nor angry with yourselves,
> for I was sent before you to save us all alive;
> you meant evil against me, but it was meant for good.
> (Reznikoff, *Poems 1918–1975*, 81)

Still, however my taste feels about it, this is nothing if not Jewish. Therefore, when read through a homeopathic lens, this flood of undiluted Jewish subject matter makes Reznikoff's Homeopathic Jewish Quotient (HJQ) very low. If everything is Jewish, then the ratio of Jewish words to all words would be 1:1, yielding the HJQ of 1. This, as we will see, will be lower than Zukofsky's HJQ, which in turn will be lower than Ginsberg's.

Here, lest my hippie heritage be seen as completely overcoming my tepidly Jewish upbringing, is the quasi-homeopathic parable that Gershom Scholem tells:

> When the Baal Shem had a difficult task before him, he would go to a certain place in the woods, light a fire and meditate in prayer—and what he had set out to perform was done. When a generation later the "Maggid" of Meseritz was faced with the same task he would go to the same place in the woods and say: We can no longer light the fire, but we can still speak the prayers—and what he wanted done became reality. Again a genera-

> tion later Rabbi Moshe Leib of Sassov had to perform this task. And he too went into the woods and said: We can no longer light a fire, nor do we know the secret meditations belonging to the prayer, but we do know the place in the woods to which it all belongs—and that must be sufficient; and sufficient it was. But when another generation had passed and Rabbi Israel of Rishin was called upon to perform the task, he sat down on his golden chair in his castle and said: We cannot light the fire, we cannot speak the prayers, we do not know the place, but we can tell the story of how it was done. And, the story-teller adds, the story which he told had the same effect as the actions of the other three. (Scholem, 350)

Back to "Ginsberg has a higher HJQ than Zukofsky." Really, isn't it simpler to reframe their difference-amid-genealogical-similarity as a difference in historical generation, as both poetic and chronological? Zukofsky grew up speaking Yiddish; two decades later, Ginsberg grew up speaking English, with his father writing rhymed and metered poems and sending them to the *New Yorker*.

Let's do a practice problem on both poets. Consider "*A*"-1. What's its HJQ? It's hard to say: "*A*"-1 is a composition with many agendas. One thing it intends is to enact a memory of a true act of art worship by the embodied author. "Desire longing for perfection" (*A*, 2) presents Zukofsky as the purest auditor of Bach's *St. Matthew Passion* in Carnegie Hall; unlike his contemporaries, the 1928 concert subscribers whose ears are so stuffed with money they can't hear a note, Zukofsky can imagine the original 1729 performance of the piece—in fact, the vivid directness with which he presents it furnishes an index to what he considers good art. In 1729 the music arose from an organic community with Kapellmeister-genius Bach set amid his fellows, the people of Leipzig, who are both audience and performers. We see Bach rushing to church to conduct the music, observed breathlessly by the "Matronly flounces, heaving, starched" (1) of Leipzig housewives, who also mention his sexual potency ("Johann Sebastian, twenty-two children!" [1]) as they themselves are also rushing to sing alto or soprano in one of the double choruses.[4] It is a consonant chord of art/community/eros. In contrast, the 1928 moment is compounded of gross, ill-assorted conflict: the Wobblies and Henry Ford; diamonds and aestheticized crucifixion; the propaganda of Mike Gold and the commodified, modern-sounding poetry of Frost, Sandburg, and Jeffers, as it is presented and condemned by Zukofsky's Poundian paratactics.

My first pass at an HJQ would be to place it around 4: Zukofsky presents himself as a Jew; but also as one of the workers (a marxist if not necessarily a Marxist); as a poet contending in the arena; and as an art lover: "Feet off the ground: / As beyond effort— / Music leaving no traces, / Not dying, and leaving no traces" (*A*, 5). So if we count the strands as Jewish, marxist, poet, art-ecstatic, we see that one quarter is Jewish, making for an HJQ of 4. (Remember, with homeopathic poetics, less is more).

But if one reads with more attention to the surface, line by line, the ratio of materials changes considerably. There is, in fact, only one line where one can reasonably infer the poet is Jewish: "It was also Passover." Wouldn't that compute to one line in a five-page poem, and therefore to an HJQ of 100 or some such? In other words, if the original "drop of medicine," to recall my earlier troubled quasi-term, were Zukofsky identifying himself, ever so briefly, as Jewish, it becomes quite amplified by its dramatized scarcity: it is the only single-line verse paragraph in the body of the poem.

But to find "*A*"-1 as having a high HJQ feels untrue to the facts. How do we factor in the erasure of Jewishness that Zukofsky half imbibed from Pound, but not just from him (Henry Adams, e.e. cummings)? The *St. Matthew Passion* has more overt anti-Semitism than anything else in Bach. Zukofsky had a nose for it.

Zukofsky collages typologically, as if all identities are analogous. The author of "*A*"-1, it strikes me, would not admit to any HJQ. When "the great Magnus" is quoted,

> *Executive*'s not the word, use *engineer*,
> Single handed, ran 'em like soldiers,
> Seventy-four yesterday, and could run 'em today,
> Been fishin' all Easter
> Nothin' like nature for hell-fire (*A*, 5)

the verbal references are meant to unify, with Magnus's hell-fire matching the same term in Bach's libretto. The last words of "*A*"-1 ("O fierce flaming pit!") belong both to the libretto and to the pit the striking coal miners are refusing to enter. Such typologies disturb any easy calculation.

Second practice problem. In his late "Multiple Identity Questionnaire" Ginsberg writes from many subject positions, but at least one of them is as a Jew:

> I'm a jew? a nice Jewish boy?
> A flaky Buddhist, certainly
> Gay in fact pederast? I'm exaggerating?
> Not only queer an amateur S&M fan, someone should spank me for
> saying that
> Columbia Alumnus class of '48, Beat icon, students say.
> White, if jews are "white race"
> American by birth, passport, and residence
> Slavic heritage, mama from Vitebsk, father's forebears Grading in
> Kamenetz-Podolska near Lvov.

I'm an intellectual! Anti-intellectual, anti-academic
Distinguished Professor of English Brooklyn College,
Manhattanite, Another middle class liberal,
but lower class second generation immigrant,
Upperclass, I own a condo loft, . . .
(Ginsberg, *Death & Fame*, 41)

Let's check the proportions, looking at the beginning of the list: jew, nice Jewish boy, flaky Buddhist, gay, pederast, queer, amateur S&M fan, Columbia Alumnus, Beat icon, White (if jews are "white race"), American, Slavic, intellectual, Anti-intellectual, anti-academic, Distinguished Professor, Manhattanite, middle class liberal, lower class, second generation immigrant, Upperclass . . .

The math gets fuzzy because the categories are put comic-polemically. And then there is the pretty shocking anti-Semitic orthography Ginsberg insists on, writing "jew" twice although he uses caps elsewhere conventionally (Vitebsk, Kamenetz-Podolska) and comically ("Another middle class liberal"). But, fuzzily, let's say that Ginsberg presents us here with a quotient of roughly three or so Jewish or Jewish-inflected identifications in a total of twenty. So, roughly, he's showing an HJQ of 7.

In spite of this small irruption of self-hating orthography (i.e., "jew"), Ginsberg here remains a Jew. He ends his written career projecting his ashes to the cemetery with his father in "Things I'll Not Do (Nostalgias)":

Never go to Bulgaria, had a booklet & invitation
[. . . .]
No more sweet summers with lovers, teaching Blake at Naropa,
Mind Writing Slogans, new modern American Poetics, Williams
        Kerouac Reznikoff Rakosi Corso Creeley Orlovsky
Any visits to B'nai Israel graves of Buba, Aunt Rose, Harry Meltzer and
    Aunt Clara,
        Father Louis
Not myself except in an urn of ashes. (*Death & Fame*, 99)

20
Dickinson – So –

Reading Dickinson makes me confront my modernist poetic upbringing from an unflattering angle. Primitive questions rearise, the stupid early ones. How good is Emily Dickinson? How good is she compared to Williams? Compared to Stein? To Pound, to Zukofsky, to Olson? To Eliot? This group—my modernist pedagogues—is heteroclite, but they do share a common blind spot when it comes to Dickinson. Yes, there is Stein's "Sacred Emily," but isn't that at most an indeterminate nod in Dickinson's direction but more probably having nothing to do with any word Dickinson wrote? Wouldn't Emily Brontë be a more likely referent? Perhaps the heteroclite group was, like me, deafened by the hymn metrics (IM mor TAL i TY, which to this day my modernist ear can never register without a micro-shock of boredom). Or perhaps they never listened. Does Pound mention her? Pound's pronouncements are memorable, but no Dickinson mention comes to mind. She's not in *ABC of Reading* or Zukofsky's *A Test of Poetry*, nor in the index of "*A*". Susan Howe's use of Williams's *American Grain* idiocy as the epigraph to *My Emily Dickinson* is chilling: "Poets? Where? They are the test. But a true woman in flower, never. Emily Dickinson, starving of passion in her father's garden, is the very nearest we have ever been—starving." Here is the inventive, socially perspicacious Williams, completely out to lunch. It's not the only time this happens with him, of course, but still, how could he miss such great poetry? Does what makes Dickinson's writing so compelling just not register in modernist terms?

Another thread of modernism-trouble that Dickinson brings is that while she didn't register with the aforementioned pedagogues, she *was* picked up on by Tate and Winters, which can make her a counter in the wrong game played by the wrong poet-critics, the modernist-tamers, whose poetry was only accessible via their cold critical anterooms.

Though I know, rationally, that her work didn't surface in any serious form until after most of the modernist pedagogy was set and that her absence from that pedagogy therefore has a simple historical explanation, still, when I read Dickinson seriously I'm troubled by a thinness at the heart of my modernist formation. Perhaps the modernists weren't just too early for Dickinson, perhaps they're just parochial. (Again: rationally, I know that poetry's house has many mansions, but still . . .)

Two instant reactions I have when reading Dickinson are exhilaration and inadequacy, which, coincidentally, are two of her most powerful subjects:

An ignorance a Sunset
Confer opon the Eye –
Of Territory – Color –
Circumference – Decay –

It's Amber Revelation
Exhilarate – Debase –
Omnipotence' inspection
Of Our inferior face –

(J 552 / F 669)[1]

These are Dickinson's stanzas, but I wrote them too, in "Essay on Style," my first collage piece. There I morphed quotations into one another (Whitehead describing an audience listening to a symphony becoming, via gradual word substitution, an account of a duck signaling her ducklings); interspersed segments of a narrative (Mozart giving a composition lesson to a bored princess); and also, consulting the sacred oracle of Chance, I just stuck things in. I opened Dickinson (the Johnson edition) at random.[2]

My Immortality-aversion was already in place, preventing me from using the last stanza: And when the solemn features / Confirm – in Victory / We start – as if detected / In Immortality –

An ignorance Dickinson
Confer upon the reading I

First Pan died
(during the reign of Tiberius, say 30 AD
[see Plutarch, "On the Obsolescence of Oracles"]);

then God died
(in the nineteenth century
[Nietzsche, *The Gay Science*]);

and then the Author
(in the latter half of the twentieth
[Barthes, "The Death of the Author"]);

but there still is,
in the twenty-first century, a
fully coherent reader. Thank you very much, as Stein would say.

Territory – Color – / Circumference – Decay – How *abstractly* Dickinson writes! She is not following Pound's advice to "go in fear of abstractions." His example, "dim lands of peace" (Pound, *ABC*, 5), is visually lax and historically bland, so of course poets should go in fear of *that*.

Whereas Territory, Color, Circumference, Decay
The first three name enlightenment tools of orientation without saying
where anything is
Decay adding the shock of dying time

How long, coherent reader, before these Moods –
Attention – Semantic Economy – Mental Energy – Blood Sugar –
Not only Decay – but vanish –
Even the memory?

Amber Revelation
might initially be the color of the sky
a window of twenty seconds, but by the time the phrase has been written
a next look up sees the color has lost all name

So now "Amber Revelation" signifies not a full moment when dynamic color filled the western sky one thought one was naming as it was happening, present-tense Revelation! The Book of Nature—at the pencil tip! How wonderfully apt the worded Mind!

but a thin – Remembered –
past thing

and "Amber Revelation"
a Revelation caught in Amber

not a bad name
for a paperweight
from the gift shop at
the Dickinson Homestead,

one of the more expensive gifts
one rung above the
I'm Nobody! T-shirt

the very strokes she set down on the paper, in the very room where she wrote, burning a lamp at night, an expensive habit, but in her situation, affordable

it Exhilarates – Debases –

Is that reading dynamic connected at all to modernist calls to clarity, excitement, energy?

It's not so much that I'm not a Dickinson scholar and haven't read her work in sufficient detail and breadth (*debased*), it's more that I find it hard to keep hold of the sense of any given poem I read. The balance tips so frequent, now

I want to investigate this fugitive sense, but it doesn't stay.

The investigation is being written, quite ostensibly, from the position of poet-critic, some stop between the depots, neither here nor there. I could insist that in this respect it rhymes, slantwise, with the position of Dickinson, the first—along with Whitman—poet-critic of the American language, except she wasn't, Cotton Mather and such types having already lathered up the language, insisting that anything written not simply be a performance within a genre,

but have an effect, perform
a material-spiritual intervention,

at least for those paying attention,
a demand requiring

exhausting regimens of framing calisthenics
each phrase having to justify each word

in the face of some transcendently opaque demand for perfect intelligibility
Omnipotence' inspection, say

Under such conditions, it's hard not to be coy: I'm
Nobody, or, conversely, grandiose:

The Soul's Superior instants
Occur to Her – alone –

– Herself – ascended
To too remote a Height
For lower Recognition (J 306 / F 630, partial quote)

This seems not Written
to circulate among those of lower – Recognition

And what are we recognizing? The work of Howe, Werner, Cameron, Smith, Jackson has shown convincingly how crucial the visual embodiment of Dickinson's writing is,[3] how sensitive her pencil was, moving across the sheets, scraps, chocolate wrappers

and Mitchell's work shows how grounded in sound her writing is, how deftly she plays with the modular possibilities provided by the corpus of hymns

But Dickinson's singularity is still daunting. Yes, intellectually she was far from isolated, immersed in an up-to-date flow of public discourse, as Reynolds, Miller, Friedlander, and others point out, showing how present contemporary discourses and debates are in her work, almost every phrase wittily engaged with its present moment, every rift loaded with the Ore of public speech genres juggled deftly

Yes a few poems published in newspapers, and yes large-scale sending of poems to friends, but Dickinson wrote almost 1,800 poems (with various degrees of finish, variation, singleness—many were first thoughts, semi-false starts, true fragments and so on, but still),
hundreds and hundreds and hundreds of, you could say,
the best poems written in America
the most intensely meant, most concentrated, sharpest, the most open poems,
choose whatever praise-terms suit
imagine she did that
then put them in her sock drawer
with no mention of them in her will

Clearly Dickinson had a phenomenal fund of poetic courage and ambition
So imagine being a poet with such a range of address, of roles to write from
and then simply letting the acts accrue outside of public time

or was she such a patrician,
that she could die as she had lived,
in fitting privacy, because she knew the necessaries would be taken care of?

or was she
in Reynolds's term
a Female Adventuress
calmly willing to wait through nonsubjective time
for armless fame to lift her writing out from among her Dimities?

The simplest justice one can do Dickinson
is to say the obvious
that she's good in a way that the *doxa* of the last hundred modern years
—whether oracled through Pound, Stein, Breton, Artaud, Olson—
can't reach with their various pointing devices

Doesn't something need to be witnessed and adjusted here
or is poetry just a generic name for a group of very different activities?

To actually be reading Dickinson is always frame breaking
and one of the first frames that breaks
is the sense of what I'm reading
what poetry is

"Publication – is the Auction" (J 709 / F 788) was written by someone who found the violence proposed by the abolitionists to be as disgraceful as the violence enacted upon slaves—is that possible?

many mansions

The first memorable encounter I had with her language was short and unmarked but nevertheless deeply unpleasant. At the Iowa Writers' Workshop in 1971 I heard a new-vetted way of confirming poetic value uttered as a kind of threat. When one poet wanted to insist on the dominating greatness of poem Y, he growled the Dickinsonism, "It takes the top of my head off." No counterargument was being solicited. It could have been, I suppose, a courageous act of polygendered solidarity, but it wasn't.

Dickinson's words are always multiple, but isn't their location always underwritten by absolutism? Isn't that the mainspring of their debasing thrill?

Can Dickinson's words circulate without being bent unrecognizably?
Can they be put in play or must they be quoted or visually reproduced with reverent resolution?
They do seem peculiarly adapted to resisting critical constructions

*

Her well-varied Noes
might be quite literal

a species of Curst be He
who moves these bones

Was her writing literally not to cross
her father's ground

Does it always select its own society?
of being – as Stein would have it –
the only one?

Reading Dickinson produces great charge, but the process is unlike what Charles Olson urges in "Projective Verse," where, as the familiar quote has it: "A poem is energy transferred from where the poet got it . . . by way of the poem itself to, all the way over to, the reader. . . . [T]he poem itself must . . . be a high-energy construct and, at all points, an energy-discharge" (Olson, *Selected Prose*, 240).

Olson is insisting
with all the virtuous volume of someone who has just discovered that poetry can have a public sphere, a possibly very big open space where one has to make sure one's voice carries,
insisting

on continuous linguistic evidence of the poetic:
All charged language all the time at all points all the way over

which is utterly slantways to Dickinson. Olson's is a utopian TVA scenario. (I placed a dam in Tennessee, and the energy transferred from it got all the way over to the reader while simultaneously the power lines were discharging freely at all points along their extension.)

With Dickinson, there is sometimes not quite a reader, or a dear dead reader, or an emphatically specific reader who is not any current reader. And it is not always decipherable where the boundaries of a poem might be among her partially segmented and stitched lifelong experiment in writing. As opposed to the declarative vividness Olson demands, Dickinson's writing is *subjunctive*. The charge in her work is, as she writes, "– so –"

Don't put up my Thread and Needle –
I'll begin to Sew
When the Birds begin to whistle –
Better stitches – so –

These were bent – my sight got crooked –
When my mind – is plain
I'll do seams – a Queen's endeavor
Would not blush to own –

Hems – too fine for Lady's tracing
To the sightless Knot –
Tucks – of dainty interspersion –
Like a dotted Dot –

Leave my Needle in the furrow –
Where I put it down –
I can make the zigzag stitches
Straight – when I am strong –

Till then – dreaming I am sewing
Fetch the seam I missed –
Closer – so I – at my sleeping –
Still surmise I stitch – (J 617 / F 681)

There's the perpetually interesting counterpoint of the rhythmic rhyme of lines 1 and 3 [Needle / whistle] placed among the inbred rhyme of 2 and 4 [Sew / – so –]. In the second pair the verb is made simple and heroic by the ballad-like voice promising to take up the struggle even though it is somehow incapacitated in the present, wounded, speaking from some dark time deep in the night before the birds whistle. (There's a realist nomenclature if there ever was one: they're not going to save the day by warbling some aesthetically salvific Song at the first streaks of dawn). That emphatic verb (I'LL beGIN to *SEW*) is rhymed with "– so –," which is of course the same sound but utterly differentiated by its syntactic and narrative functions. When will it be time to Sew? When it's "– so –," when the night is past and the birds begin to whistle, then some other condition will obtain, and the stitches will be much better. "– so –" is promissory: a slightly drawn-out, speculative noise, a utopia that one must believe in but cannot live in.

The stanzas embody what they say they can't actually be doing in the present moment; they embody the "– so –" state: when sight isn't crooked, when the mind is plain, when the poet is strong, when the magical stitching will take place. And of course it *is* taking place: we *are* reading it in the present, even though it is referring to some subjunctive time.

The enounced poet of this poem (the "speaker") is not the Homeric rhapsode (in Greek, "the stitcher") displaying the heroes' wounds. But even though she writes that she is in an incompetent state, unable to see, to think straight, or put anything together in any semblance of order, nevertheless, the poet as enunciator (i.e., the bard) presents, in the third stanza, the wished-for, inevitable magic sewing:

Hems – too fine for Lady's tracing
To the sightless Knot –
Tucks – of dainty interspersion –
Like a dotted Dot –

It's not likely Dickinson knew the poem, but this stanza seems close to the elfish displays of preternaturally perfect sensuousness in Christina Rossetti's "Goblin Market." Cf., "Would you like Summer? Taste of our's! / Spices? Buy – here! / Ill! We have berries, for the parching!" (J 691 / F 272)

Where Olson wants language that's perfect copper wire, fiber-optic cable, firewire, Dickinson makes language interior to itself, too fine to see, too intelligible to be known—you can only read it, "Like a dotted Dot –." You can't understand "dotted" without first hearing the "Dot." Syntactic time goes backward: a Dot is not perfect until it's dotted. A more radical gesture occurs inside the word *so*, with its unsynthesizable collocation of sew/sow

"– so –" marks the poetically redeemed world that she posits in her poems

I'm "wife" – I've finished that –
That other state –
I'm Czar – I'm "Woman" now –
It's safer so –

How odd the Girl's life looks
Behind this soft Eclipse –
I think that Earth feels so
To folks in Heaven – now –

This being comfort – then
That other kind – was pain –

But why compare?
I'm "Wife"! Stop there! (J 199 / F 225)

A primary condition Dickinson's poetry courts is "so":
an exhilarated state which does not easily include the reader

But why compare?
Stop there?

*

Originally, yes. But my wife recently got her grandmother's copy of the 1915 *Poems by Emily Dickinson.* 1915 means it's more or less contemporaneous with the first issues of *Poetry* magazine, *Des Imagistes, Tender Buttons.* Here is Poem X. Even in its antique dress it is very much worth the reader's time.

In A Library

A precious, mouldering pleasure 't is
To meet an antique book,
In just the dress his century wore;
A privilege, I think,

His venerable hand to take,
And warming in our own,
A passage back, or two, to make
To times when he was young.

His quaint opinions to inspect,
His knowledge to unfold
On what concerns our mutual mind,
The literature of old;

What interested scholars most,
What competitions ran
When Plato was a certainty,
And Sophocles a man;

When Sappho was a living girl,
And Beatrice wore
The gown that Dante deified.
Facts, centuries before,

He traverses familiar,
As one should come to town

And tell you all your dreams were true;
He lived where dreams were sown.

His presence is enchantment,
You beg him not to go;
Old volumes shake their vellum heads
And tantalize, just so.
(*Poems by Emily Dickinson*, 22–23)

21
Punctuation-Watching for Beginners

I know when I've fallen in love   I start to write love songs

. . . . . .

Also I seem to start dropping punctuation

Jackson Mac Low, "58th Light Poem:
For Anne Tardos—19–20 March 1979"

I'm using "punctuation-watching" on analogy with "bird-watching" and I am one of the novice birders my title addresses. In looking at how punctuation was dealt with by modernist, objectivist, and postmodern poets, it is clear that something was happening: the relative absence of conventional punctuation—commas, semicolons, periods, question marks, capital letters at the beginning of lines—can be seen without reading. Scan the pages of *Spring and All*, "As a Wife Has a Cow: A Love Story," late Niedecker, late Olson, late Zukofsky, etc., for such marks and you'll find few. The preponderance of punctuation-less words is obvious; but what this means is difficult to disentangle: Outside of Stein's "Poetry and Grammar" and Olson's "Projective Verse," quasi-exceptions which I will discuss later, there was little mention of punctuation throughout the poetics, a surprising omission in a general milieu that encouraged discussion of the nuts and bolts of writing. There wasn't much said about punctuation, but, in general, the writing practices show an unsystematic avoidance of it.

When the pages are read, differences show up: punctuation will be carefully rationed at times; other times its relative scarcity reads as more haphazard. In the different poetics stories, words are always the hero; but punctuation is never the enemy. This makes generalization about what was going on unlikely. In what follows, I'll be empiric: ah, a semicolon—let's see what it does. I'll venture local generalizations, but I won't be finding new widely legible conventions. Behaviors will vary.

At times punctuation avoidance looks systematic: there are no commas or periods in Oppen's *Primitive* or in Zukofsky's *80 Flowers*. But more often it is semi-systematic: conventional punctuation will suddenly appear in a mostly punctuation-free passage. Then again there are the outright exceptions to this larger trend: Eliot and Reznikoff both were observant about commas and such; Moore was punctilious. Finally, there is Pound, whose theory and practice were, to say the least, highly influential; but with regard to punctuation, the theory was silent and the practice deeply inconsistent. In many places Pound was punctuation-friendly, arguing that poetry should be "at least as well written as prose" (Pound, *Selected Letters*, 48) and recommending the novelist's virtues to poets: "His true Penelope was Flaubert" (*P/T*, 549) as he wrote in *Mauberley*, praising the exacting craftsman who, as the legend has it, spent the morning putting in a comma which he then spent the afternoon taking out. In his own poetry, one of Pound's signature effects, as here at the beginning of Canto 71, is a comma-ful urbanity:

> A German ambassador once told me he cdn't bear St Paul
> he was, he said, so hard on fornication. (*C*, 414)

Contrary to such ostentatiously conventional displays, Pound also produced, as I will be discussing, influential examples of punctuation-less poetry. And he used a third mode as well: carelessness. In fact, in the couplet just cited, the two lines do not act alike with regard to conventional punctuation: the second foregrounds it, but the first avoids it. There is no period after "St" and in conventional prose there would be a semicolon or colon after "Paul"; the insistent abbreviation "cdn't" suggests a business environment, where we might, for that moment, be reading a memo.

For a clear example of his carelessness, take these lines from the *Pisan Cantos*:

> Kuthera, here are Lynxes and the clicking of crotales
> There is a stir of dust from old leaves
> Will you trade roses for acorns
> Will lynxes eat thorn leaves?
> What have you in that wine jar? (*C*, 505)

Though the first two lines sound like complete sentences, there are no periods. What are the varying left margins doing? Why no capital for the second "lynx"? Why no question mark after "acorns"? Such things happen throughout Pound's poetry. (Try to find a rationale for his use of capital vs. lowercase at the beginnings of lines in *The Pisan Cantos*.) If Pound is taken as paradigmatic, then his carelessness about such matters might lead to the conclusion that there had been little change since the eighteenth century, when punctuation was not something authors paid attention to. As Janine Barchas writes, "bibliographers term dashes, along with italics, punctuation, ornamentation, and capitalization, 'accidentals,' a term which captures the common eighteenth-century practice of leaving these details to the discretion of the compositor" (157).

This would be the lowest level: where punctuation doesn't stack up as a category but simply remains a pile of tedious chores for the help to deal with. Or perhaps the carelessness has a specific class resonance, like a nineteenth-century

British aristocrat using "ain't," or a Renaissance courtier's sprezzatura. Both work as descriptions of Pound (a gentleman can be both punctilious and careless).

Our punctuation-watching tour began in the jumbled field of Pound's practice, but I'll now turn to more orderly territories. It is possible, in fact, by marshaling some of the evidence, to make a case for the waning of conventional punctuation as an inevitable result of poetic advance. The trajectories of the poetry of Niedecker, Oppen, and Zukofsky from early to late can suggest that the teleological goal was a state of words freed of punctuation. First, a short poem of Niedecker's from *New Goose* (1946):

> I said to my head, Write something.
> It looked me dead in the face.
> Look around, dear head, you've never read
> of the ground that takes you away.
> Speed up, speed up, the frosted windshield's
> a fern spray. (Niedecker, 100)

Commas, periods at the end of sentences, capitals at the beginning of sentences and after a verb of saying—except for the absence of quotation marks, this is fully punctuated. Her later poems, as we will see in a moment, avoid these marks. Such a progression makes for good Greenbergian formalism, where, as an art becomes more advanced, it (heroically) jettisons materials and effects from other media.[1] Advanced painting sticks to the possibilities of paint on a flat surface; advanced poems are made of words.

This is the implicit point of a story Williams tells in his *Autobiography*. A stuffy customer is voicing old-fashioned doubts: "But Mr. Hartpence, what is all that down in this left hand lower corner?" Williams continues:

> Hartpence . . . carefully inspected the area mentioned. Then, after further consideration, "That, Madam," said he, "is paint." . . . This story marks the exact point in the transition . . . from the appreciation of a work of art as a copying of nature to the thought of it as the imitation of nature. . . . It is still the failure to take this step that blocks us in seeking to gain a full conception of the modern in art. In painting Cézanne is the first to have consciously taken that step. (240)

This has Williams's typical enthusiasm: an art dealer's remark becomes the "exact point" where an aesthetic breakthrough manifests itself. The implicit moral is that the artist focuses on the proper materials for the art to advance; the discerning audience shouldn't look for what's not there. If we analogize paint and words, then to make a poem purely of words is the ambitious poet's task.

Williams soon makes this explicit: "Gertrude Stein found the key with her conception of the objective use of words" (241).

The *Autobiography* was a retrospect from the late 1940s; in his poetic practice decades earlier, Williams can be seen working implicitly toward a condition of words mostly freed from punctuation.[2] The ever-inconsistent Williams, having reached this form in *Spring and All*, worked in it for a decade then gradually moved away from it. But the new convention remained legible and easy to use: capitalization indicates a new sentence.

In her later work, Niedecker often used this new convention. Take, for instance, "Wintergreen Ridge":

Man
        lives hard
                on this stone perch

by sea
        imagines
                durable works

in creation here
        as in the center
                of the world

let's say
        of art
                We climb

the limestone cliffs
        my skirt dragging
                an inch below

the knee
        the style before
                the last

(247–48)

At first blush this can seem to support the neat dichotomies of a Greenbergian formalism, where words are the vivid, primary material needing to be freed from the pedantic conventions of punctuation. But I don't think that is what is happening. The dichotomies are messier. It's hard to establish an articulated opposition between words and punctuation. Yes, in these two cases and in similar ones, the ostensible period is avoided. But its function is fully present. There is no opposition in either poem between words and the syntax of sentences. One could say there are invisible periods here. When the page displays "of art / We climb," we should understand (in the older convention): "of art. / We climb." We are bidden to keep track of the sentences unfolding; noticing sentence boundaries imparts a specific rhythm to the words.

I read the Niedecker lines as forming a sentence like so: Man lives hard on this stone perch by the sea, imagines durable works in creation here, as in the center of the world, let's say, of art. The concluding two lines end the sentence with an afterthought, in which I hear a touch of archness, rebuking the self-centered grandiosity of artists. The final words could be represented like so: the world, let's say . . . of art. The implication is that maybe Man's imagination of durable works should assume a less heroic scale. Maybe instead of thinking about eternal duration, we in the moderately sized art world should be mindful of our actual passage through time in our increasingly unstylish costumes, our slightly long skirts retarding our ascent.

In poetics, this has been the long century of the word as such, of the materiality of the signifier, and I understand that reading invisible punctuation can seem untoward. But in this next ostensibly punctuation-less Niedecker poem, some such reading procedure seems called for:

> Why can't I be happy
> in my sorrow
>
> my drinking man
> today
>
> my quiet
> tomorrow
> (230)

The words here have the stripped-down (but not simple) look that is something of a dress code for one strand of late Objectivism—Niedecker, Oppen, and, to an extent, Zukofsky. But it is hard to avoid the implied articulation of these three couplets. The first is a question demanding a paradoxical resolution. It might be self-address, which would have a somewhat plaintive accent: "*why* can't I be happy?" Or: "why can't *I* be happy?" Or it can be taken as aggressively addressed to some other who doesn't yet understand the paradox of being happy in sorrow: "why *can't* I?" In either case, the next two couplets supply the halves of the supporting argument via a quick narrative. First, "my drinking man / today," indicates an unpleasant state of affairs lasting all day. That certainly explains the sorrow. But, luckily, this sorrow will lead to the happiness spelled out in the last couplet: "my quiet / tomorrow." There's an implied colon or even an equals sign between the last two couplets: my drinking man today = my quiet tomorrow. The semi-parallelism emphasizes the transmutation. Both couplets begin *my [adjective]* and both end with a single-word line narrating the time. The parallelism amplifies the difference: "my drinking man" in the first couplet makes us expect a [my adjective + noun] pattern in the second; instead, we get a blank: "my quiet" . . . what? Nothing. Tomorrow the man will not be in evidence (he'll be too wasted); there will just be *my quiet*. The delayed rhyme, sorrow/tomorrow, which completes the poem, signals the validity of the happy-in-sorrow paradox. ("Happy" here is relative: overall the scene of the poem is fairly grim, but at least the stoic argument for happiness the couplets suggest has its clear logic.)

What is such a reading suggesting about punctuation? That readers can supply their own invisible punctuation? That the syntax and rhetoric formerly signaled by conventional punctuation can be indicated via line and stanza breaks and capitalization? Is it all just a matter of fashion? Are we to conclude that punctuation is passé and does not appear in the more fashionable pages, but, meanwhile, the transactional regimes of syntax and rhetoric that punctuation used to signal continue on apace?

Another set of early and late examples, from Zukofsky, poses a related conundrum, where words and punctuation, at first obviously separate, become hard to disentangle on closer reading. At first scan, the opposition, and thus the implied teleology, seems clear enough: "*A*"-1 (1928) uses conventional punctuation; *80 Flowers* (1978) does not.

Early Zukofsky:

The next day the reverses
As if the music were only a taunt:
As if it had not kept, flower-cell, liveforever,
        before the eyes, perfecting.
—I thought that was finished:
Existence not even subsistence,
Worm eating the bark of the street tree,
Smoke sooting skyscraper chimneys,
That which looked for substitutes, tired,
Ready to give up the ghost in a cellar—
Remembering love in a taxi:
(*A*, 4–5)

Late Zukofsky, "Mountain Laurel":

Known color grown mountain laurel
broadleaf of acid earth margin
excite green winter years hoarfrost

mooned pod *honesty* open unvoiced
May-grown acute 5-petal calicoflower cluster
10-slender rods spring seed sway
trefoil birds throat *Not thyme's*
spur-flower calico clusters laurelled well
(*Complete Short Poetry*, 235)

But a strict Greenbergian progress away from punctuation toward untrammeled words dissolves when I read the passages. To be sure, they work very differently: the first moves line by line, the second word by word; this makes the first a dramatic monologue or dialogue, while the second is a dense lyric made of single words, each of which is a small museum of Zukofsky's concerns.[3] But though the parts differ, the articulation of the parts in both passages has common characteristics.

To say that the first has punctuation and the second does not is to ignore the urgent signaling going on in the second via italics, capitalization, and word boundaries. Although the form is insistent—eight lines of five words means we are reading forty words—we are not simply examining single words when we read the poem. The italicized words "*excite*" and "*honesty*" jump out as sharply insistent in some way; and the italics of the last line and a half, plus the initial capital, make "*Not thyme's / spur-flower calico clusters laurelled well*" into a new statement, something said, some gnomic moral that the birds sing (Zukofsky likes the Shakespeareanism of "*throat*" as a verb of pure song). This effect is reinforced by the capital *n* of "*Not*," which is the now-conventional sentence without a period from *Spring and All.* As for word boundaries, specific, unusual choices are being made throughout. Each word counts a great deal here and is necessarily put under pressure, often resulting in compounding ("May-grown," "5-petal," "10-slender") or fusion ("*calicoflower*"). But why compound in one case and not the other? Why "calicoflower" but then "*spur-flower*"? Why "calicoflower" but then "*calico clusters*"? Why are some compounds natural and descriptive ("May-grown," "5-petal") but others highly abstract ("10-slender")? And then, at just one point, there's the "little word"[4] *of*, a connective which belongs to the world of dramatic, phrase-using beings.

I read a continuous insistence on highly specific articulation of words here: something quite punctuation-like in intention. But except for the *Not* announcing a sentence without a period, all of this punctuation-like behavior—the intensive signaling of the italics, hyphens, word-boundary decisions—remains proto-conventional. Possibly "*excite*" in the third line is meant as a command: "O Mountain Laurel" (addressed in the first two lines), "*excite* the winter . . ."; but there are many other possibilities, all of them tricky.

The similarity I see between this poem and the earlier one is this: the ostensible punctuation in "*A*"-1 and the punctuation-like signaling of the late poem are both para-conventional. (Here, I seem to have slipped into a different metaphorical frame: rather than some birdlike occurrence, punctuation is now a matter of behavior; it is a collection of possible signals given by some poetic actor.)

When I say that the punctuation signals in "*A*"-1 are para-conventional, I mean that it is hard to tell what a particular gesture is intending. Why is there no punctuation between "the reverses / As if" but in the next line there is a colon: "a taunt: / As if"? The general paratactic rhythm of the passage is clear, as is the description of a down day after the aesthetic bliss of the previous night; but I can't tell how colons, commas, and dashes make any particular difference at the end of the lines.

In both early and late work, I'm saying, there's a richness (overload) of intention that the two regimes of punctuation—the first conventional, the second ad hoc—are of only equivocal help in conveying.

What does this mean? Am I saying that punctuation—in this new, stretched sense of all typographic behavior used to articulate the relation of the words and lines to one another—is fundamentally distinct from words? (This would be the opposite of what the Niedecker poems suggested to me.) Am I saying that words should always be used freshly, that they are the workable locus of novelty, but that punctuation should always be conventionally legible? That a word should never just be itself, and that an act of punctuation should always be clearly itself?

In the interest of empiricism, I will let my contradictory generalizations stand.

To turn now to Stein and Olson, the quasi-exceptions I mentioned earlier. They both discuss punctuation vociferously, but in neither case did their emphasis establish a convention.

The absence of punctuation is what buoys the forceful wit of the opening sentence in "Poetry and Grammar": "What is poetry and if you know what poetry is what is prose" (*GS II*, 313). A pedagogical paraphrase might run like so: What is poetry? And if you know what poetry is, what is prose? But readers who are well versed in Stein will wince: her own sentence is so much livelier, more forceful, more vividly paradoxical. "What is poetry and if you know what poetry is what is prose" explodes the questions it poses: it's both prose *and* poetry.

"Poetry and Grammar" is mostly not about punctuation, but rather about words arranged in categories and charismatically judged (nouns are salvageable; adjectives are dreck). Stein is both charming and decisive about this. The charm has a tone of knowing fantasy, a bit like Ratty in *The Wind in the Willows* leaning forward to say, "Weasels—well, you can't really trust them." Adjectives are just not interesting; they are a class of word one might just as well forget. Commas are especially distasteful; they are servile: "They really have within them deeply within them fundamentally within them the comma nature" (319). More scornful notice of the comma: "And what does a comma do, a comma does nothing but make easy a thing that if you like it enough is easy without the comma. A long complicated sentence should force itself upon you, make you know yourself knowing it and the comma, well at the most a comma is a poor period that it lets you stop and take a breath but if you want to take a breath you ought to know yourself that you want to take a breath" (320–21). (In the interest of length, I won't continue, but reading the surrounding pages of the lecture reveals a remarkably sustained articulation of just how unpleasantly pathetic commas are.)

Stein is obviously not thinking of Olson's "Projective Verse"; nevertheless, there's an accidental rejoinder here, fifteen years early. Where Olson makes the breath of the poet heroic, a fact that must be registered on the page, Stein has already taken into account the reader, allowing her to breathe autonomously.

Olson and Stein are particularly disparate. Nevertheless, watch how the comma gets treated in "Projective Verse." It is the moment where Olson is praising the typewriter (surely one of the least prophetic but still influential moments in modernist/postmodern poetics!) as "a machine" for "scoring" poetry. I've read and taught it for years, but I'd never noticed how Olson dismisses the comma: "If a contemporary poet leaves a space as long as the phrase before it, he means that space to be held, by the breath, an equal length of time. . . . If he wishes a pause so light it hardly separates the words, yet does not want a comma—which is an interruption of the meaning rather than the sounding of the line—follow him when he uses a symbol the typewriter has ready to hand" (*Selected Prose* 246). And then he presents, on its own line: "What does not change / is the will to change."

Olson heroizes the slash (the Poundian sign par excellence of masculinization), but note the micro-shudder as the comma is dismissed as nonpoetic, having reference to meaning rather than the more primal, actual sound. But heroic as this exhortation was, it never became conventional. After "The Kingfishers," Olson himself never used the slash again in a poem.[5]

A key antecedent for Olson is Pound—the mystic, Eleusinian, musical, charismatic Pound. This side of Pound is emphatically, but implicitly, anti-punctuation: the Chinese ideograms; the insistence that, at its peak, poetry has all the energy of the natural and the divine worlds. Here, in *ABC of Reading*, is Pound writing about melopoiea:

> The best smith, as Dante called **Arnaut Daniel**, made the birds sing IN HIS WORDS; I don't mean that he merely referred to birds singing—In the canzone beginning
>
> l'aura amara
> Fals bruoills brancutz
> Clazir

> Quel doutz espeissa ab fuoills.
> Els letz
> Becs
> Dels auzels ramencz
> Ten balps e mutz
> etc.
>
> And having done it in that one strophe he kept them at it, repeating the tune, and finding five rhymes for each of seventeen rhyme sounds in the same order.
>
> Having done that he constructed another perfect strophe, where the bird call interrupts the verse.
>
> Cadahus
> En son us . . .
> (*ABC*, 53)

Two points: Daniel's tour de force is to unite natural, actual, real birdsong with the virtuosity of his musical-verbal dexterity (five end rhymes, seventeen rhyming syllables in the stripped-down stanza). And in the description of some lines (Cadahus / En son us . . .) from a second Daniel poem, Pound insists that the words simply *are* birdcalls: "another perfect strophe, where the bird call interrupts the verse."

The punctuation-free, minimal, foreign, and hence authentically natural look of what Pound is celebrating had wide influence, deriving both from the visual layout of the *ABC of Reading* and from the many pop-up visual anomalies in *The Cantos* (ideograms, blacked-out lines, etc.). Creeley was one thoroughly influenced, it seems to me. The punctuation-spare look of *For Love* and *Words* seems interestingly close to Daniel as Pound presents him. Here is the last stanza of "Kore":

> "O love,
> where are you
> leading
> me now?" (*RC I*, 206)

There is much more to say, but the waning afternoon (we're back to the birding frame) is preemptory in calling a halt to this particular outing. Tomorrow if the weather holds we'll look at some of Stein's practice, behaviors that her lecture, smart and intriguing as it was, said nothing about. Here's "Winning His Way" (1931), where she uses periods to try to make words into sentences:

> What is poetry. This. Is poetry.
> Delicately formed. And pleasing. To the eye.
> What is fame. Fame is. The care of. Their. Share
> And so. It. Rhymes better.
> (Stein, "Winning His Way," 7)

And here, quite differently, at the conclusion of "As a Wife Has a Cow: A Love Story," she listens to see how syntactically stacked she could make a sentence: "Have it as having having it as happening, happening to have it as having, having to have it as happening. Happening and have it as happening and having it happen as happening and having to have it happen as happening, and my wife has a cow as now, my wife having a cow as now, my wife having a cow as now and having a cow as now and having a cow and having a cow now, my wife has a cow and now. My wife has a cow" (*GS I*, 503) . . . until the end, of course, when she avails herself of the short complete sentence and its pleasures.

Notes

Chapter 2

1. For a more in-depth consideration of these matters, see Middleton, 1–25.

2. A stronger version of such "noncommutative" rhyme (where A rhymes with B and C, but B and C don't rhyme with each other) occurs in the last stanza of the long version. In four of the six-line stanzas, lines 2 through 5 rhyme a a b b. In the last stanza, the A rhymes are hand/in and the B rhymes are and/hand. In other words, "hand" is both an A and a B rhyme: to exaggerate for paradox, "hand" doesn't rhyme with "hand."

3. In the earlier versions of the poem, from the initial publication in *Others* through the 1932 version published in *The New Poetry*, edited by Harriet Monroe and Alice Henderson (and used in Louis Zukofsky's *A Test of Poetry*), the beginning is: "I too, dislike it." While "I, too, dislike it" is grammatically correct, it loses the ingenuousness of the earlier "I too, dislike it," which to my ear and eye is a compromise formation, almost as if Moore is chiming in: Me too, I dislike it.

4. For almost a century modernists of quite distinct stripes have articulated their poetics against academia. Pound: "Watch the Beaneries" (*Kulchur*, 344); "Teach? at Harvard? / Teach? It cannot be done" (*Cantos*, 453), etc.; Stein: "that is the trouble with . . . teaching, the things not that can be learnt but that can be taught are not interesting" (*Everybody*, 220); Olson calls an academic conference an "abomination," a "false & dirty thing . . . nothing more than a bunch of commercial travellers from the several colleges" (*Poems*, 233); Spicer: "I learned [to be objective about poems] from the English Department (and from the English Department of the spirit—that great quagmire that lurks at the bottom of all of us) and it ruined ten years of my poetry" (Spicer, 61).

5. I can't remember where I read this.

6. For "poethics," see Retallack, *The Poethical Wager*.

7. "With / daring" and the following poem, *Eureka!*, were part of a series of postcard poems instigated by Ken and Ann Mikolowski, edited by Alice Notley, and published posthumously as *A Certain Shaft of Sunlight*.

8. Hegel in *Phenomenology of Spirit* writes that at night all cows are black; Horace in "The Art of Poetry" that the aim of the poet is to delight and to instruct.

Chapter 3

1. I discuss this in "That Deep Romantic Chasm," a review essay on Jeffrey Robinson's *Unfettering Poetry: The Fancy in British Romanticism*, in *European Romantic Review* 22.1 (February 2011).

Chapter 4

1. Unless we count the name of the Dallas radio station: KLIF.

2. An experimental method from the French group OULIPO, where each noun in a text is replaced by another noun seven items distant from it in the dictionary; e.g., "morning" becomes "moron." Automatized comedy/estrangement.

Chapter 5

1. The reference is to the first line of section V of "Propertius": "Now if ever it is time to cleanse Helicon."

I hear the first line as unironic, an homage to the tone of Pound's poem. I'm not appropriating Pound's language, I'm re-siting his address to set it down in my present.

2. "Something to be read in normal circumstances" ("Propertius," section I). This is the opposite of Pound's "ball of light" typeface (Pound, *Guide to Kulchur*, 55) in which context melts away. I'm celebrating Pound the secular, civic love poet, and saying no thanks to Pound's gods, both pagan and fascist.

Rather, my vote goes to his assiduous courting of public space,
though soon he would be driven to distraction

by stroboscopic unrequited glimpses of systematicity
which he mistook for totality

—hence Mussolini and those swamps (ever draining, never to be drained)
inexhaustibly inciting panic. But that's later.

In "Propertius" he was addressing "normal circumstances"
because he no longer had any

and missed the good old days
of 1912 and 1913 when he was just beginning to write in modern English.

"Propertius" is his most extended stretch
of consecutively phrased poetry in that language.

3. See Baudelaire's "The Painter of Modern Life": "By 'modernity' I mean the ephemeral, the fugitive, the contingent, the half of art whose other half is the eternal and the immutable" (Baudelaire, 102).

4. "Propertius," section II.

5. I have discussed Pound's fascination with Gaudier-Brzeska in *The Trouble with Genius* (51). Gaudier's display of instantaneous comprehension of a Chinese ideogram, "Of course you can *see* it's a horse" (Pound, *ABC*, 21), expresses the nub of Pound's impatience with discourse—with ordinary reading (see Perelman). Pound writes of Gaudier-Brzeska as utterly attractive: "I have written more than once that Gaudier-Brzeska was the most complete case of Genius I have ever encountered. Put it creative genius, fully equipped, but Gaudier was a danger to everyone in the room" (Pound, *Selected Prose*, 459). The example of Gaudier-Brzeska's sculpture served as a model for Pound's sense that great writing consisted of chiseling away all excess. It is no coincidence that Pound's account of condensing a sixty-line poem into the two lines of "In a Station of the Metro" occurs in his memoir of Gaudier-Brzeska (86–89).

Evidence for Pound's intense homosociality is not hard to find: his notorious "Sage

Homme" (Pound, *Selected Letters*, 70), for instance; or this, in his description of himself and Eliot deciding to turn away from Imagisme: "at a particular date, in a particular time in a particular room, two authors, neither engaged in picking the other's pocket, decided that the dilution of *vers libre*, Amygism, Lee Masterism, general floppiness had gone too far and some counter-current must be set going" (Pound, "Harold Monro," 590). But a queer Pound is an implausible figure.

6. This attitude toward World War I is not all that different from the one expressed in Stein's contemporary "Lifting Belly": "Lifting belly is anxious. / Not about Verdun. / Oh dear no." (*GS I*, 415); see Perelman, 153.

7. This is almost a direct quote from the opening of Canto III (Pound, *Cantos*, 11).

8. This is teasing Pound's well-known castigations of Milton's Latinate syntax, where Pound excoriates "Him who disobeys me disobeys" (Pound, *ABC*, 51).

9. There are few other places where Pound pulls out all the stops like this.

10. That Pound, the sworn enemy of flimsy credit schemes, would use "draft" (i.e., a promissory note) to describe the first and final installments of *The Cantos—A Draft of XXX Cantos, Drafts & Fragments*—is a profound irony, which Richard Sieburth pointed out some decades back ("In Pound We Trust"). My use of Keats's well-known epitaph ("Here lies one whose name was writ in water") is intended to underline my sense of this irony. I will discuss Rachel Blau DuPlessis's notable de-ironization—i.e., calling her long poem *Drafts*—in the next chapter.

11. Cf. Canto CXIII, 800 (Pound, *Cantos*).

12. Cf. "A Pact" (Pound, *P/T*, 269).

13. Cf. "Propertius," section I.

14. Cf. Pound's well-known letter to Harriet Monroe: "Objectivity and again objectivity, and expression: no hindside-beforeness, no straddled adjectives (as 'addled mosses dank'), no Tennysonianness of speech; nothing—nothing that you couldn't, in some circumstance, in the stress of some emotion, actually say" (Pound, *Selected Letters*, 49). Pound's insistence that poetry be speakable does have its commonsense virtues: stale Edwardian poeticisms were a tedious element of the poetry scene in 1915. But in the larger frame of his career, this desire for the person and the work to coincide leads to Pound's own tedious totalitarian syntheses.

Chapter 6

1. For the importance of the word *drafts* to *The Cantos*, see note 10 in the previous chapter.

2. A personal term Creeley persistently used to name his pantheon of crucial poets; to my ear, it also implies that they are always present, are always company for him.

3. As a start, see *Against Expression*, edited by Kenneth Goldsmith and Craig Dworkin.

4. This is why the sharp line Pound and Williams often draw between prose and poetry is useless when it comes to their own work: *Spring and All* and *ABC of Reading* are more fruitfully approached as writing.

5. This is not to say Creeley did not know *The Cantos*. In a 1951 letter, he lists his favorites: "XXX, XIII, XLVII, XLV, and the section marked *libretto* on the end of LXXXI" (Creeley, *Selected Letters*, 85).

6. See Bush, *The Genesis of Ezra Pound's Cantos*.

7. Jena Osman, Susan Stewart, Gil Ott.

8. "On *Drafts*," *Blue Studios*, 211–12.

9. ". . . the historical sense compels a man to write, not merely with his own genera-

tion in his bones, but . . . the whole of the literature of Europe from Homer" (Eliot, *Selected Prose*, 940).

10. "The beautiful lips slightly scornful"? See the discussion of Reznikoff's "Hellenist" in Chapter 20.

11. "About thirty years ago, seated on one of the very hard, very slippery, thoroughly uncomfortable chairs of the British Museum main reading room . . . I lifted my eyes to the tiers of volumes and false doors covered with imitation bookbacks which surround that focus of learning. Calculating the eye-strain and the number of pages per day that a man could read, with deduction for say at least 5% of one man's time for reflection, I decided against it" (*Guide to Kulchur*, 53).

See my discussion in Chapter 10.

12. "The Futurist Manifesto," http://bactra.org/T4PM/futurist-manifesto.html.

Chapter 7

1. William Carlos Williams, *Collected Poems, Vol. I*, 372. This collection will be cited in the text as *WCW I*. Other writings by Williams will be cited as follows: *WCW II* = *Collected Poems, Vol. II*, ed. Christopher MacGowan (New York: New Directions, 1988); *FD* = *The Farmers' Daughters* (New York: New Directions, 1957); *IM* = *Imaginations*, ed. Webster Schott (New York: New Directions, 1970); *IW* = *I Wanted to Write a Poem: The Autobiography of the Works of a Poet*, ed. Edith Heal (Boston: Beacon Press, 1958); *P* = *Paterson*, ed. Christopher MacGowan (New York: New Directions, 1992); *L* = *Selected Letters of William Carlos Williams*, ed. John Thirlwall (New York: New Directions, 1957).

2. "Books: Shantih Shantih Shantih," *Time*, March 3, 1924, http://www.time.com/time/magazine/article/0,9171,881419,00.html.

3. "Writing Test Sample: Grade 8, Narrative Writing," *Written.co* (February 24, 2011), http://written.co/2011/02/writing-test-sample-grade-8-narrative-writing/.

4. David E. Chinitz speaks of Williams's "Thirty Years' War on Eliot" (Chinitz, 144). On Williams's interest in Duchamp, see Sayre.

5. William Rose Benet and Conrad Aiken, eds., *An Anthology of Famous English and American Poetry* (New York: Modern Library, 1945).

6. Williams never defined the variable foot clearly. His letter to John C. Thirlwall is one of his most sustained discussions. He points to his own poem "The Descent" (*WCW II*, 245), mentions Gerard Manley Hopkins and Whitman as antecedents, and speaks of Einstein's relativity—but does not offer a definition (*L*, 334–36).

7. Doyle, 239. When the remarks are reprinted in *Poetry and the Age*, the italics are removed: see Randall Jarrell, *Poetry and the Age* (London: Faber, 1953), 230. For Jarrell's earlier rave, see Doyle, 174–79. Williams continues to be accused of fundamentally confusing life and art. In a current anthology, Lawrence Rainey complains of "Williams's truculent and dogmatic belief that poetry could offer unmediated access to the world" (Rainey, 500).

8. See Solt and Cushman.

9. In the latter stages of his career, Williams often set his lines in staggered groups of three. E.g.:

The descent beckons
        as the ascent beckoned.
                Memory is a kind
of accomplishment, (*WCW II*, 245)

This is often referred to as his stair-step line.

10. Williams, who was echoing a Pound letter, had already made a similar observation in *The Great American Novel* (*IM*, 167).

11. Charles Olson, *Selected Writings*, ed. Robert Creeley (New York: New Directions, 1967), 84. In the Poundian shorthand Olson employs, fr = from; abt = about.

12. Here, I am referring to the titles Williams used later; in *Spring*, the poems were merely numbered.

13. Robert Grenier, "On Speech," *This* 1 (1971), n.p. Grenier is referring to Williams's "To me, all sonnets say the same thing of no importance" (*WCW II*, 54).

Chapter 8

1. See Chapter 7 for a discussion of this.

2. For a discussion of Stein and Duchamp, see Perloff 137–54.

3. The first is from Stein, *Everybody's Autobiography*, 298; the second, originally, in "Sacred Emily," *GS I*, 395. In *Toklas*, the initial article obscures the proper name: "a rose is a rose is a rose in a rose," *GS I*, 798.

4. "Stein and Toklas put a well-mannered, mature face on lesbian sexuality. . . . They embodied American ideals of domesticity and family" (Corn and Latimer, 237).

5. See Malcolm and Will; contra, see Bernstein.

6. See Corn and Latimer, Chapter 5.

7. *Yale Poetry Review*, no. 7 (December 1947): 2–3.

8. In the Library of America publication, which will be the publication of record for the foreseeable future, "bomb" is enclosed in parentheses, which slightly masks the editorial provenance of the word. The 1947 *Yale Poetry Review* publication uses brackets, making the editorial patching more visible. Thanks to Nancy Kuhl of the Beinecke Rare Book & Manuscript Library at Yale University for granting access to the original.

9. *Reflection on the Atomic Bomb*, ed. Robert Bartlett Haas (Los Angeles: Black Sparrow Press, 1973).

10. *Camera Work*, Special Number, August 1912. http://library.brown.edu/cds/mjp/render.php?id=1427745507802127&view=mjp_object

Chapter 9

1. A version of this essay appeared in the *Journal of the Poetry Society of America* (April 2000) as part of a discussion of complexity in poetry.

2. This story may be apocryphal, but it is an interesting illustration of the needy master contemplating possible gaps in the totality of his adoration. Robert Frost, at the height of his fame, read to an audience of thousands at the Michigan Union in Ann Arbor. The auditorium was packed but, nevertheless, a few empty seats high up were visible from the podium, and the organizers had to quickly procure additional bodies before the reading could go on.

Chapter 10

1. Pound is referring to the Eleusinian Mysteries in ancient Greece.

2. When quoting from Pound's *Pisan Cantos* in this essay, I will give canto and line number.

3. See Chapter 6.

4. There are many instances in Creeley's poems of the troubadour stance—the good Dr. Jekyll in this mini-allegory. Mr. Hyde appears as well, most famously in "The Warning": "For love—I would / split open your head and put / a candle in / behind the eyes" (*RC I*, 140).

5. Cf. Keats's criticism of Coleridge's "irritable reaching after fact," 536.

6. This excerpt omits the Chinese characters.

7. Burton Hatlen, "Pound's *Pisan Cantos* and the Origins of Projective Verse," in *Ezra Pound and Poetic Influence*, ed. Helen M. Dennis (Amsterdam: Rodopi, 2000), 131–52.

8. Remembering Bush's point that the opening of 74 was a late addition, it seems possible that "a bang" is registering the atomic bomb—obliquely to be sure.

9. The first slash indicates a line break; the slash after "yr" is part of Pound's abbreviation of "your."

Chapter 11

1. I will cite Mullen's books as follows: *The Cracks Between What We Are and What We Are Supposed to Be* (Tuscaloosa: University of Alabama Press, 2012) = *CB*; *Recyclopedia*—which collects *Trimmings*, *S*PeRM**K*T*, and *Muse & Drudge*—(St. Paul, MN: Graywolf Press, 2006) = *R*. The cover I discuss is from *Muse & Drudge* (Philadelphia: Singing Horse Press, 1995); *Tree Tall Woman* (Galveston, TX: Energy Earth Communications, Inc., 1981) = *TTW*.

2. The three quotes are from this source: John Rickford, "Rachel Jeantel's African American Vernacular English use in the Zimmerman trial/verdict," Language Log, entry posted August 1, 2013, http://languagelog.ldc.upenn.edu/nll/?p=5574#more-5574.

3. In Major, "Spaginzy spagades" is defined as "Pig Latin for 'Negro'" (437) and "splibby" as "good feeling, 'soul'" (439). For Mullen's use of Major's book, see *CB*, 200, 209.

4. I am following Mullen's usage here and not capitalizing black and white.

5. Chapter 10, "Pound's Cage."

6. See Schulze for an excellent account of the trope of health in the early twentieth century.

7. See the previous chapter.

8. See Chapter 9 for a discussion of another poem from *Tree Tall Woman*, "Father (Part 1)."

9. However, Mullen has recently made quite clear her disapproval of Stein's cavalier racialism, not just in "Melanctha" but also in *Tender Buttons*. See *CB*, 20–28.

10. For a perspicacious overview and detailed readings of *Muse & Drudge*, see Shockley, 82–118.

11. In "A Conversation with Harryette Mullen" we learn that a nubia is "a fleecy collar that Victorian women wore around their necks," but such pinning down is precisely not the point of what Mullen is doing.

12. The line "tighter than Dick's hatband" (*R*, 164), for example, refers to a condom.

13. For "unwobbling pivot" see Confucius. For "cohere" see Canto CXVI: "I cannot make it cohere"; "i.e. it coheres all right / even if my notes do not cohere" (Pound, *Cantos*, 810–11).

Chapter 13

1. "A man cannot say, 'I will compose poetry.' The greatest poet even cannot say it; for the mind in creation is as a fading coal" (Shelley, 549).

2. The bulk of the definition was written by Harold Bloom for the 1965 edition and was reprinted in 1974; the "evident subjectivity" clause was added by another hand in 1993.

3. Bloom's dramatization of his own (flamboyantly subjective) critical agons is in ironic counterpoint to the warning against critical subjectivity offered here.

4. See Perelman, 118–21.

5. To be fair, Jameson may have been thinking of *The Tennis Court Oath* here. Nevertheless, his pronouncements on postmodernism have been, to say the least, influential; and it is still not uncommon to read that Ashbery's writing is without meaning.

6. Note the perfect bathos of that title.

7. John Ashbery, email to author, May 28, 2008.

Chapter 14

1. See Plotnitsky for a rebuttal of the kinds of gesture that Sokal made; Guillory provides a capacious view of the intellectual landscape at the time.

2. "While the publication of the hoax article was enabled by the failure of the editors to detect its spurious physics, its deeper embarrassment arose from Sokal's capacity to reproduce postmodernism as a discursive *bloc*, in effect, the ideology of a party in the culture wars" (Guillory, 473).

3. My account is taken from Heyward's great book.

4. Ashbery mentioned this to me in conversation—without referring to Ern Malley.

5. The attitudes of the hoaxers were not purely polemical. Alongside the appetite for and loathing of modernist absurdities there is the complex self-criticism entailed by the fact that *Ecliptic* begins with "Dürer: Innsbruck, 1495," a poem McAuley had himself written in earnest a year before (see Lecercle, 136–150).

6. For a much fuller account of literary hoaxes, see Ruthven.

7. These hoax poets are close to, but distinct from, pseudographic figures such as Fernando Pessoa's heteronyms. Another near but distinct category would be phantom archeological poetry such as Armand Schwerner's *The Tablets*.

8. See Groom for a detailed discussion of the importance of Ossian and Chatterton to the development of Romanticism.

9. See the discussion of Ashbery's use of bathos (proto-Flarf) in the previous chapter.

10. This line is omitted in Pound's *Poems and Translations*, ed. Richard Sieburth (New York: Library of America, 2003); the omission is mentioned in a note (1306).

11. At a panel talk on pseudonymy/pseudography that I participated in with Kent Johnson, Tan Lin, and Joshua Schuster at the Kelly Writers House on April 23, 1999, Johnson defended "Yasusada" (without acknowledging authorship) as an act of "imaginative sympathy."

12. See de Bary.

Chapter 15

1. William Carlos Williams, *Collected Poems, Vol. I*, ed. A. Walton Litz and Christopher MacGowan (New York: New Directions, 1986), 72. This collection will be cited in the text as *WCW I*. Other writings by Williams will be cited as follows: *A* = *Autobiography* (New York: New Directions, 1967); *WCW II* = *Collected Poems, Vol. II*, ed. Christopher MacGowan (New York: New Directions, 1988); *FD* = *The Farmers' Daughters* (New York: New Directions, 1957); *IM* = *Imaginations*, ed. Webster Schott (New York: New Directions, 1970); *P* = *Paterson*, ed. Christopher MacGowan (New York: New Di-

rections, 1992); *RI* = *A Recognizable Image*, ed. Bram Dijkstra (New York: New Directions, 1978).

2. For the poem: https://media.sas.upenn.edu/pennsound/authors/Williams-WC/15_Princeton_03-19-52/Williams-WC_21_The-Sea-Elephant_Princeton_03-19-52.mp3; the commentary: https://media.sas.upenn.edu/pennsound/authors/Williams-WC/15_Princeton_03-19-52/Williams-WC_22_Comment-2_Princeton_03-19-52.mp3.

3. Again, I am ignoring the case of rehearing a piece, where I anticipate certain passages I know will be arriving next.

4. Of course, one can read faces, paintings, skies, etc. And *parole in libertà*, *calligrammes*, and the variousness of Lettrist writing require quite other notions of reading. But for this discussion, I am intending a plain denotative sense of reading: sequential processing of marks on paper.

5. The actual practice of Western music loosens or even attacks this precision: think of Cage and post-Cagean procedures. This turning-away from exactitude can be traced back to the *Sprechstimme* of Cage's teacher, Schoenberg. And prior to that there are the traditions of cadenza improvisation (Mozart, Beethoven) and filling in figured basses (Bach).

6. Here, I should note Steve Evans's term, "the phonological braid," made of vocal timbre, text, and technology.

7. See Havelock and Lord.

8. http://media.sas.upenn.edu/pennsound/authors/Williams-WC/27_UCLA_May-1955/Williams-WC_25-Sea-Elephant_UCLA_May-1955.mp3.

9. Pig Cupid is from Mina Loy, "Songs to Johannes" (Loy, 53).

Williams's sea elephant is mostly male, though the gender story is tangled. Halfway through, Williams mentions a beard (and that could be ambiguous); he next ventriloquizes the sea elephant as female (if you accept the low-key allusion to Aphrodite rising from the sea); and then, near the end, the sea elephant is triumphantly hetero, disporting with his harem, while always remembering to eat.

10. This is another Keatsian facet of Williams, who was never shy about hosting another consciousness: cf. one of Keats's less famous sound bites on negative capability: "if a Sparrow come before my Window I take part in its existence and pick about the Gravel" (Keats, 74).

Chapter 16

1. Alice Notley, *Doctor Williams' Heiresses* (Berkeley: Tuumba Press, 1980), n.p. Subsequently *DWH*.

Chapter 17

1. *Talks* (*Hills* 6/7), Bob Perelman, ed. (San Francisco: 1980); and *Writing/Talks*, Bob Perelman, ed. (Carbondale: Southern Illinois University Press, 1985).

2. I discuss this at length in *The Marginalization of Poetry: Language Writing and Literary History*. See the second chapter especially.

3. David Antin, *Talking at the Boundaries* (New York: New Directions, 1976), 56.

4. Margreta De Grazia, "Sanctioning Voice: Quotation Marks, the Abolition of Torture, and the Fifth Amenedment," *Cardozo Arts & Entertainment Law Journal* 10, no. 2 (1992).

5. See Ellen Zweig's "Where Is the Piece? An Account of a Talk by David Antin," in *The Poetry Reading: A Contemporary Compendium on Language and Performance*, eds. Stephen Vincent and Ellen Zweig (San Francisco: Momo's Press, 1981), 174–86.

6. Antin's remarks are germane: "I knew the neo-formalist concerns of most of the language group, as well as what I would call the political modernism of notions of a writerly resistance to a coercive, institutionally controlled 'readerly' language, etc., which took the form of hostility to 'narrative' and 'representation' and intermittently to the idea of 'referentiality.' Since I came out of a very similar modernist (experimentalist) background and had moreover a doctoral education in just such modernist derived linguistics as inspired many of the language poets, I was curious to examine what I was looking for in 'narrative' in spite of my own history" (From a letter to the author, November 10, 1996).

7. Jack Kerouac, *Visions of Cody*, introduction by Allen Ginsberg (New York: McGraw-Hill, 1972), 171.

8. It is a fascinating moment. Kerouac has added "(*demurely downward look*)" as a description of Cody, who is talking about his inability to "get it down"—to write. Kerouac can, of course, get it down: does that make him more masculine than the suddenly "demure" Cody? Cody senses something like this, since he objects to the description of himself he reads the following night. Michael Davidson discusses this passage in *The San Francisco Renaissance: Poetics and Community at Mid-century* (Cambridge: Cambridge University Press, 1989), 73–76.

9. Ron Silliman's later description certainly seems to be factoring into Eleanor Antin's complaints (among others): "Poets model the discussion / portion of a talk after the territorial behavior / of male elephant seals, each striving / to be the dominant alpha bull." *What* (Great Barrington, MA: The Figures, 1988), 112.

10. I have outlined this issue from another angle in *The Marginalization of Poetry*, where I discuss the differing implications of the titles of the magazines each was involved in editing: Watten and *This*; Bernstein and *L=A=N=G=U=A=G=E*. *The Marginalization of Poetry* (Princeton: Princeton University Press, 1996), 19–20.

11. To re-cite the blurb: "I've been a poet, critic, linguist, and engineer, and though this knowledge informs the book, it is not the work of a professional."

Chapter 18

1. This chapter was originally given as a talk at the "Zukofsky at 100" conference at Columbia University in September 2004.

2. I will refer to Zukofsky's books via the following abbreviations: "*A*" = A; "*A*" 1–12 = A 1–12; *Complete Short Poetry* = *CSP*; *Pound/Zukofsky* = *P/Z*; *A Test of Poetry* = *T*.

Chapter 19

1. This piece originally appeared in *Radical Poetics and Secular Jewish Culture*, eds. Miller and Morris.

2. To be fair, Whitman did describe *Leaves of Grass* as a "language experiment," and work like *An American Primer* shows his continuing interest in language. Still, an overwhelming desire for the physical seems basic to his work.

3. See Rothenberg, "Harold Bloom: The Critic as Exterminating Angel"; see also "Canonicity" in this volume.

4. My unsystematic readings in music history suggest that Zukofsky's picture of an organically whole Bach-in-Leipzig is as idealized as Milton's depiction of Eden. Actual Leipziggers were getting tired of "old Bach" and his fusty counterpoint, which was forestalling the superior excitement of the emerging gallant style (eventually to flower with Haydn, C.P.E. Bach, Mozart).

Chapter 20

1. It strikes me that some readers may have the Johnson edition (J) and some the Franklin (F), so I'm citing both.

2. *7 Works* (San Francisco: The Figures, 1977).

3. And Mitchell shows convincingly how sturdy was the contract her ear kept with hymn metrics across the vicissitudes of whatever writing surface.

Chapter 21

1. I am using the term "Greenbergian formalism" loosely; in my usage it is more an influential notion than a particular pronouncement of Clement Greenberg. See https://dictionaryofarthistorians.org/greenbergc.htm.

2. See the discussion of "To Elsie" in Chapter 7.

3. Michelle Leggott's *Reading Zukofsky's 80 Flowers* shows how tightly Zukofsky could pack things.

4. Zukofsky (sardonically? democratically?) claimed that his epic concerns focus on the little words "a" and "the," which contain enough for a lifetime's work.

5. A few poems incorporate the slash, but conventionally, as marking a line division.

Works Cited

Adams, Hazard. *Critical Theory Since Plato*. New York: Harcourt Brace Jovanovich, 1971.

Aiken, Conrad and William Rose Benet, eds. *An Anthology of Famous English and American Poetry*. New York: Modern Library, 1945.

Allen, Donald M., ed. *The New American Poetry*. New York: Grove Press, 1960.

Andrews, Bruce. *I Don't Have Any Paper So Shut Up (or, Social Romanticism)*. Los Angeles: Sun & Moon Press, 1992.

———. *Lip Service*. Toronto: Coach House Books, 2001.

Antin, David. *Talking at the Boundaries*. New York: New Directions, 1976.

———. Letter to Bob Perelman, November 10, 1996.

Aristotle. *Poetics*, in *Critical Theory Since Plato*. Edited by Hazard Adams. Rev. ed. Fort Worth: Harcourt Brace Jovanovich College Publishers, 1992.

Ashbery, John. *The Tennis Court Oath*. Middletown: Wesleyan University Press, 1962.

———. *The Double Dream of Spring*. New York: Ecco Press, 1976.

———. *Houseboat Days*. New York: Viking, 1977.

———. *Some Trees*. New York: Ecco Press, 1978.

———. *Girls on the Run*. New York: Farrar, Straus, and Giroux, 1999.

———. *Chinese Whispers*. New York: Farrar, Strauss, and Giroux, 2002.

Barchas, Janine. *Graphic Design, Print Culture, & Eighteenth-Century Novel*. Cambridge: Cambridge University Press, 2002.

Barthes, Roland. "The Death of the Author." In *The Rustle of Language*, translated by Richard Howard, 49–55. Berkeley: University of California Press, 1989.

de Bary, Brett. "After the Apocalypse: Hara Tamiki's Writings on the Bombing of Hiroshima." *Journal of the Association of Teachers of Japanese* 15, no. 2 (Nov, 1980): 150–69.

Baudelaire, Charles. "The Painter of Modern Life." In *Modernism: An Anthology of Sources and Documents*, edited by Vassiliki Kolocotroni, Jane Goldman, and Olga Taxidou, 102–8. Chicago: The University of Chicago Press, 1998.

Bernstein, Charles. "The Academy in Peril: William Carlos Williams Meets the MLA." In *Content's Dream: Essays 1975–1984*, 244–51. Los Angeles: Sun & Moon Press, 1986.

———, ed. *Gertrude Stein's War Years: Setting the Record Straight: A dossier*. In *Jacket2*. https://jacket2.org/feature/gertrude-steins-war-years-setting-record-straight.

Berrigan, Ted. *Red Wagon*. Chicago: The Yellow Press, 1976.
——. *Nothing for You*. New York: Angel Hair Books, 1977.
——. *In a Blue River*. New York: Little Light Books, 1981.
——. *A Certain Slant of Sunlight*. Oakland: O Books, 1998.
——. *The Collected Poems of Ted Berrigan*. Edited by Alice Notley with Anselm Berrigan and Edmund Berrigan. Berkeley: University of California Press, 2005.
——. "An Interview with John Cage." *http://epc.buffalo.edu/authors/berrigan/cage.html* (accessed October 18, 2015).
Bloom, Harold. *Agon : towards a theory of revisionism*. New York: Oxford University Press, 1982.
Bochner, Jay. *An American Lens: Scenes from Alfred Stieglitz's New York Secession*. Cambridge: MIT Press, 2005.
Brathwaite, Edward Kamau. *X/Self*. Oxford: Oxford University Press, 1987.
Bunting, Basil. *Complete Poems*. New York: New Directions, 2000.
Bush, Ronald. *The Genesis of Ezra Pound's Cantos*. Princeton: Princeton University Press, 1992.
——. "'Quiet, Not Scornful'? The Composition of *The Pisan Cantos*," in *A Poem Containing History: Textual Studies in The Cantos*. Edited by Lawrence S. Rainey. Ann Arbor: University of Michigan Press, 1997.
Cage; John. "Writing Through the Cantos." In *Postmodern American Poetry*, edited by Paul Hoover. New York: Norton, 1994.
Cage, John, and Joan Retallack. *Musicage: Cage Muses on Words, Art, Music*. Middletown: Wesleyan University Press, 1996.
Cameron, Sharon. *Choosing Not Choosing: Dickinson's Fascicles*. Chicago: University of Chicago, 1992.
Camp, James, X. J. Kennedy, and Keith Waldrop, eds. *Pegasus Descending: A Book of the Best Bad Verse*. Providence, RI: Burning Deck, 2003.
Carruthers, Mary. *The Craft of Thought*. Cambridge: Cambridge University Press, 1998.
Chinitz, David E. *T. S. Eliot and the Cultural Divide*. Chicago: University of Chicago Press, 2005.
Colbert, Stephen. *The Colbert Report* (July 23, 2013.) Interview with Kenneth Goldsmith. Web. *http://thecolbertreport.cc.com/videos/5tqazj/kenneth-goldsmith*
——. *The Colbert Report* (April 4, 2013). Commentary on Boston Marathon bombing. *http://thecolbertreport.cc.com/videos/ifpmy1/intro-4-16-13*
Coleridge, Samuel Taylor. *Biographia Literaria*. Vol. 1. Edited by James Engell and W. Jackson Bate. Princeton: Princeton University Press, 1983.
Corn, Wanda M. and Tirza True Latimer. *Seeing Gertrude Stein: Five Stories*. Berkeley: University of California Press, 2011.
Creeley, Robert. *The Collected Poems of Robert Creeley 1945–1975*. Berkeley: University of California Press, 1982. (*RC I*)
——. *The Collected Essays of Robert Creeley*. Berkeley: University of California Press, 1989.
——. *The Collected Poems of Robert Creeley 1975–2005*. Berkeley: University of California Press, 2006. (*RC II*)
——. *The Selected Letters of Robert Creeley*. Edited by Rod Smith, Peter Baker, and Kaplan Harris. Berkeley: University of California Press, 2014.
Creeley, Robert, and Charles Olson. *The Complete Correspondence*. Vol. 1. Edited by George Butterick. Santa Rosa: Black Sparrow Press, 1980.

———. *Charles Olson & Robert Creeley: The Complete Correspondence*. Vols. 7 and 8. Edited by George F. Butterick. Los Angeles: Black Sparrow Press, 1987.

Culler, Jonathan. *Structuralist Poetics*. Ithaca: Cornell University Press, 1975.

Cushman, Stephen. *William Carlos Williams and the Meaning of Measure*. New Haven: Yale University Press, 1985.

Davidson, Michael. *The San Francisco Renaissance: Poetics and Community at Mid-century*. Cambridge: Cambridge University Press, 1989.

De Grazia, Margreta. "Sanctioning Voice: Quotation Marks, the Abolition of Torture, and the Fifth Amendment." *Cardozo Arts & Entertainment Law Journal* 10, no. 2 (1992).

Dennis, Helen M. "The Official Proceedings of the 17th International Ezra Pound Conference." Amsterdam: Editions Rodophi B.V., 2000.

Dickinson, Emily. *Poems by Emily Dickinson*. Edited by Mable Loomis Todd and T. W. Higginson. Boston: Little, Brown, and Co., 1915.

———. *The Complete Poems*. Edited by Thomas H. Johnson. Boston: Little, Brown, and Co., 1960.

———. *The Poems of Emily Dickinson*. Variorum Edition. Edited by R. W. Franklin, in three volumes. Cambridge: Harvard University Press, 1998.

Doyle, Charles, ed. *William Carlos Williams: The Critical Heritage*. London: Routledge, 1980.

Dunbar, Paul Laurence. *The Collected Poetry of Paul Laurence Dunbar*. Edited by Joanne M. Braxton. Charlottesville: University of Virginia Press, 1993.

DuPlessis, Rachel Blau. *Drafts 1–38, Toll*. Middletown: Wesleyan University Press, 2001.

———. *Blue Studios*. Tuscaloosa: University of Alabama Press, 2006.

———. *Torques: Drafts 58–76*. Cambridge: Salt Publishing, 2007.

———. *Purple Passages: Pound, Eliot, Zukofsky, Olson, Creeley, and the Ends of Patriarchal Poetry*. Iowa City: Iowa University Press, 2012.

———. *Surge: Drafts 96–114*. Cromer: Salt Publishing, 2013.

Dworkin, Craig, and Kenneth Goldsmith, eds. *Against Expression: An Anthology of Conceptual Writing*. Evanston: Northwestern University Press, 2011.

Eliot, T. S. "Charleston, Hey! Hey!" in *The Nation & Athanaeum* 40, no. 17 (January 29, 1927).

———. *Selected Prose*. Edited Frank Kermode. New York: Harcourt, 1975.

Evans, Steve. "The Phonotextual Braid." *Jacket2*, http://jacket2.org/commentary/phonotextual-braid.

Fillmore, Lily Wong. "The Second Time Around: Cognitive and Social Strategies in Second Language Acquisition." PhD diss., Stanford University, 1976. Quoted in Alison Wray, *Formulaic Language and the Lexicon*. Kindle Locations 2180–81. Kindle Edition.

Forché, Carolyn, ed. *Against Forgetting: Twentieth-Century Poetry of Witness*. New York: Norton, 1993.

Friedlander, Benjamin. "Auctions of the Mind: Emily Dickinson and Abolition." *Arizona Quarterly* 54, no. 1 (Spring 1998): 1–26.

———. *One Hundred Etudes*. Washington, DC: Edge Books, 2012.

Gaskill, Howard, ed. *The Reception of Ossian in Europe*. New York: Thoemmes Continuum, 2004.

Ginsberg, Allen. "Wichita Vortex Sutra." In *Collected Poems 1947–1980*, 394–411. New York: Harper & Row, 1984.

——. *Death & Fame*. New York: HarperCollins, 1999.
——. *Spontaneous Mind: Selected Interviews, 1958–1996*. Edited by David Carter. New York: HarperCollins, 2001.
Goldsmith, Kenneth. "Against Expression: Kenneth Goldsmith in Conversation." *http://www.poets.org/poetsorg/text/against-expression-kenneth-goldsmith-conversation*
——. "Being Boring." *http://wings.buffalo.edu/epc/authors/goldsmith/goldsmith_boring.html*
——. Comment on "The Body of Michael Brown." Facebook post. *https://www.facebook.com/kenneth.goldsmith.739/posts/354492771403205 3*
——. *Day*. Great Barrington: The Figures, 2003.
——. Reading at the White House, May 11, 2011. *https://www.youtube.com/watch?v=hMSvrIPhA4Y&feature=kp*
——. *Uncreative Writing: Managing Language in the Digital Age*. New York: Columbia University Press, 2011.
——. *Seven American Deaths and Disasters*. New York: Powerhouse Books, 2013.
——. *Sports. http://wings.buffalo.edu/epc/authors/goldsmith/Goldsmith_Sports.pdf.*
Graves, William. "The Bathetic." *Talks (Hills 6/7)*. Edited by Bob Perelman. 1977.
Grenier, Robert. "On Speech." *This* 1 (1971).
Groom, Nick. *The Forger's Shadow: How Forgery Changed the Course of Literature*. London: Picador, 2003.
——. "Romanticism and Forgery." *Literature Compass* 4, no. 6 (2007): 1625–49, *http://onlinelibrary.wiley.com/doi/10.1111/j.1741-4113.2007.00485.x/abstract*
Guillory, John. "The Sokal Affair and the History of Criticism." *Critical Inquiry* 28, no. 2 (Winter 2002): 470–508.
Handelman, Susan. *The Slayers of Moses: The Emergence of Rabbinic Interpretation in Modern Literary Theory*. Albany: SUNY Press, 1982.
Hatlen, Burton. "Pound's *Pisan Cantos* and the Origins of Projective Verse." In *Ezra Pound and Poetic Influence*, edited by Helen M. Dennis. Amsterdam: Rodopi, 2000.
Havelock, Eric. *The Literate Revolution in Greece and Its Cultural Consequences*. Princeton: Princeton University Press, 1982.
H. D. *An End to Torment: A Memoir of Ezra Pound*. New York: New Directions, 1979.
Hejinian, Lyn. *The Language of Inquiry*. Berkeley: University of California Press, 2000.
Heyward, Michael. *The Ern Malley Affair*. London: Faber and Faber, 1993.
Howe, Susan. *My Emily Dickinson*. Berkeley: North Atlantic Books, 1995.
Jackson, Virginia. *Dickinson's Misery: A Theory of Lyric Reading*. Princeton: Princeton University Press, 2005.
James, William. *The Principles of Psychology*. Vol. 1. New York: Dover, 1950.
Jameson, Fredric. "Periodizing the 60s." In *The Ideologies of Theory*. Vol. 2. Minneapolis: University of Minnesota Press, 1988.
Jarrell, Randall. *Poetry and the Age*. London: Faber, 1953.
Joyce, James. *Dubliners*. New York: Penguin, 1993.
Keats, John. *The Letters of John Keats*. Edited by Maurice Buxton Forman. Vol. 1. Oxford: Oxford University Press, 1931.
——. *Poetical Works*. Edited by H. W. Garrod. Oxford: Oxford University Press: 1956.
——. Letters to John Taylor (February 27, 1818) and to George and Thomas Keats

(December 21, 1817). In *Critical Theory Since Plato*, 3rd ed, 536. Edited by Hazard Adams and Leroy Searle. Boston: Thomson Wadsworth, 2005.

Kerouac, Jack. *Visions of Cody*, introduction by Allen Ginsberg. New York: McGraw-Hill, 1972).

Koch, Kenneth. *Collected Poems*. New York: Knopf, 2007.

Kruchenykh, A. and V. Khlebnikov. *The Word as Such*. In *Words in Revolution: Russian Futurist Manifestoes, 1912–1928*, edited by Herbert Eagle, 57–62. Cornell: Cornell University Press, 1988.

Lazer, Hank. *Opposing Poetries*. Vol. 2, *Readings*. Evanston: Northwestern University Press, 1996.

Lecercle, Jean-Jacques. *Interpretation as Pragmatics*. New York: St. Martin's Press, 1999.

Lee, Charles and Wyndham Lewis, eds. *The Stuffed Owl: An Anthology of Bad Verse*. New York: NYRB, 2003.

Leggott, Michelle. *Reading 80 Flowers*. Baltimore: Johns Hopkins Press, 1989.

Lehman, David, ed. *The Oxford Book of American Poetry*. Oxford: Oxford University Press, 2006.

Lewis, Wyndham. *Time and Western Man*. London: Chatto and Windus, 1927.

Liebregts, Peter. *Ezra Pound and Neoplatonism*. Teaneck, NJ: Farleigh Dickinson University Press, 2004.

"Longinus." *On the Sublime*. Translated by W. Hamilton Fyfe. Cambridge, MA: Loeb Classical Library, 1946.

Louÿs, Pierre. *The Songs of Bilitis*. Translated by Alvah C. Bessie. Mieoloa: Dover Publications, 1988.

Loy, Mina. *The Lost Lunar Baedeker*. Selected and edited by Roger L. Conover. New York: Farrar, Straus, and Giroux, 1996.

Mac Low, Jackson. *The Complete Light Poems*. Edited by Anne Tardos and Michael O'Driscoll. Victoria, TX: Chax Press, 2015.

Macpherson, James. *The Poems of Ossian and Related Works*. Edited by Howard Gaskill. Edinburgh: Edinburgh University Press, 1996.

Major, Clarence. *Juba to Jive: A Dictionary of African-American Slang*. New York: Viking Penguin, 1994.

Malcolm, Janet. *Two Lives*. New Haven: Yale University Press, 2007.

Mariani, Paul. *William Carlos Williams: A New World Naked*. New York: McGraw-Hill, 1981.

McGrath, Charles. "How Many Stephen Colberts Are There?" *The New York Times*, January 4, 2012. http://www.nytimes.com/2012/01/08/magazine/stephen-colbert.html.

Mellow, James R. *Charmed Circle*. New York: Praeger, 1974.

Middleton, Peter. *Distant Reading: Performance, Readership, and Consumption in Contemporary Poetry*. Tuscaloosa: University of Alabama Press, 2005.

Miller, Cristanne. *Reading in Time: Emily Dickinson in the Nineteenth Century*. Amherst: University of Massachusetts Press, 2012.

Miller, Stephen Paul, and Daniel Morris, eds. *Radical Poetics and Secular Jewish Culture*. Tuscaloosa: University of Alabama Press, 2010.

Mitchell, Domhnall. *Measures of Possibility: Emily Dickinson's Manuscripts*. Amherst: University of Massachusetts Press, 2005.

Moore, Marianne. *Collected Poems*. New York: Viking Press, 1967.

Mullen, Harryette. *Tree Tall Woman*. Galveston, TX: Energy Earth Communications, Inc., 1981. (*TTW*)

———. "Harryette Mullen in Calgary, Alberta." *Boo* 7 (Vancouver, 1996). n. p.

———. *Recyclopedia*. St. Paul: Greywolf Press, 2006. (*R*)

———. "A Conversation with Harryette Mullen." http://wings.buffalo.edu/epc/authors/mullen/interview-new.html

———. *The Cracks Between What We Are and What We Are Supposed to Be*. Tuscaloosa: University of Alabama Press, 2012. (*CB*)

National Poetry Foundation website. https://nationalpoetryfoundation.wordpress.com/.

Niedecker, Lorine. *Collected Works*. Edited by Jenny Penberthy. Berkeley: University of California Press, 2002.

Nietzsche, Friedrich. *The Gay Science*. Translated by Walter Kaufman. New York: Vintage, 1974.

Notley, Alice. *Songs for the Unborn Second Baby*. New York: United Artists, 1979.

———. *Doctor Williams' Heiresses*. Berkeley: Tuumba Press, 1980.

O'Connor, William Van and Edward Stone, eds. *A Casebook on Ezra Pound*. New York: Thomas Y. Cromwell Company, 1959.

O'Hara, Frank. *Collected Poems*. New York: Knopf, 1971.

Olson, Charles. *Charles Olson & Ezra Pound: An Encounter at St. Elizabeths*. Edited by Catherine Seelye. New York: Grossman Publishers, 1975.

———. *The Collected Poems of Charles Olson*. Edited by George F. Butterick. Berkeley: University of California Press, 1987.

———. *Collected Prose*. Edited by Donald Allen and Benjamin Friedlander. Berkeley: University of California Press, 1997.

Oppen, George. *New Collected Poems*. Edited by Michael Davidson. New York: New Directions, 2002.

Ostriker, Alicia. "'Howl' Revisited: The Poet as Jew." *American Poetry Review* 26, no. 4 (July/August 1997): 28–31.

Padgett, Ron. *You Never Know*. Minneapolis: Coffee House Press, 2001.

Perelman, Bob. *7 Works*. Berkeley: The Figures, 1978.

———, ed. *Talks (Hills 6/7)*. San Francisco: 1980.

———, ed. *Writing/Talks*. Carbondale, IL: Southern Illinois University Press, 1985.

———. *The Trouble with Genius*. Berkeley: University of California Press, 1994.

———. *The Marginalization of Poetry: Language Writing and Literary History*. Berkeley: University of California Press, 1996.

———. "Pound's Legibility Today: Pedagogy and/or Initiation." In *Ezra Pound and Referentiality*, edited by Hélène Aji. Paris: Presses de l'Universite de Paris-Sorbonne, 2003.

———. *Iflife*. New York: Roof Books, 2006.

———. "That Deep Romantic Chasm," a review essay on Jeffrey Robinson's *Unfettering Poetry*. In *European Romantic Review* 22.1 (February 2011).

———. "A Williams Sound-Script: Listening to 'The Sea-Elephant.'" *Jacket 2* (Spring 2013). http:jacket2.orgarticlewilliams-soundscript.

Perloff, Marjorie. "Can(n)on to the Left of Us, Can(n)on to the Right of Us." In *Poetic License: Essays on Modernist and Postmodernist Lyric*, 7–30. Evanston: Northwestern University Press, 1990.

———. *Frank O'Hara: Poet Among Painters*. Rev. ed. Chicago: University of Chicago Press, 1997.

——. "In Search of the Authentic Other: The Poetry of Araki Yasusada." In Yasusada, *Double Flowering*, 148–68.

——. "Of Objects and Readymades: Gertrude Stein and Marcel Duchamp." *Forum for Modern Language Studies* 32, no. 2 (1996): 137–54.

——. *The Poetics of Indeterminacy: Rimbaud to Cage*. Evanston: Northwestern University Press, 1983.

Pessoa, Fernando. *Fernando Pessoa & Co*. Translated and edited by Richard Zenith. New York: Grive Press, 1998.

Plotnitsky, Arcadi. "'But It Is Above All Not True': Derrida, Relativity, and the Science Wars." *Postmodern Culture* 7, no. 2, 1997.

Plutarch. "On the Obsolescence of Oracles." https://www.loebclassics.com/view/plutarch-moralia_obsolescence_oracles/1936/pb_LCL306.347.xml.

Pope, Alexander. "Peri Bathous: or, Martinus Scriblerus, his Treatise of the Art of Sinking in Poetry." *Alexander Pope*. Edited by Pat Rogers, 195–238. New York: Oxford University Press, 1993.

Pound, Ezra. "Harold Monro." *Criterion* XI, no. 45 (July 1932).

——. *The Spirit of Romance*. New York: New Directions, 1952.

——. *ABC of Reading*. New York: New Directions, 1960. (*ABC*)

——. "Doctor Williams' Position." In *Literary Essays of Ezra Pound*. Edited by T. S. Eliot, 392–94. New York: New Directions, 1968.

——. *The Unwobbling Pivot / The Great Digest / The Analects*. New York: New Directions, 1969.

——. *Gaudier-Brzeska*. New York: New Directions, 1970.

——. *Guide to Kulchur*. New York: New Directions, 1970. (*GK*)

——. "Homage to Sextus Propertius." In *Personae*, 207–30. New York: New Directions, 1971.

——. *Selected Letters 1907–1941*. Edited by D. D. Paige. New York: New Directions, 1971.

——. *Selected Prose 1909–1965*. Edited by William Cookson. London: Faber, 1973. (*SP*)

——. *The Cantos of Ezra Pound*, 12th printing. New York: New Directions, 1991. (*C*)

——. *Ezra Pound: Poems and Translations*. Edited by Richard Sieburth. New York: Library of America, 2003. (*P/T*)

——. *The Pisan Cantos*. Edited by Richard Sieburth. New York: New Directions, 2003. (*PC*)

—— and Louis Zukofsky. *Pound/Zukofsky: Selected Letters of Ezra Pound and Louis Zukofsky*. Edited by Barry Ahearn. New York: New Directions, 1987.

Preminger, Alex and T. V. F. Brogan, eds. *The New Princeton Encyclopedia of Poetry and Poetics*. Princeton, NJ: Princeton University Press, 1993.

Rainey, Lawrence, ed. *Modernism: An Anthology*. Oxford: Blackwell, 2005.

Retallack, Joan. *The Poethical Wager*. Berkeley: University of California Press, 2003.

Reynolds, David. *Beneath the American Renaissance; The Subversive Imagination in the Age of Emerson and Melville*. Cambridge: Harvard University Press, 1988.

Reznikoff, Charles. *Poems 1918–1975*. Los Angeles: Black Sparrow Press, 1996.

——. *Testimony*. Los Angeles: Black Sparrow, 2015.

Rimbaud, Arthur. *A Season in Hell*. Translated by Louise Varese. New York: New Directions, 1952.

Rossetti, Christina. "Goblin Market." In *The Complete Poems*, 5–19. London: Penguin Classics, 2001.

Rothenberg, Jerome, ed., with Harris Lenowitz and Charles Doria. *A Big Jewish Book: Poems & Other Visions of the Jews from Tribal Times to Present*. Garden City, NY: Anchor Books, 1978.

———. "Harold Bloom: The Critic as Exterminating Angel." Originally in *Sulfur* 2 (1981); now available at http://www.webdelsol.com/Sulfur/Rothenberg_text1.htm (accessed October 19, 2015).

Rukeyser, Muriel. *Out of Silence: Selected Poems*. Evanston: TriQuarterly Books, 1992.

Ruthven, K. K. *Faking Literature*. Cambridge: Cambridge University Press, 2001.

Sayre, Henry M. "Ready-Mades and Other Measures: The Poetics of Marcel Duchamp and William Carlos Williams." *Journal of Modern Literature* 8, no. 1 (1980): 3–22.

Scholem, Gershom. *Major Trends in Jewish Mysticism*. New York: Schocken Books, 1954.

Schulze, Robin G. *Becoming Marianne Moore: The Early Poems, 1907–1924*. Berkeley: University of California Press, 2002.

———. *The Degenerate Muse*. Cambridge: Cambridge University Press, 2013.

Schwerner, Armand. *The Tablets*. Orono: National Poetry Foundation, 1999.

Shockley, Evie, *Renegade Poetics: Black Aesthetics and Formal Innovation in African American Poetry*. Iowa City: University of Iowa Press, 2011.

Shakespeare, William. *King Lear*. In *Complete Works*. Edited by Alfred Harbage. Baltimore: Penguin Books, 1969.

Shelley, Percy Bysshe. *The Complete Poems of Percy Bysshe Shelley*. New York: Modern Library, 1994.

———"A Defense of Poetry." In *Critical Theory Since Plato*. Edited by Hazard Adams and Leroy Searle. 3rd edition. Boston: Thomson Wadsworth, 2003.

Shoptaw, John. *On the Outside Looking Out: John Ashbery's Poetry*. Cambridge, MA: Harvard University Press, 1994.

Sidney, Philip. "An Apology for Poetry," in Adams.

Sieburth, Richard. "In Pound We Trust: The Economy of Poetry / The Poetry of Economics." *Critical Inquiry* 14 (Autumn 1987): 142–72.

Silliman, Ron. *What*. Great Barrington: The Figures, 1988.

Smith, Martha Nell. *Rowing in Eden: Rereading Emily Dickinson*. Austin: University of Texas Press, 1992.

Smith, William Jay. *The Spectra Hoax*. 2nd edition. Ashland: Story Line Press, 2000.

Sokal, Alan. "A Physicist Experiments with Cultural Studies." *Lingua Franca* (May/June 1996): 62–64.

———. "Transgressing the Boundaries: Toward a Transformative Hermeneutics of Quantum Gravity." Originally published in *Social Text* 46/47 (spring/summer 1996): 217–52.

Solt, Mary Ellen. *Toward a Theory of Concrete Poetry*. Edited by Antonio Sergio Bessa. Buffalo: OEI, 2010.

Spicer, Jack. *The Collected Books of Jack Spicer*. Edited by Robin Blaser. Los Angeles: Black Sparrow Press, 1975.

Stein, Gertrude. *Paris France*. New York: Charles Scribner's Sons, 1940.

———. *Wars I Have Seen*. New York: Random House, 1945.

———. "Winning His Way." In *America a Prophecy*. Edited by Jerome Rothenberg and George Quasha. New York: Vintage, 1974.

———. *Everybody's Autobiography*. Cambridge: Exact Change, 1993.

——. *Writings 1903–1932*. New York: Library of America, 1998. (*GS I*)
——. *Writings 1932–1946*. New York: Library of America, 1998. (*GS II*)
——. "Henri Matisse" and "Pablo Picasso." In *Camera Work*, Special Number, August 1912: 23–25; 29–30. http://library.brown.edu/cds/mjp/render.php?id=1427745507802127&view=mjp_object
Stendhal. *Racine and Shakespeare*. Translated by Guy Daniels. New York: Crowell-Collier Press, 1962.
Sutherland, Keston. "The Trade in Bathos." *Jacket* 15 (2001).
Terrell, Carroll F., ed. *A Companion to The Cantos of Ezra Pound*. Berkeley: University of California Press, 1980.
Tolson, Melvin B. *Harlem Gallery and Other Poems*. Edited by Raymond Nelson. Charlottesville: University of Virginia Press, 1999.
Treat, John Whittier. *Writing Ground Zero: Japanese Literature and the Atomic Bomb*. Chicago: University of Chicago Press, 1995.
Vincent, Stephen and Ellen Zweig, eds. *The Poetry Reading: A Contemporary Compendium on Language and Performance*. San Francisco: Momo's Press, 1981.
Wagner, Linda, ed. *Interviews with William Carlos Williams*. New York: New Directions, 1961.
Walcott, Derek. *Omeros*. New York: Farrar, Strauss and Giroux, 1992.
Ward, Geoff. *Statutes of Liberty: The New York School of Poets*. 2nd edition. New York: Palgrave, 2001.
Werner, Marta L., ed. *Emily Dickinson's Open Folios: Scenes of Reading, Surfaces of Writing*. Ann Arbor: University of Michigan Press, 1995.
Whitman, Walt. *Complete Poetry and Collected Prose*. New York: The Library of America, 1982.
Wikipedia, "Bathos." http://allthetropes.wikia.com/wiki/Bathos
Will, Barbara. *Unlikely Collaboration: Gertrude Stein, Bernard Faÿ, and the Vichy Dilemma*. New York: Columbia University Press, 2011.
Williams, William Carlos. "The Poem as a Field of Action." In *Selected Essays of William Carlos Williams*, 280–91. New York: Random House, 1954.
——. *The Farmers' Daughters*. New York: New Directions, 1957.
——. *Selected Letters of William Carlos Williams*. Edited by John Thirlwall. New York: New Directions, 1957.
——. *I Wanted to Write a Poem. The Autobiography of the Works of a Poet*. Edited by Edith Heal. Boston: Beacon Press, 1958.
——. *Autobiography*. New York: New Directions, 1970.
——. *Imaginations*. Edited by Webster Schott. New York: New Directions, 1970. (*IM*)
——. *A Recognizable Image*. Edited by Bram Dijkstra. New York: New Directions, 1978. (*RI*)
——. *Collected Poems*. Vol. I. Edited by A. Walton Litz and Christopher MacGowan. New York: New Directions, 1986. (*WCW I*)
——. *Collected Poems*, Vol. II. Edited by Christopher MacGowan. New York: New Directions, 1988. (*WCW II*)
——. *Paterson*. Edited by Christopher MacGowan. New York: New Directions, 1992. (*P*)
Woolf, Virginia. *A Room of One's Own*. San Diego: Harcourt Brace & Co., 1989.
Wordsworth, William. "Preface to *Lyrical Ballads*." In Hazard Adams, *Critical Theory Since Plato*, 482–92. New York: Harcourt Brace Jovanovich, 1971.

——. *William Wordsworth – The Oxford Authors*. Edited by Stephen Gill. Oxford: Oxford University Press, 1984.

Yale Review, no. 7 (1947). New Haven.

Yasusada, Ariki. *Doubled Flowering*. New York: Roof Books, 1997.

Zavatsky, Bill. "Everything You Always Wanted to Know about Poetry." In *The Whole Word Catalogue* 2 (1977). Reproduced on Academy of American Poets website, http://www.poets.org/viewmedia.php/prmMID/16062.

Zukofsky, Louis. "*A*" 1–12. Kyoto: Origin Press, 1959.

——. "*A*". Berkeley: University of California Press, 1978.

——. *Complete Short Poetry*. Baltimore: Johns Hopkins University Press, 1991.

——. *A Test of Poetry*. Middletown, CT: Wesleyan University Press, 2000.

Index